Alexander Robinson

A Study of the Saviour in the Newer Light

A Present Day Study of Jesus Christ. Second Edition

Alexander Robinson

A Study of the Saviour in the Newer Light
A Present Day Study of Jesus Christ. Second Edition

ISBN/EAN: 9783337027704

Printed in Europe, USA, Canada, Australia, Japan

Cover: Foto ©Lupo / pixelio.de

More available books at **www.hansebooks.com**

A STUDY

OF THE

SAVIOUR IN THE NEWER LIGHT

" How God anointed Jesus of Nazareth with the Holy Ghost and with power ; who went about doing good, and healing all that were oppressed of the devil ; for God was with him."—ACTS x. 38.

A STUDY

OF THE

SAVIOUR IN THE NEWER LIGHT

OR

A PRESENT-DAY STUDY OF JESUS CHRIST

BY

ALEXANDER ROBINSON, B.D.

FORMERLY MINISTER OF THE PARISH OF KILMUN,
ARGYLESHIRE

SECOND EDITION, REVISED FORM

WILLIAMS AND NORGATE

14, HENRIETTA STREET, COVENT GARDEN, LONDON
20, SOUTH FREDERICK STREET, EDINBURGH; AND
7, BROAD STREET, OXFORD

1898

LONDON
G. NORMAN AND SON, PRINTERS, FLORAL STREET
COVENT GARDEN

PREFACE

THIS work was published in a slightly different form in October 1895. While there were not wanting persons far from inconsiderable who sympathised with its aims and appreciated its contents as of solid value, its general reception was as unfavourable a one as, perhaps, any book ever ordinarily meets with. Especially, a serious offence was taken at it by the Church of Scotland, of which I had been, at the time of publication, an accredited preacher for between nine and ten years. And it became the occasion of an ecclesiastical "Case," which lasted over a period of eighteen months. It was condemned by the General Assembly of 1896, and ordered to be withdrawn. The General Assembly of 1897, again, put to me as the author the question, whether I would "repudiate" its teaching, and, having received a negative answer, cut me off from the recognised ministry of the Established Church. Meanwhile, the work as a publication had only had a few months' life, having been withdrawn entirely from sale, under legal advice, during the early judicial proceedings, and later withdrawn in submission to the Church's own command.

What was the cause of the offence being taken, and of the "Case"? There was nothing in the book that was not both devotional and in support of the high moral ideals which are associated with the name of Christianity; how, then, did it arouse such hostility?

One cause of offence, doubtless, was the free criticism
of the New Testament documents. A sentiment
seemed generally to assert itself, which drew a distinction between the gospels and even the rest of
the Bible, regarding them as the one ground which
ought to be secured from any intrusion that might
disturb the mind of the ordinary worshipper. Another
matter, however, which plainly offended was the
attempting, however reverently, on the part of a minister
of the Church, to trace a development of human thought
and human purpose in Him to whom the Church had
for so many centuries ascribed the being of the Second
Person in the Godhead. In vain had I, in the preface
and the last chapter, claimed that the course of the
study was not opposed to the essentials of the Church's
doctrine, that the complete human nature of Jesus had
all along been asserted by the Church, and that the
conception of the Divinity of Jesus was not opposed to
but seen through the humanity of Jesus. In vain also
did I, when the Case commenced, seek opportunity for
a direct presentation and a separate estimation of the
plea on which I hoped to justify my action, namely
an appeal to the disavowal by the early Church of
such views as denied a complete human nature on the
part of Jesus. The course of procedure which was
required in the Case proved not to admit of such
a free and full investigation as I had hoped for.
Only at the second General Assembly was I successful
in presenting what I considered to be an untrammelled
defence of my position ; and this late defence, allowed
" ex gratia," was for technical reasons found not
admissible for consideration by my judges. The book
stood condemned by the General Assembly of 1896 as
subversive of the doctrine of the Church. Only some

thirty to forty in that assembly of several hundreds had dissented from this judgment.

Anxious not to break with the Church which I had loved to serve, until driven to such a course by honour itself, and remembering my ordination promises of subjection, I had in the first year strained other considerations to render as great a submission as conscience would allow; and when the continued withdrawal of the book from circulation was informally proposed to me a day before the judgment was formally pronounced, I had acquiesced thus far, being persuaded at the time that the corporation of which I was a member had the right to demand the withdrawal of a particular published form of my study. I had done this also with the greater readiness in that, under the handling of the book by its assailants, there had come clearly to my notice certain faults of taste in many of its expressions, due to strong feeling which had not yet been chastened by experience of publication. Especially a bitterness in controverting the long popular ascendancy of the Fourth Gospel over the other three gospels, and in defending as against that gospel the far more sympathetic representation of the Saviour's character which prevails in the other three gospels, occasioned me a keen regret. The book had been but a short time the subject of attack when I realised that this bitterness not only was itself an intemperance, but also suggested to the reader a slighting of the Fourth Gospel's real value and importance. Was it entirely without excuse? When I think of the eight chapter of John, and then think of the real Jesus, told of in the Sermon on the Mount and the Parable of the Prodigal Son, when I remember the crushing weight of such a verse as John iii. 36, and then call up to imagination the glories of the Divine Government as the real Jesus disclosed it, I still must remain convinced that the Fourth Evangelist has been a hard "schoolmaster," far from adequately representing his Master and King. But nevertheless he deserved very serious respect, as one who had both awakened the spirits of many to the truth, and had made an inestimable contribution to the construction of formal knowledge.

During the year that followed, however, I realised that in the acquiescence which I had thus given I had yielded too much—too much by a hair's-breadth in the terms I had consented to use, too much by a serious lapse as the real significance of the engagement into which I was understood to have entered was brought into clearness by after reflection. I had intentionally consented to make a difference, and had intentionally consented— though reluctantly—to give such a submission to the demands of the Church as involved a postponement of all further action. But the experience of the following year brought home to me rigorously that, in having at a critical moment allowed these intentional acts to be expressed by an unreserved acquiescence in a withdrawal of the book from circulation, I had, first, left my position before the public in an uncertainty which could only be injurious, and, second, had virtually done more than I had intended, namely signed away to the Church that general power in relation to my published book, which, as an individual, it was my duty as well as my right to retain. I had, indeed, made two slips. One of these was the failing to emphasise the temporary character of my engagement, the other was the failing to claim the liberty of a re-issue which would preserve the *identity* of the book. On realising this, I had it before me to try and recover

honourably the seemingly small but really considerable ground which I had lost; and as the result of
much reflection I resolved, at all hazards, while preserving my deferential attitude, to ask for a complete
end of all definite compact. Accordingly to the General
Assembly of 1897 I spoke as follows:—" Now after
a year's thought the matter of withdrawal has presented itself to me somewhat differently, and I have
a more careful response to place before this Assembly.
It is this, While I do not wish the first published form
to be republished at any time, I respectfully ask that
no special compact whatever in this matter be understood as continued; and in asking this I appeal to the
delicate appreciation of individual responsibility, as
well as to the recognition of a Protestant individual
liberty, which both must be found in the minds of my
judges. The book being, in many copies, in the hands
of a certain public as an utterance of mine, which
utterance in its essentials I am unable to disown, I
neither dare nor will for any price barter away such
liberty as may from this moment be mine, of retaining
control as to what published form may bear my own
latest signature."

Though I thus claimed freedom from all continued
compact, I was willing to continue my attitude of
deference to the extent of a very thorough-going
revision—even being agreeable to a change of title, if
the re-issue of the work under the same title might
be objected to by competent authorities within the
Church. And even though I have been, by the action
of the second General Assembly, set free from all
obligation to the Church as at present established, I
still wish to act in the spirit of my former deference
and submission. Accordingly I have subjected the

work to the most careful revision, and, before re-issuing, have let such time elapse as seemed to me becoming. in the circumstances.

I now, however, let the book go freely into the hands of the public again, in its revised form, desiring to do justice, first, to certain inquirers interested in its subject and its treatment, to whom I have incurred some responsibility through the issue of the first edition; second, to myself, as being so far, owing to the withdrawal, judged by the public largely at second hand; and, third, to the great causes of Knowledge and Religion, in regard to which causes such faults of expression as have seemed to me to have been truly found would be ill confessed if not publicly corrected, and in behalf of which causes no man, I apprehend, has the right to offer arrested and undone work if the opportunity still remains to him to restore and complete. In other words, I republish my book, considering it right to do so, with such corrections and improvements as seem to me to be demanded, partly with the wish to make equally accessible to all and to rectify, where there may be necessity, an already published utterance, and partly with my original purpose, namely, to help in the advance of inquiry and knowledge regarding the most important of all subjects, therein also helping in the reconstruction for modern times of our benign Christian faith.

For I do remain convinced of the importance of the work to which this purpose is applied. The modern movements which this book has tried to take account of are there around us; I cannot understand a Protestant Christian position which does not attempt to relate these movements to our historic faith. Negative movements are there—some among special investigators, such as that, for example, which is interpreting anew the origin of the Gospel of John, and explaining anew the divergences of that work from the other gospels, others among multitudes of thoughtful persons outside as well as within the band of special theological scholars, such as that, for example, which is measuring anew the amount of importance attributable to the reality of miracles, in the prevalent sense of the word. Positive movements are also there, notably the increased consideration of men and women for the fate of their fellows, involving a corporate instead of an individual cry for help, and, combined with this, the increased estimate of the importance of a faith in nothing less than a Divine care for all. And how have these movements of both kinds been dealt with, for the time, by those who condemned this book? Since the publication of the earlier form, the comment of assailants regarding the whole conception and general view of the book has been largely in accordance with the words which I quoted in my earlier preface from Michelet's life of Luther, depicting the mistaken confidence with which the original Protestant movement was viewed by the Church. "Ever since the thirteenth century," says Michelet speaking of the Papacy, "men had been disputing with it, had been railing against it, but apparently with no effect. The world, it imagined, had been quietly and permanently lulled to sleep by the dull and uniform clatter of the schools. It seemed as though scarcely anything new remained to be said about the matter."* Similarly now the complacent comment is, All these things were said long ago by the "Deists," the old "Rationalists," the "Tübingen

* Engl. Tr. p. 18, c. 2.

School," and so forth, and they have long ago been answered. But let it be that there is some little grain of truth in such asseverations. It is a lifeless, a deplorably somnolent, course to follow, this merely "answering" discoveries and developments. The "answers" may indeed render a service in moderating the work of advance; but the discoveries remain, and the unfoldings of thought nourish and delight the few who cultivate them. The sound method of preserving the dear articles of our faith is not by "answering," but by adapting the expressions of faith to the developments of thought and the discoveries in knowledge.

Especially mistaken, I must still maintain, was the assault on the reverent study of the Saviour's *human* nature. That assault was not in accordance with the true genius of our religion. Indeed, meaning no shadow of offence towards those who hastily joined in it, I cannot but think it was an unconscious assertion of that *representationist* class of religion to which both the Jewish and the Christian religions have in every fresh awakening opposed themselves. The true Christian position is recognition of the Eternal and Incomprehensible as manifested in a human life that was entirely real.* And with this it combines recognition of a human ideal as embodied and figured in the same human life. Surely if the real human nature of the historical Jesus were more appreciatively comprehended—the real human nature, with the human anguish, the human endeavour, and the human victory—there would be also a better comprehension of how there was more than the human at work all through, and of how there is more than the human still to trust in, and both the hope in Jesus and the salvation of our race by Jesus would

* See Westminster Confession, viii. 2 elucidated by ii. 1.

enter on a new stage of achievement more glorious than any that had preceded it.

The work appears essentially the same as before. Also the re-writing is merely in special places; and those who appreciated the earlier form may find little difference in the later. The slightness of the change, however, is ascribable to the continued fixedness of my views on the subject in general, and does not, I think I may maintain, take away from the spirit of my submission to the temporary and formal withdrawal· While willing to revise, and to meet all reasonable criticism, I have thought anything like a complete recasting to be both uncalled for and in all respects inadvisable. I have made alterations (1) in the way of removing that mischievous element of bitterness which I have mentioned, (2) in the way of giving expression to a very few real changes of opinion on details, of which a notable case is the interpretation of the "bridegroom" sayings in the gospels, and (3) in the direction of improving some of the expressions— especially of avoiding all unessential statement of the kind which has proved itself to irritate and offend the earnest of certain modes of thinking.* Instead of a short introductory note and some short supplementary explanations regarding the gospels, I have essayed a critical introduction to the whole work. I have also divided one chapter into two ; and two sets of material I have enlarged so as to make two chapters which may

---

* I have pleasure in acknowledging obligation to many persons who, both in public and in private, have criticised the details of expression in the earlier form. While the censures of these have not all seemed to me to be just, a number of them have prompted improvements which I have made gladly. At the head of these critics stands my old teacher, Professor Dickson, for whose discussion (adverse) I hereby express indebtedness.

be looked on as almost entirely new, namely "The
Bread of Life" and "The Divinity of Jesus." I wish
that from this time those few bitter expressions which
I have apologised for and eliminated be considered as
re-called, and, on their account, inasmuch as otherwise
this new publication is virtually the same book as the
earlier, I wish the earlier form of my book to be
considered as entirely superseded by this later.

Under the head of the third line of alteration which
I have just spoken of, comes the somewhat more
restrained expression on the subject of "miracle."
I should like to make clear, in regard to this subject,
two things; first, that, my aim not being to unsettle
faith, but to promote faith, I do not wish to remove
from any one's thought any association which is really
helping faith; second, that my antagonism is not
directed against the belief in miracles, but against the
belief that faith in God as revealed in Jesus Christ
requires the miracles of the past to prove it, and
against that wrong conception of miracles according to
which it is supposed that in miracles God interrupts,
as if by after-thought, His own government, or more
properly, His own overruling. *Miracle* is a relative
term, but a term expressing a sound conception. Its
value is truly estimated only as one adheres to and
does not go beyond its derivative meaning of *a
wonderful thing.* A miracle, properly speaking, is an
occurrence which, being beyond the knowledge of the
universe attained by a particular age or by particular
individuals, calls forth recognition and worship of the
Supreme Overruler. It may be partly explainable by
further knowledge; but it was, none the less, a miracle
or wonderful thing for those who first regarded it, and
their consequent sentiment of worship was based on

no delusion, but on a sound and wise ascription
of everything which excites admiration and gratitude
to the Supreme as ultimate explanation. The most
ordinary class of miracles is that of answers to personal
prayer; and such miracles it is both error and loss to
slight or disbelieve. The most extraordinary miracles
ever related are the New Testament miracles of visions
of the dead as risen ; and to explain, in some measure,
or to analyse these, is not to take away from their
trueness and importance. *Particular miracle-narratives*,
however, are to be considered in distinctness from
the general consideration of the term miracle. They
are ever coloured by the ways of thinking and by
the ways of communication of the particular age or
particular individuals that witnessed the miracle.
They thus are made up in part by the record of a
real event and in part by a natural upbuilding of local
and temporal thoughts. It is permissible for an after-
age to analyse these particular miracle-narratives,
subtract the local and temporal thoughts, and express
the original event through the help of thought more
cosmopolitan.

The title of the book is virtually the same as before.
The subject is Jesus Christ, called "the Saviour" by
all of us who seek to serve Him, both those within the
Churches and those without the Churches—Jesus
Christ, the Saviour, viewed reverently by the aid of
"the newer light." By "the newer light" I mean the
illumination which during this century has brought a
better understanding of the Divine Nature than was
possessed in the earlier ages of our country's history—
that illumination which has produced one kind of
awakening in the thoughts of our own Erskine,
Campbell, Maurice, Kingsley, Macdonald, and the rest,

another in the New Testament Criticism of Germany, and still another, combining the natures of these other two, in such works of both science and piety as the great life of Jesus by Keim, and a lately born already expanding class of works in our own country. If the historical views stated in this book are even in the main correct, we who gratefully receive the illumination of which I have just spoken are justified in the conviction not only that that illumination has been brought about in the growth of thought through the overruling of an ever-kind Providence, but also that its emergence even thus late can be traced back to the earthly life and the historical personality which these pages are seeking earnestly to bring before the understanding. The newer is better than the older not as if there were nothing in common between the two, but because the same historical power which first so far opened to the eye the life that is beyond the surface of things has in later times still steadily borne on that life, so as to disclose its qualities the more clearly. The newer light has shone not only on the unseen life still around us, but also on the historical life of Jesus and on the four gospels; and it has disclosed most important fresh phenomena in both. In the former it has disclosed a far richer picture of heroic and saintly human character, a strength of personality, and a perfection of gentleness, purity, and compassion, which all both awakens a new devotion and admiration towards the Man Jesus, and also both strengthens and increases the content of the theological doctrines connected with Him. In the latter it has disclosed the distinction between the representation and the reality, between four literary and doctrinal accounts and a Figure seen through them all and behind them

all, so great, so sublime, that none of the representations
is adequate for it.   This book is *a study* of the Saviour
in the newer light.

While the work is a direct study, based on the four
gospels themselves, I have to repeat my acknowledgment of an indebtedness much beyond what is
indicated by the detailed references which I give in
the margin, to the great labourers in sacrifice and love
whose gifts for the traveller in the regions of Biblical
Study are like those of the inventors of the steam
engine and the railway line.   Specially, without
presuming to interpret them, I mention my obligation
to Professor Holtzmann, to Keim, the illustrious
German historian of the life of Jesus, to Pfleiderer,
whose venerable voice was lately heard among ourselves, and to Weizsäcker, Wittichen, Weiss, Wendt,
Hausrath, and O. Holtzmann, along with others
nearer home, whose names, if I do not mention them,
I none the less cherish in gratefulness.

My little book will have a success more than worthy
of it, and compensating for much painful experience
in connection with its first attempts to live, if in ever
so few minds and ever so humble it even suggests
the healthfulness, the charm, and the beneficence of
that freer study of Theology which has arisen in our
time, and of its one special department, the reverent
but critical study of the Bible.   Can it be that my
fellow-ministers, by so large a majority as appeared,
have no sympathetic response for my purpose?   Can
it be that a line of inquiry and discovery so pure
and elevating in subject matter, and so bright in hope
and promise for the dearest human interests, as that
which this book attempts to follow, will continue to be
regarded as menacing anything that in real experience

has been found sacred? May one not, rather, entertain a wish to see much increase, beyond even what of late years has emerged, both of general interest and of direct labour in relation to the field of thought with which this book has to do ?   There is surely desirable an increase of activity which would involve many distinct personal efforts, differing according to the many kinds of talent, attainment, and points of view, united in earnestness and in the belief that through the Christian revelation the Most High has indeed become rationally known and rationally knowable.

In conclusion, I trust that there will not be repeated by any true Christian the allegation of this book being an instrument in the service of unbelief. It is published in the service of the gospel, whether it is really rendering good service or ill-service. God forgive us all, of one side and the other side, such errors as in our endeavours we may stumble into! The book is not addressed to, and need not be read by, such persons as are already satisfied with their enlightenment and their attainments. But those who may love and worship the Master while recognising the changes and advances in modern thought, I respectfully ask, as I did before, to accompany me in a pilgrimage of thought, through the representations of intervening years, towards the real earthly life of Him who in these late days is still the source of light and the centre for faith.

January, 1898.

CONTENTS

CONTENTS

PART III

THE LAST DAYS

PART IV

CONCLUSION

APPENDIX

INTRODUCTION

KNOWLEDGE of the Saviour is based on the four
gospels. The four gospels have come down to us in
manuscripts of which the earliest dates from the fourth
Christian century. Both the previous history and the
origin of the works have to be determined by the nature
of their own contents, by such allusions to them as
may be found in other ancient writings, and by the
general estimate which may be arrived at after comparison of both these elements.

That the gospels are early writings can be easily
established from such sources of information. For
certainty on this point it is enough to appeal to the
gospels themselves, along with the indubitable evidence
which exists of their having been known and revered
in early Christian times. It has been proved beyond
question that so early as the second century the gospels Collective
evidence
were venerated much as they have been in the later in the
Christian ages ; and their language, manner of thought, works of
Westcott,
and points of view join with that consideration in Tregelles,
&c.
placing them, broadly speaking, very near the time of
the events with which they deal. Also it can be very
well made out that there are few additions and few
blemishes in the forms in which we have them. But
for what is beyond this general position the evidence is,
at first sight, disappointing. Of evidence regarding
the particular origin of the gospels, from other works,
contemporary or immediately succeeding, modern
investigators have found but a meagre supply. Indeed,

1

putting aside mere quotations and references that may give indications in a general way, there is only one piece of testimony which has in recent times been much built upon. It is found in the Church History of Eusebius, written early in the fourth century, and consists of a quotation from *Papias*, who was bishop of Hierapolis in Asia in the early part of the second century. It runs thus: "And the Elder (*presbyteros*, previously alluded to as John) said this, Mark, being the interpreter of Peter wrote accurately as many things as he called to mind, not, however, in the order in which they were either spoken or done by the Christ (or the words may mean, not, however, in order, being the things either spoken or done by the Christ). For he neither heard the Lord nor followed him; he later followed Peter, as I have said, and the latter was accustomed to form his teaching for particular needs, not making a collection of the Lord's words (*kuriakon logon*, or in another reading *logion*, sayings). So that Mark did not do any wrong having thus written some things as he called them back to mind. For of one thing he took care, not to pass over anything of what he heard, or to falsify anything in it." And of Matthew, adds Eusebius, this was said by Papias, "Matthew, then (*oun*), in the Hebrew dialect wrote together the sayings (*ta logia*), and every one interpreted them as he was able ".

Another passage, however, little less ancient, has an importance, though its direct evidential value must be pronounced to be limited. *Irenaeus*, bishop of Lyons, writing later in the second century, gives this account of the four gospels :—

"Matthew put forth a gospel scripture among the

Died 340.

Eus. Bk. iii. c. 39.

Died 202, or about that time.

Hebrews in their own dialect, while Peter and Paul were preaching at Rome and founding the Church.

"After the departure of these (apostles), Mark, again, the disciple and interpreter of Peter, also himself handed on to us through writing what had been preached by Peter.

"Luke, again, the follower of Paul, set down in a book the gospel preached by that (apostle).

"Then afterwards John, the disciple of the Lord, who leaned on his bosom, also himself put forth the (or, a) gospel while staying at Ephesus in Asia ". *Ir. on Heresies, iii. 1.*

Now while this passage does not, like the extract from Papias, name an authority more ancient than the writer himself, and while, further, Irenaeus generally speaking does not show the careful accuracy that inspires great confidence, the passage has this importance, that it must be looked at as in some way expressing the belief of the Church in Irenaeus's time.

The view thus expressed by Irenaeus, conjoined with the belief in our received gospels being the four works alluded to by him, remains to this day the view of many Christians, including the learned and the pious as well as the more careless. But among those who have inquired earnestly into the special subject, at least within Protestant Christianity, the view has been in most cases greatly departed from. Soon after the Sacred Books became the property of the public, there began a rigorous scrutiny which, first appearing only in isolated quarters as negative criticisms and rival theories, has gradually been forming itself into certain distinct scientific conclusions ; and these conclusions, it seems not too much to say, are ever more and more gaining acceptance. Even one of the most conserva-

Weiss,
Leben
Jesu, I.,
p. 101.

tive of recent Biblical scholars, speaking specially of the relations between the fourth gospel and the other three, characterises the ancient way of dealing with the matter as "naïve". The modern mind has asked, Do the gospels themselves, when seriously examined, admit of that ancient view being taken of them? And the answer which, as may be affirmed, is ever extending and ever growing more decided is at least in part a negative one.

Two statements may be hazarded as expressing what may now be called preliminary scientific certainties, namely :— .

(1) The *likeness* between the first three gospels is of such a kind that one is forced to modify the idea of their being entirely independent witnesses.

(2) The *unlikeness* between the fourth gospel and the other three is of such a kind that one is forced to modify the idea of its being a witness at all of the history pure and simple.

An alarm, not unnatural, has arisen in many quarters over these positions. And this alarm often gives way to the contemptuous question, Could it be that, if such things were true, Christendom would only now be finding them out? The question is easily answered by a proper understanding of the development of history.

English
works
giving
various
details,
Woods in
Studia
Biblica,
Gould in
Interna-
tional
Critical
Com-
mentary,

And the alarm may yet find a better refuge, namely in the discovery that all our dearest convictions and faiths are not destroyed but the more securely built up by the newer knowledge of the gospels.

Of the two scientific positions just stated the first is based on these discoveries :—

(*A*) That the first three gospels, though written in a different language from that which, almost beyond question, was ordinarily spoken by the actors in the occurrences, are in large portions almost word for word the same as one another,

(*B*) That in their differences certain principles can largely be detected, pointing to one original and explaining the departures from the original,

(*C*) That the choice of occurrences is very nearly the same, though there must have happened much more of importance, and

(*D*) That the arrangement is greatly the same, though it is sometimes of an unusual kind.

The other position is based on such discoveries as these :—

(*A*) That in John the whole manner of thought and the whole manner of expression ascribed to Jesus are different from the case of the other gospels—the thought being in the one case ethical and religious, in the other metaphysical, and the expression being in the one case terse and imaginative, in the other argumentative and using the terms of a philosophy prevailing in the period,

(*B*) That the subjects ordinarily handled by Jesus are generically different—in the one case the Divine Presence, the Fatherhood of God, and the message to the unfortunate and the sinful, in the other the Person of the Son, the distinction between the elect and the world, and the message to the elect,

(*C*) That the opponents are differently viewed—the Pharisees and Scribes being the opponents in the one case, with Herod as an ally, while in the other case the Jews as a nation seem to stand opposed to Jesus,

(*D*) That the character of Jesus on the human side is

[marginal notes:] Campbell, First Three Gospels, &c. &c.

Ex. see Mt. xi. 21, work in Chorazin, &c. (Holtzmann). Specl. ex. Mt. xiv. and Mk. vi. See also Mt. xvii. and Mk. ix.

The so-called Alexandrian philosophy. See, in Engl. the works of Tayler, Davidson, Matthew Arnold, Haweis, and of German works specially those of Holtzmann, O. Holtzmann, Hausrath, Keim (tr.).

also see
Schürer in
"Contem-
porary Re-
view,"
Sept. 1891.

different in the two cases—it being at least difficult to reconcile the figure in the eighth chapter of John with the figure in the incidents of the earnest scribe and the meeting with Zacchaeus, or with the speaker of the Sermon on the Mount and the parable of the Prodigal Son,

Ex. Mk. ii.
1-12, in Jn.
v. 1-16, Mk.
vi. 3, in Jn.
vi. 42, Mk.
viii. 29, in
Jn. vi.
68-69.

(E) That while thought, expression, and subjects are different, the subjects of the other three gospels appear largely in John as a kind of disregarded background, and

See above-
mentioned
works.

(F) That the narrative in John has details of time and place irreconcilable with those given by the others.

All these considerations have to be taken along with the broad result of comparison, that if a choice must be made between the other three gospels and the fourth in regard to historical credibility, both internal and external evidence decide in giving the preference to the other three gospels.

The older
view of the
Fourth
Gospel is
defended
notably
by Lut-
hardt,
Meyer,
Weiss,
Godet,
Sanday;
but these
able
writers
make
important
conces-
sions.

From these preliminary positions with their negative character, a multitude of truth-seeking pilgrims have advanced by many paths, the description of which could fill many volumes, leading, as there is good reason now almost to assert, in the direction of certain fixed positive positions.

In defining these positive positions, it is necessary to say at the outset that they hardly include the case of the Fourth Gospel. While there is ample evidence of a tendency to go beyond the negative conclusion above stated, and find still a purely historical contribution in the Fourth Gospel, there cannot be said to be unanimity as to the way in which this further attainment is to be reached. And so, many of the most competent critics and scholars have been inclined to put the Fourth

Gospel quite aside for the historical question, and lay the firmer hold on the data of the other three. We shall be driven to enquire more closely into this matter further on. Meanwhile it is enough to say that for lovers of the Fourth Gospel this treatment loses its offence when there is fully recognised the thought which is in some degree common to all modern scholars, namely, that that work is essentially a *Christian Study*, that not historical facts but doctrines are its theme, and that, if it does not give the exact words and actions of the historical Jesus, still the majority of its ideas, albeit expressed in a literary form of the evangelist's own, have their origin in an inspiration from the Eternal Life that in Jesus was specially manifested.

It is, however, in regard to the other three gospels, called generally the SYNOPTIC gospels, that fixed positive ground may with much justification be claimed to have been reached. It may now be almost asserted that the movement of Protestant Christian thought is towards the acknowledgment, already come to by many most accomplished and unwearied investigators, that, while the first three gospels have not been quite independent of one another in their origin, they represent *two* original independent written sources. And the two sources thus recognised are identified by many with the two works alluded to in the extract already quoted from the bishop Papias. So that the testimony of Papias, unlike that of Irenaeus in his fuller statement, is in this acknowledgment almost fully accepted, it being only noticed that of the works he alludes to the second is not our Matthew, but a Hebrew or Aramaic work by the Apostle Matthew now lost, while the other is either our Mark or a work which our Mark has very closely followed.

To sketch briefly how this view has been come to—
the interdependence of the first three gospels being
started from, various hypotheses have been resorted to
in order to explain it. And while many of the most
illustrious modern scholars have defended one or other
of such hypotheses so strenuously as to seem to be of
irreconcilable difference of opinion, their united labour
has all been bringing to light certain facts on which
the view just stated is based by its supporters.

That we have in our Gospel according to St. Mark,
as it stands or very nearly as it stands, a very ancient
document made use of by the authors of the first gospel
and of the third, is a conclusion based on such facts as
these :—

(*A*) That a natural development of events is seen
in Mark where Matthew and Luke are plainly more
artificial,

(*B*) That the human character of Jesus is much more
prominent in Mark than in either of the other two,
and

(*C*) That in many particular cases of likeness and
difference there can be shown, from comparison of the
text alone, and with a clearness hardly admitting the
possibility of mistake, an altering process on the side
of Matthew.

To bring these out in some small detail,—

These considera-tions brought out in detail in above-mentioned works. See also Rush-

(*A*) The special example of the natural development
of events in Mark is the gradual assuming of the office
of the Messiah on the part of Jesus, with his forbidding
the name to be applied at first, and the gradual
conviction on the part of the apostles. This may be
said to be absent from Luke, and by Matthew it is at
least neglected, in his didactic setting forth of Jesus in

the character of the Messiah from the beginning. The common order prevailing in Matthew and Mark is most departed from in the earlier portion of the narrative. And the difference there between the two gospels becomes quite intelligible when it is supposed that the First Evangelist, in his aim of artistically setting forth Jesus as the Messiah, has neglected the gradual manner in which he was recognised as such, and has made the narrative as before him in Mark yield a little, first to the presentation of the new law from the Mount, then to an establishing in detail of the fact that Jesus raised the dead, and restored the blind and the dumb, leading up to the message of Jesus to John the Baptist, and lastly to the ceremonious sending forth of apostles. The state of matters that exists would not be so intelligible were it supposed that Matthew was first, and that Mark, following Matthew, had omitted the Sermon on the Mount, had postponed the story of Jairus's daughter, had omitted the message to John, had broken up the sayings to disciples, and, having done all this, had given a narrative still so spontaneous and so true to ordinary laws of growth and advance as that which meets us in the Second Gospel. And even if it were at all admissible to resort to the idea that Mark was so great a literary artist as himself to impart the development to his narrative, this would be met by the fact that the development appears also in Matthew, but there with interruptions, suggesting not a less elaborated form, but a new form disregarding the point of development. All this, further, is supported by the way in which Matthew resumes Mark's order after it has been departed from, with the phrases "at that time" and "when Jesus had ended these sayings"—

brooke, Synopticon. Very exhaustive treatment in Holtzmann's Introduction and Commentary

See Mk. viii. 29 and Mt. xvi. 15 ff. and cp. Mt. xii. 23. xiv. 33.

xii. 1, vii. 28.

strongly suggestive of a selection of material. **The** *general* example of the natural development of events seen in **Mark is to be** found in the circumstantial occurrence in Mark of sayings virtually **the same as** some of those which in Matthew **and** Luke are set within formal speeches.

See Mk. iv. 21-22, xi. 25, xiii. 11.

(*B*) As regards the **human** character, while all three represent Jesus as having **been moved by** human feelings, and even as having been subjected to human limitations, Mark brings in, where **the others do not,** that he was "moved with compassion," that he looked round "with anger," that the spirit "driveth" him, that he "could not be hid," and that he received *approval* from the earnest scribe.   These touches might indeed be referred by some to a process of pictorial finishing which **has been** ascribed to Mark in general; but against such **a way of** explaining them are many considerations. For one thing, the whole tendency of the early literature can be seen to be **towards emphasing** the Divine in Jesus, not the **human ; and as this** tendency **is by** no means absent from the **Gospel of** Mark itself, one cannot well maintain **the** author to have **been** an exception with respect **to it.** Besides, these **touches are** so well supported **by** the spirit of Jesus's sayings in all three gospels, as having been true to the history, that it is far more natural to believe them to have emerged **with an** original narrative than to suppose them to have been added afterwards by ever so clever a hand.

For the others see Mt. xiv. 13 and Lk. vii. 9 ; but for Mk. alone see i. 41, iii. 5, i. 12, vii. 24, xii. 34 ; also v. 30 and x. 21. See Weizsäcker, Untersuchungen, pp. 51-62. Cp. Keim, I., 129 (Engl. tr.).

See Mk. ix. 3, xv. 39, &c.

(*C*) A special case under heading *C* is the end of the account of the Baptist's death, with Jesus's learning of it.   Generally there fall to be noticed under this head, (*a*) the quotations from **the Old** Testament, showing a

Mk. vi. 29-30, Mt. xiv. 12-13. (a) Mt. iii.

didactic purpose in Matthew, coming in more spontaneously in Mark, (b) the abridgments in Matthew,
(c) the differences that suggest misunderstanding on the
part of Matthew, and (d) the differences that suggest
an advance of reflection and doctrine on the side of
Matthew, especially the shielding of apostles. A
similar state of matters may be made out as between
Mark and Luke; but it is hardly necessary to have
recourse to textual comparison in the case of Mark and
Luke; for the posteriority of Luke is sufficiently proved
by its doctrinal arrangement, and, posteriority being
granted, the author's use of at least either Mark or
something very like Mark follows from the likeness
between the two gospels.

It being, then, first recognised that Matthew and
Luke have used either our Mark or a document which
our Mark has closely followed, it is a simple movement
of thought which next recognises a second written
source besides Mark. Matthew and Luke have likenesses not only where they follow Mark, but also where
they give material that Mark has not preserved. And
this state of things can be explained neither by the one
having used the other nor by both having followed oral
tradition, as the independence of presentation in the
case of each author is too great for the former supposition, and the fixedness of the material is too
decided for the latter. A common written source,
therefore, remains as the only explanation. Various
questions, indeed, have been discussed and differently
answered in regard to this other source : Was it only
known to the two authors in Aramaic, or was it a
Greek work or a Greek translation ? Did the two have
it in the same form, or had it already, before they

1-3, Mk. i.
1-4, Mt.
xiii. 13-17,
Mk. iv.
12; (b)Mk.
vi. 5, vi.
39-40, ix.
14-29. x.
32,Mt.xiii.
58, xiv. 19,
xvii.14-20,
xx. 17; (c)
Mt. iv. 21-
22, Mk. i.
19-20, and
special
case
above; (d)
Mk. iv. 38,
xii. 35, Mt.
viii. 25,
xxii. 42;
Mk. ix.
38-42.
x. 35, xvi.
7, Mt.
xviii. 5-6,
xx. 20 (cp.
v. 24),
xxviii. 7.
For Mk.
and Lk.
see Mk. i.
1-4, Lk.iii.
1-6, Mk.xi.
1, Lk. xix.
29.

See Mt.
v.-vii. and
Lk. vi.,
ix.-xix.

See above
mentioned
works;
also those
of Weiss,
Wendt,
Weiz-
säcker, &c.

began their work, assumed different forms? Did Mark himself also use it, as well as the authors of Matthew and Luke? Did it contain only sayings of Jesus ("logia"), or something of narrative also? While these questions, except the last, are principally just questions for scholars, and hardly affect the work of this book, it is necessary to take up some position in regard to them; and so it comes to be said here, the work of the following pages will proceed from this basis: That the differences between Matthew and Luke, though it is possible they are partly explainable by the existence of different forms of the original work, are mostly to be attributed to the distinct purpose which guided the authors as they selected and wove together from what was before them (this the course of the book must itself bear out); that Mark had not used the other source (this being a cumbersome idea, and incompatible with Mark's omission of so much important material); and that the original work was of a fragmentary character, containing narrative as well as sayings, though the latter was its main content (this being demanded by the differences in many places; for example, by the emphatic turns in Matthew, made much of by Dr. Keim in arguing for the priority of Matthew). Also it will be here presupposed that Luke, besides the original document, had also before him our Matthew (this being demanded by a comparison of the Sermon on the Plain with the Sermon on the Mount, the arrangement being evidently the First Evangelist's, and the " Plain " as opposed to the " Mount " having, as one is much persuaded to believe, an intentional significance).

These two documents, the Gospel of Mark and the

Mt. iv. 13, xiv. 13, xvi. 21; cp. Mk. i. 21, vi. 31, and viii. 31.

lost work by the Apostle Matthew, are sufficient to
have given origin to at least the substance of our first
three gospels. There arises, however, at this point
the further question: Are all the contents of these
gospels to be referred to the two sources now
considered? To this it may be answered, first, as
specially regards Luke, it is a difficult question to
decide whether the author may not have possessed
also a third written source, from which has come the
important material which he presents in excess of the
other two. He may have had such a source. But
it is possible to account for his extra material without
this. A comparison between the three records of the
Trial and Sufferings of the Saviour very strikingly
suggests that in regard at least to that part of the *See the parallel columns in the works of C. Campbell and Rushbrooke, above mentioned.*
history the Third Evangelist *preferred* the Apostle
Matthew source, whereas the First Evangelist preferred the account in Mark. And this further suggests
that it may have been the same all through, which
would again suggest that the Third Evangelist very
fully reproduced the Apostle Matthew source, whereas
the First Evangelist did so with more reserve. This
would account for the extra pieces in Luke, viewing
them as coming from the Apostle Matthew source.
And with this agrees the fact that many of the pieces *Cp. certain conclusions of Wendt, p. 79. § 5, &c. of "Die Lehre Jesus," part I. He instances vii. 36-48. x. 25-37. &c., as passages*
in question are very specially of a universalistic
character, which, while making intelligible their having
been grasped at and preserved by the publican Matthew,
also may well have made them unattractive to the First
Evangelist, with his palpably legalistic purpose. Nor
is this inconsistent with the fact that it was the First
Gospel, not the Third, which received from the Church
the name of the Gospel according to Matthew; for

showing a preference on the part of Lk. for the Matthew source over Mark.

this name may have become affixed to it before the Third Gospel was generally received, if not, indeed, before it was written. Beyond the special case of Luke, further, there is no need to suppose any other written source than the two, except for the separate birth accounts of Matthew and Luke, and for the separate concluding portions of the resurrection accounts in Matthew and Luke. It is, however, finally, to be recognised that a general oral tradition not

See Weizsäcker spec.

only must have interposed between the apostolic testimony and at least the Gospel of Mark, if it did not also give special forms to the Apostle Matthew collection, but must have been a concomitant factor, along with these two earlier written sources, in the production of the two later gospels besides. And this not principally in a floating condition. The oral tradition, as

See spec. Holtzmann and Caspari. See Acts xxi. 8, Ephes. iv. 11.

has been pointed out by scholars, must have been specially crystallised in didactic forms used in the services and assemblies of the Church.

What result, then, does all this lead to in regard to the credibility of the gospels as indicating historical events? The first three gospels, we have seen, are themselves very early works, and are based on two works. Of these two works the one in all probability rests on the testimony of the Apostle Peter, while the other is directly the work of the Apostle Matthew; at any rate they reach to apostolic times. As, then, their whole contents show the earnestness that asks for credence, credibility may surely be admitted for them. The interposing of the oral tradition, indeed, may seem to weaken the position — especially as there are good grounds for maintaining that this tradition, in its

Espec. in Mk. xiii.

Church forms, actually interwove foreign material in

some cases. This, however, is met, as far as concerns and in Mt xxiv. and xxv. the main facts of Jesus's life and the substance of Jesus's teaching, by the undoubted earliness of the works, which might be compatible with mistakes in detail, but hardly with any serious error. And this is greatly confirmed by the fact that, in spite of what has above been acknowledged, we can still look upon the three gospels as, for practical ends, *three independent witnesses*. That the traditional idea of independence has to be modified, we have seen. And it may appear as if our three witnesses are resolved altogether into two for the case of the teaching, and possibly even into one for the case of the framework of events, inasmuch as it may be maintained that the Apostle Matthew source was a mere collection of sayings. It has been said above, however, that in this work the latter opinion will not be recognised; and the remark may be See Holtz-mann, Einlei-tung, p. 350. hazarded that the prevailing scholarship and criticism are not likely to bear out that opinion. But further, what is mainly to be noticed is that the earliness of the works involves an independence on such important matters as the substance of the teaching and the framework of events. Indeed, in view of this, the very fact of their community brings the independence on such cardinal matters into relief. What we have is a case of three writers, of whom two had the other's work before them, which two freely departed from the other's work in many respects and to a very considerable degree, but nevertheless *acquiesced in regard to a strongly marked substance of teaching and a general framework of time, place, and order of occurrences*. This substance of teaching, thus, and this framework are, in a way, more emphatically attested than if they had appeared in three spontaneous writings ; for they have stood the test of vigorous handling, and, where other matters have been taken liberties with, have remained fixed, under the hands of three men living at a time when knowledge of them was still fresh.

It may be objected, indeed, to the last point that, as regards the framework of time and place, the same argument might be applied to the Fourth Gospel, which is also an early work, and that, inasmuch as it has broken down this framework, the testimony of the other three is weakened.   But this is, first, to be answered confidently by pointing out that the Fourth Evangelist, having a special end in view, shows a complete carelessness on the subject of time and place, quite different from the simplicity of narrative of the other three, and putting him, as regards this question, out of the list of witnesses.   And further, the course of the study will show that, recognising this carelessness, one can detect the Synoptic framework in the Fourth Gospel also.

So, many earnest workers have recently laboured to present the picture of the Saviour's life and teaching by means of reproducing the original documents, and subtracting those elements which comparison and criticism plainly declare to be the accretions of tradition or of

C. Witti-chen and Prof. Wendt of Heidel-berg.

doctrinal purpose.   And at least two of these workers have, with unwearied labour and masterly ingenuity, aimed at even a high measure of accuracy in this task.

Now if the life of Jesus were a mere ordinary life, our introductory survey might stop here.   The state of matters which we have had before us in regard to the gospels, is enough for a very sure knowledge to be based on it regarding a quite certain figure in the past.

And such reproducing and corrective labour as has just
been alluded to, even if in many points possibly mistaken, is enough to present us both with a considerable
amount of information of virtually absolute certainty,
and also with much more that, if not quite sure, is
as certain as what is known regarding any other
historical figure so far removed from us in time. But
inasmuch as the life has not been an ordinary life—
inasmuch as it been a power in the world such as no
other life has been, and has been accepted as indicative
of a circle of facts in the profounder regions of
reality, there arise, at this stage, the following critical
considerations:—

(1) So far as we have come, certainty as to the
teaching that fell from the sacred lips and certainty as
to what was accomplished by the sacred will are
subjected to the decision of an intricate external
investigation; and convincing in great degree as the
investigation has shown itself, its certainties remain
probable certainties, the mind leaping from received
documents to a lost document, and again from the lost
document itself to the audience of the Master. Such
a way of arriving at a fixed position does not satisfy
religious faith. And so, thus far modern knowledge,
while making away with the old standing ground of
verbal inspiration, does not provide us with a new rest
for the heart's devotion.

(2) The stage we have reached, with its purely
objective evidence, leaves least completely attested
precisely some of the sayings and actions of the
Saviour which have most appealed to our race, namely
those coming to us in single presentations in the
Gospel of Luke.

2

(3) The consigning of the Fourth Gospel to the purely doctrinal sphere, while satisfactory and salutary taking it as a whole, is not the end of the matter as regards its details. The recognition of purely historical information independently conveyed in it, cannot be abandoned.

Now here there presents itself the very important question, Are these defects to be made right by further advance in objective investigation? or, taking the three considerations separately, may we hope that the first want will yet be met by accumulation of identical results and a strengthening of unanimity? may we hope that the second will be met by the discovery of further external testimony, or of further phenomena in the testimony which we possess, bringing to all of the important passages a similarly adequate quantity of securities? and may we hope, as regards the last difficulty, that the work of certain mediating labourers will yet prevail in the case of the Fourth Gospel, and that in it too an independent source, tangible and fixed, will receive as willing a recognition as the Mark source and the Apostle Matthew source?

Most notable, Wendt, and in England Arnold, Haweis; but the special views of these are not adopted here in the sequel.

Doubtless there is still much to be hoped for in the advance of objective labour. And especially in regard to the Fourth Gospel question, it may be here stated that this work, in this form as in its earlier form, will recognise within the Fourth Gospel an independent historical document, which the evangelist has enlarged on as a text for his doctrinal presentation. A very notable question in relation to the existence of such an independent source, is the question whether the author of the Fourth Gospel made use of the earlier gospels. For if he did, then it may with great force be maintained that these other gospels were sufficient to provide the historical material which forms his starting-point. And on few subjects have scholars of all shades of thinking shown more unanimity than in holding that he was at least acquainted with the Synoptic Gospels. In the earlier form of this work the contrary opinion was maintained ; and in restating it acknowledgment must be made of what, not without reason, may be deemed continued rashness or fool-hardiness. The ground on which the generally rejected opinion rests, that the evangelist did not make use of the earlier gospels, is this, that in the cases where the same occurrences as are told of in the other gospels unmistakably appear in the Fourth Gospel in a new dress, the ideal clothing so transforms them that, were we to believe the evangelist had before him such complete works as our other gospels, or even the narratives adopted by our other gospels in anything like the form they now possess, we should be accusing him of an arbitrariness, a wilful disrespect, and a heedless license, in regard to generally accepted representations, all to an extent which can scarcely be considered suitable to the promptings of a lofty purpose; and that he allowed himself such is surely, in view of the earnest-ness of his work, hardly credible. This point is, indeed, in some way met by supposing that it was only at second-hand that the evangelist knew those other gospels, or that, in writing, he had them only before his memory. Here, however, an attempt will be made to bring out, as the study proceeds, that the original of the Fourth Gospel was a fragmentary collection of material preserved by the Apostle John (hence the tradition), keeping in touch with the repetitions of

Cp. Jn. vi. 70-71, w. Mk. viii. 33; Jn. viii. 52-58, w. Mk. xii. 18-27; Jn. x. 40, w. Mk. xi. 27-33, &c. Wendt, "Die Lehre Jesu," I., 332.

See Jn. xix. 35, xxi. 24.

2 *

Peter and the other disciples long enough to preserve
a certain community of diction with these, then com-
mitted to writing still in its fragmentary condition,
and finally used by the philosophical writer, whoever
he may have been, who has left to future ages a work
so complex and so hard to explain.

Even holding, however, that we are possessed of this
further source, our difficulties are not diminished; for
now, added to the intricate but comparatively definable
work of severing the original sayings and events from
three presentations very like one another, there comes
a new, far more subtle work of severance, namely, no
less than a severance of the original material in the
Fourth Gospel from a superimposed body of doctrine,
which has taken the very greatest literary liberties
with the narrative for the sake of expressing its own
thoughts.   And so, bringing in the Fourth Gospel to
help us, we only, in an already intricate path towards
certainty, find more intricacies of a greater degree of
difficulty.

But just at this point of seeming bewilderment, we
are forced into an altogether new set of methods of
knowledge, which clear the whole situation.   The very
irritation and the very sense of absurdity which must
arise over the discovery that many pre-suppositions
found to be so healthful and so stimulating as applied
to practical life are so difficult to confirm scientifically,
suggest the thought, *There must be a new set of scientific
principles altogether* which are available to supplement
the objective labour thus far considered.

There are principles of a different kind which must
now be mentioned as available for accurate knowledge
of the historical life of Jesus.   They are partly such as

might be resorted to in regard to any life in the past ; but partly also they have a special existence in relation to the one life. They are these :—

(1) The general Impression made by Jesus on the world, as seen specially in the early Christian writings, but further also in subsequent history, is a canon not only for the determination of the significance of his life, but also for interpreting the records of his life. This principle may rightly be looked at as a scientific equivalent for the Traditional Authority of the Catholic Church. *Cp. Weizsäcker in his Untersuchungen.*

(2) The recorded events as a whole present a *picture*, satisfying all laws of logic, of which, however, the component parts are scattered among the four gospels ; and it is reasonable and permissible to find the history through the adaptation of these parts, as their being capable of making a complete picture and their having originated in a scattered condition is inconceivable. This principle was illustrated in the earlier form of this book by the case of a *puzzle*—surely no unworthy illustration, if one but remembers how search is exacted under the Divine Government in regard to all sacred objects of knowledge—of a puzzle, say a child's picture of some Bible scene, in which the scattered portions are to be put in their places.

(3) The character as a whole presents a picture also, this time not in the material aspect of the picture, but in the aspect of its genius, coming before us as a unique, fresh entity, which no man ever can have imagined out of the combinations of fancy ; and it is reasonable and permissible to prune and correct particular records of sayings by the rule of the character as a whole. This principle might be so far *Cp. Holtzmann in the Introduction to his Commentary, and the general treatment of the Critical School, as Pfleiderer, &c.*

applied in the case of any character; but with **respect**
to that character which **comes before us in the gospels**
it has special applicability, inasmuch as the stronger
a character is **the** more must its outcomes show
unity.

On these principles, **as** filling up the **gaps in**
objective research, the **following** study reverently
proceeds. And they are sound principles. Application
of them may, indeed, at times **look like** subjective
dealing with the sources of information. **And** really
all application of them is to an extent subjective. **It**
is the receiving of the objective impression along **with**
a sympathetic and reconstructive action on the part **of**
the mind or subject. But this subjective action will be
of true value in any particular case only where it is no
mere individual **action, but has** been stimulated by the
universal movements **of thought; and** similarly any
small contribution to knowledge **that any** individual
may be enabled to present, must **itself stand the** test of
the general declaration, as being **in accord or not in**
accord with the combined testimony **of objective**
evidence and general sympathetic understanding. **In**
the case of the life of Jesus Christ, indeed, what must, in
very great part, both prompt any valuable work and also
help largely to test it, will be that general Christian
recognition which is expressed not in popular unproved
fancies, **nor even in the** phrases of creeds, **but** in the
ideals **of both public** and private Christian aspiration
and practice. All judgment, **short of that** based on
the darkest pessimism and pyrrhonism, will admit that
the ethical ideal which **is** binding together Christian
communities, both **in outward** institutions and in
secret experiences of self-examination and self-restraint,

is a witness to historical reality as regards the person of the Initiator.

The principles in question, further, are essentially the same principles as those professed for a wider range of sacred study by Protestant Christianity, and the application of them is the application to the historical life of the same principles that Protestantism demands for the whole circle of sacred truth; for the Protestant centre of authority is not the Bible as external testimony, but the Bible as illumined through spiritual influence which has traversed the universal Christian consciousness.

And finally as relates to these principles, while the objective conclusions above specified are not to be under-estimated, being indeed the presupposition and the preparation for the others, these have the power which the objective conclusions have not, of bringing virtual unanimity and certainty on the matter before us. That this is so can be seen from the fact that different contributors to the newer knowledge, whose special contentions regarding the sources of the gospels may vary considerably, are found, in respect to the life and teaching of Jesus, arriving at very much the same results. It is not, indeed, to be pretended that these latter principles, any more than the objective labour, can reproduce the teaching of the Saviour in verbal exactness, or can give any more than an undetailed presentation of the outward events; but they can give to the general comprehension of these a restful certainty, and for particulars which, without our principles, are insufficiently evidenced, they give the right either, if these particulars are repellent, to remove

For ex. cp. Holtzmann with Keim, or Prof. Bruce with Keim.

them decisively, or, if they are needed for the unity and vitality, to set them firmly in their proper places.

It remains to add to this introduction a few more special preliminary considerations.

First, it is to be noted that the gospels have all a *structure*, which has been built not for the end now before us, of seeing the history alone, but for the more complex end of setting forth the Messiah and the Gospel. Accordingly, in searching for the history, it is necessary to notice the structure carefully before attempting to abstract the historical material from it. The different evangelists have in common this plan: To show (*a*) the centralising of the Divine in the human in Jesus, (*b*) the main teaching of the Saviour, (*c*) the opposition of the authorities, (*d*) the farewell charge of the Saviour, (*e*) the death, and (*f*) the Resurrection. But having this plan in common, they use their material differently for building according to the plan. Thus, the first floor of the structure, the centralising of the Divine, is presented differently by all four evangelists; and very specially such diverse choice of material is seen in the case of the fourth floor, the farewell charge, the Synoptic writers and the Johannine writer having chosen a different set of sayings of the Master from one another altogether, to regard as the groundwork of his farewell charge. This state of matters makes a special call on the Subjective Canons above specified. It has brought about that there are to be reckoned with, in the gospels, not merely the discrepancies and the obvious divergencies which have overtaken the representations, but also a certain *artificialising* both of the

Cp. Jn. xiii.-xvii., w. Mk. xiii. ; and Mt. xxiv.- xxv.

events and even of the personality of Jesus. This artificialising we may observe quite consistently with retaining a respect for the evangelists. For the end of seeing the history pure and simple, there must be resorted to, to begin with, the criterion of *lifelikeness;* and the above-mentioned canons restrain and guide this criterion in its application to the special subject.

Again, it is to be noted that each of the gospels has a special bias and a special purpose. The emphasising, if not the discovering, of this is the glory of the famous " Tübingen School " of fifty years ago ; and while many of the theories and particular conclusions of the great Dr. Baur and the other representatives of the School have been set aside, it is a grave error to underestimate this matter of the " tendencies " in the gospels, which they brought into the foreground. Of particular influences creating bias the leading scholars of the present day have laid stress on two, namely, first, the immense veneration of the Israelite for the Old Testament, substance and form, along with the mystical interpretation of both its predictions and its narratives, and, second, the already growing types of apostolic teaching. These have affected all the evangelists more or less; and both these and other influences have worked with the evangelists' original activity, so as to make four special lines of tendency. Thus, the Evangelist Mark, seeking to show simply that Jesus was the Messiah, gives his narrative in such a way as to bring forward, without either straining or departing from fact, the *power* of Jesus's personality. The First Evangelist, again, emphasises the *purity* or the *moral kingship* of Jesus.

Prof. Bruce's book, " With Open Face," may be consulted on the characteristics of the Evangelists.

But strictly faithful to truth as his representation must be pronounced to be in essentials, he permits himself a background of scholarly detail, which is national and, more or less, arbitrary. He presents Jesus's appearance as a continuance from the old dispensation, and in doing so strains Old Testament quotations to prove, in the ways of his time, that this appearance was in every detail foreseen, gives the teaching in a collective view as a Sermon from the Mount, like the old Law from the Mount, and transmits some of the sayings in legalistic forms, or with legalistic interpretations, unknown in Mark, separating, for the future, the guilty from the innocent, the cursed from the blessed. The Third Evangelist, next, in marked distinction from the First, though not in essential divergence, brings out the *compassion* of Jesus, and the compassion of the Sovereign Power whom Jesus revealed. Then lastly the Fourth Evangelist, influenced by philosophical views as the others are not, seeks to set forth the genuineness of Jesus's life as a special outcome of the Eternal and Unchangeable. In doing this, he ignores far the greater part of the historical life and teaching. Where are the parables in the Fourth Gospel? where are the Good Samaritan, the Lost Sheep, and the Sower? where are the name of our Heavenly Father, the message to the unfortunate and the sinful, the beatitudes, the sitting at meat with publicans, and the love for enemies? The Fourth Gospel has sacrificed history to doctrine, and were we to read the work as purely historical, we should find even the character which we worship perplexingly transformed from the majestic simplicity that belonged to it as we are assured from reading the other gospels.

See espec. ii. 23 and xxvii. 9.

Spec. cp. Mt. xxv. 46, w. Mk. ix. 49.

See vi. 29, v. 20-22, vi. 44, viii. 21-24, 33-44, 55.

Let all respect be paid to this gospel. But let those who refuse to have it corrected, for historical questions, by the earlier representations, remember that they are becoming responsible for defending the literal historicity not only of the fourteenth and seventeenth chapters, but also of the eighth chapter. Really, the eighth chapter of John contains a doctrinal dialogue of early Christian times, set in a particular literary form. The achievement, as the aim, of the Fourth Evangelist is one other than historical; it is the presentation of the metaphysical aspects of the Saviour's life. In this he stands as a prophet. While, indeed, his dualistic view of human beings is no more beyond criticism *per se* than it is as a representation of the teaching of Jesus, his view, on the other hand, of the Divinity of Jesus, as amounting to the Incarnation of the " Logos ", or Eternal Reason, while it has developed, has not been surpassed.

And lastly, the discrepancies in the gospels, rightly viewed, minister to the credibility of the history. The very variety of form in which the facts appear establishes these facts, whether they have been general or particular. And here, it may be remarked, that where it is possible, by the sacrifice of a few very unessential adornments to see one event, general or particular, in several different stories, such a line of interpretation greatly ministers to the credibility. Some attempts in this direction in the earlier form of this work excited considerable disfavour. But was it just? Is it not the truth that a very limited number of episodes in the public ministry of Jesus Christ have come down to us in the Divine Government, all the more certain from their persistent appearance in the many coloured presentations of an imaginative and unscientific but earnest people?

It will be the aim, however, in the following pages, to help to show that enough is certainly known of Jesus to justify the profound doctrines and faiths which have become associated with his appearance, and also, it is hoped, in some small way to show that in Him the human heart finds One to whom it turns unreservedly as to the Captain of Salvation.

PART I.

BEFORE THE MINISTRY.

CHAPTER I.

THE HIDDEN THIRTY YEARS.

THE earthly life of Him whose name for us is "above every name" is, with the exception of some few months at the end of it, hidden from our sight. The four books in the New Testament that tell of the earthly life of Jesus neither are nor profess to be biographies of him. They are messages of "good news," which the writers wish to be read through his life and teaching. And the good news is conveyed in the language and imagery of their own time. Both for the end of truly understanding this good news and for the end of inquiring scientifically into the manner of its emergence, it is legitimate to apply to the four books a careful investigation, in which the doctrinal, the artistic, and the temporary elements become, for the moment, disregarded, and the bare facts of the history are set alone in the foreground. But of the facts of the history only a few have been preserved. And of particular facts only those remain to us which, belonging to the public ministry of our Lord, ranged over the last few months of his earthly life.

Two things, however, are possible to all who intelligently read the gospels. One of these is to get a sufficiently clear view of those last months in the life of the Master; the other is to reconstruct reverently, not in a particular way, but in a general way, the history of what went before.

The Gospel of Matthew, indeed, and the Gospel of Luke both present, at their opening, pictures having to do with the earlier life; they present pictures of the sacred infancy, intermingled in representations of beings having higher rank than men, and surrounded by a halo of brightness greater than that which shines on this world, preparing for the introduction of a career that, while human, was at the same time more than human. But these pictures in their details go back beyond the earthly history; and indeed there is little in them that can be abstracted from the pre-earthly and adjudged to the sphere of earthly history. Their place for consideration, therefore, is at the end, not at the beginning, of the work we have entered on. At the present stage all that comes to be done in regard to them is to be influenced in the spirit of inquiry by the sight of them as we pass, to call to mind that the life we are studying has won the acceptance of such representations, to listen, for a moment, in fancy to the angels' song, and let the eye, for a moment, rest on the words of its unparalleled theme.

See App. I. 1.

Lk. ii. 42-52. The Gospel of Luke also, besides its picture of the infancy, has given us one narrative of the earlier life of Jesus. Isolated, the only record in the New Testament of Jesus not yet become a teacher, stands the account of the boyhood incident in the Temple. But the very isolation of this account emphasises the

meagreness of our information. It is all we have ; and
it is itself little more than a flash, having hardly more
in it than what sympathy and reverence might have
themselves imagined.

For the real history of Jesus's life (excepting the last
few months of it) recourse must be had to indirect
methods. Fortunately, if generalities be alone aimed
at, there are indirect methods which can be followed
with a perfect confidence. We have a principle to go
on which, as regards generalities, is sufficient to give
us a clear view. This principle is simply to make the
later life, which we do know, tell also of the earlier life,
which otherwise we do not know. There are two ways
in which we can apply this principle. (1) We can, in
a few cases, find expressed references to the earlier life
in what is recorded of the later life. But (2) we can
also see generally in Jesus's own later words and
actions implicit indications of what the earlier life must
have been. In this second application, the principle
agrees with a demand which Jesus himself made of his
contemporaries. Jesus asked repeatedly that he might
be judged by his contemporaries according to his
actions, as "the tree is known by his fruit." This Mt. xii. 33.
suggests the principle by which we ourselves may learn
of the earlier life of Jesus. If we can go in thought
from the fruit to the tree, we can similarly go from the
later growth to the earlier growth. "Of thorns," said Lk. vi. 44.
Jesus, "men do not gather figs, nor of a bramble bush
gather they grapes." Similarly we can say that from
a mature fig or a mature grape we can judge that in
the earlier growth there was, whatever else may have
been seen, a young fig or a young grape. Allowing
that some of Jesus's sayings and actions might proceed

from what had come to him through experience, there is nevertheless a general character to be found in them which must have been there also in the former stages of his life; and there are certain words and deeds telling of spiritual qualities which cannot have been of late acquisition, but must have developed along with his whole heart and mind.

See Mk. i. 24; Jn. i. 45; Acts x. 38, &c. and espec. Jn. i. 46, and the note on Acts, in App. VIII. Jn. iv. 43, 44, is not of sufficient clearness to be of any weight. See also Mk. i. 9, Jn. vii. 41, 42. 52, and Mt. xxi. 11.

Proceeding, then, upon this principle of making the later known throw light on the earlier unknown, we meet as the first certain fact this, that he belonged to NAZARETH, a little inconsiderable town, beautifully situated, some three days' journey north of Jerusalem. Whether or not his belonging to Nazareth included his having been born there, need not be decided. The infancy pictures above alluded to, as literally read, make him out to have been born not in Nazareth, but in Bethlehem. On the other hand, it is not to be concealed that the evidence which comes from the rest of the New Testament suggests very strongly the other state of matters. What we have for certain is that by his contemporaries and by the immediately succeeding generation he was known as Jesus of Nazareth.

Mk. vi. 3; Mt. i. 16; Jn. i. 45, vi. 42.

We can believe him to have, as he grew up, lived with his parents Joseph and Mary, and with several sisters and brothers, in the relation of strong mutual

Renan, p. 60, c. 3.

affection. Some scholars, indeed, have believed rather that the relation between him and his family was a strained one. But this conclusion is chiefly based on

Mk. iii. 21, 31-35.

one little incident which, we shall see when we come to it, really points, if carefully viewed, quite in the opposite direction as regards the earlier part of his life. Certainly a personality so commanding as we shall see his to have been must at times have asserted itself

so as to cause little misunderstandings; and the story
of the boyhood temple incident in the Gospel of Luke, Lk. ii. 41-
whether it indicates a special occurrence or not, repre-[52.]
sents assuredly what may have often happened. But
the general course of Jesus's home life was, we may be
quite sure, smooth and pleasant. For our belief in this,
the character of Jesus, as we shall see it further on, is
enough. And we have, to help to confirm it, first, the 1 Cor. ix.
very incident just mentioned, as carefully read; then 19, &c.; Gal. i.
further, the fact that after his death the whole family Acts i. 14.
seem to have been among his disciples; not to speak Jn. xix.
still further of the story of Jesus's dying words about his 26, 27. Cp.
mother, given in the Fourth Gospel, which is likely to xv. 4-6
be based on a trustworthy enough tradition.[(Keim).]

We can believe him, further, to have grown up, in
relation to those beyond his family, a bright-natured
boy, living the simple oriental life among other boys,
giving to them and receiving from them many a
simple kindness with a simple happiness. Ecclesiastical
tradition, indeed, would make it painfully otherwise.
The "apocryphal gospels" represent him as having been Apocry-
an over-bearing boy, using miraculous power for arbitrary phal Gos-
ends. In fact, they dare to represent him in places as and Rev-
having been a merciless being in the shape of a boy, by Wal-
even at times blasting and killing the living children ker.
of earth. But ecclesiastical tradition had grown
morbid in this, being influenced by an ignorant conception of the divinity of Jesus; the "apocryphal
gospels" have no value as evidence. The real Jesus,
so far from blasting, dearly loved the children of
earth. What we must go upon is mainly this one
lovely utterance of the later Jesus himself: "Judge Lk. vi. 37,
not, and ye shall not be judged: condemn not, and [38.]

ye shall not be condemned : forgive, and ye shall
be forgiven : give, and it shall be given unto you ; good
measure, pressed down, and shaken together, and
running over, shall men give into your bosom. For
with the same measure that ye mete withal shall it be
measured to you again." This sacred utterance tells
of experience as well as of inspiration. We learn from
it that Jesus, in his earlier life, had *given to others* both
tangible things and the intangible treasures of respect
and sympathy, and had tasted in return the joys of
kindness and generous companionship. And indeed
we learn from it that Jesus had been specially of the
giving spirit, and not only that he had been specially
of the giving spirit, but that he had had a special power
of getting value out of what was of that spirit in others.

Mk. xii.
34; Jn. i.
47. See
also
Lk. xi. 5-8;
Mt. vii.
9-11.

This latter point is further supported by some incidents
in the public ministry, in which we see him rejoicing in
the goodness of others. He seems to have formed this
habit of noticing what was good in others, and to have
found in it both much happiness and also encouragement to himself for lofty faith and practice. Jesus, we
can say, from his early years, was most gentle, most
considerate, and most generous, and, on the other hand,
such as to see in those around him that which made
him love and reverence everybody.

Out of such a boyhood he grew, we can further
believe, into a similar manhood. Only it must be
recognised that as he grew older there was a reserve
about him which, while not interfering with his simple
life of giving and taking, must have made a greater
than ordinary barrier of thought and feeling between
him and his fellows, and caused him to begin to
experience a peculiar loneliness of spirit. That he did

possess such a reserve we should know from the very
uniqueness of nature in him which was afterwards to
be shown. And it is further borne out by the fact that,
in the time of the ministry, we find he had a habit of *E.g.,* Mk.
i. 35.
retiring at times from human fellowship to commune
with the Divine Presence—a habit which no doubt
would be formed by him as his unique inner promptings
began to mature in him. We cannot believe, however,
that this reserve ever entirely cut him off from companionship. His whole after-teaching was of a life of Lk. vi. 38:
Mt. xxii.
companionship. His whole ideal was companionship, 39.
as elevated and purified. And his actions in the time *E.g.,* Lk.
xix. 5, 6.
of the ministry show an easiness both in making
acquaintances and in recommending himself to them,
which can only have developed through continual
society and intimacy.

Of the intellectual life which he lived as boy and man
we can say this much, that it was devoted from the
first to the subject of religion. Such a religious genius
as afterwards meets us tells of a mind that can never
have known but the one ruling interest. That indeed
he had an eye for the objects of the outside world we
know from his sayings; but there is nothing to show
that any one class of these objects formed for him a
special interest. All the outside world spoke to him of
the Divine Life, and the Divine Life was his one
interest. Beyond this we can hardly look into his
intellectual life at all; and we need not wish to do so.
What is allowed us in relation to his intellectual life is
to see the intellectual creations which, in his time of
public ministry, he gave to the cause of religion; and
these, when we come to them, will enable us to form

some judgment as to the character of the intelligence which lived in him. To seek to see in particular how his mind had been employing itself before he gave those creations to the cause he loved, is a thing we need not wish to do. It would be like seeking to peer into the time of struggle of an artist or inventor, and follow him through the strivings, the promptings, the suggestions, and the discoveries by which he became possessed of his mental treasures ; and it would be little better than mere curiosity that would seek to do this. That Jesus learned religion through being taught the Hebrew Scriptures we can be sure of, in general from the fact of the number of quotations and allusions used by him in his speeches, and in particular from his adopting for himself the name of " Son of man." That his mind moved to an extent along the paths of the time which made the Jews a chosen people, the Scriptures a unique authority, the observance of legal points the main interest of religion, and the coming of a deliverer of the nation the main hope of religion—this too may be set down as certain, seeing various actions and words in the time of the ministry show that he was not completely separated from these. That, once more, he received certain ideas and certain guidance from the different prevailing Jewish parties of the time—the Pharisees, the Sadducees, and the Essenes—this too is more than probable, though to determine how far this may have been the case in detail takes us more into the sphere of speculation. But how and when he super-imposed on all that he learned and so far appropriated an altogether new world of ideas—free, ethereal, eternal—this we cannot tell. All we know is that during the

More subtle influence also may be traced. Cp. for ex. Mk. iv. 32 with Dan. iv. 21 and perh. Mt. xxii. 5 and Lk. xiv. 18-20 w. 1 Macc. iii. 56, &c. A special study might be made of Isaiah in this connection.

E.g., Mk. vii. 27, ii. 25, x. 19, xii. 35 ; Lk. xi. 42.

A full and admirable discussion of this point is to be found in Keim, vol. ii. pp 164-166, 179-188. (Engl. Tr.)

thirty years before he appeared in history there was
going on within him an intellectual process in which
he was receiving into his mind religion as distorted and
overgrown, and was changing it, through the power
that was in him, so as one day to send it forth again as
religion pure and lovely

One special interest indeed which he must have
possessed is to be mentioned, though we can see that
it, like every other, was subordinated to the interest of
religion, and that is the interest in healing diseases.
We can see that Jesus viewed the healing of diseases Lk. vi. 36;
as being victories of God over the spirit of evil; but Mk. ii. 5.
the success which he undoubtedly attained in regard
to the matter in the time of his ministry suggests that
he had given the matter some practical study. No
doubt much of his success was due to the faith aroused
on the part of the people in himself, and in the kind
God in whose name he acted. But the mere faith is
not enough to explain his success, as it could only well
be aroused after some genuine action of healing taking
place. No doubt also, the healing ministry of a life
which stands now "at the very centre of the world's Farrar.
history" must have had as its mainspring a personal
power which it is wisest for us not to attempt to
scrutinise. But personal power in no case dispenses
with means, and even to this sacred human life there
must be attributed procedure which was human even if
in a true sense unshared. What we are to believe of
the hidden time of Jesus's life in regard to this subject
is that, while on the one hand he was awakening to the
consciousness of a personal command over suffering,
he at the same time disciplined himself in the know- Cp. Jn.
ledge of the subject in general, and so sanctified his xvii. 19.

See Lk.
vi. 21, x.
18; Mt.
xvii. 15-
20.

personal **attributes for** the mission on which **he** afterwards entered, **in** which his own healing acts became illustrations of **his** message, that for all suffering there is a Divine Conquering.

Of the outer life that **he lived, we** are given by the

Mk. vi. 3. evangelist Mark this one **point,** that **he** became a carpenter. When and for **how** long, we know not; but all ordinary probability suggests that he would begin this trade early in life, and **continue it till the** time in which **he** went away from **his own town to** enter on his Mission. The fact that **he was known in his** own **town** simply as "the carpenter" suggests that he had not varied his occupation, and had **not in** any way **had a course of life** eventful enough to excite special attention. **And the fact** that little reference **to** this trade is **to be found in his** after-sayings must be held to be not in **disagreement with this, but** in full accordance with it. It is perfectly **explainable** by the delicacy of his disposition, which **would make** him choose, so far as possible, symbols taken from other sources than his own special occupation; and we may consider, further, how he would naturally have a shrinking from dwelling much on what he had come to know was very different from his real calling in **the** world. We may believe he was indeed to popular knowledge just "the carpenter" through all the **more** mature part of the hidden thirty years.

Mk. v. 7
shows this
truth to
have been
declared
by him in
the earli-
est time of
the minis-
try.

Amid **a** life of simple companionship **Jesus** early, we may suppose, became assured of that truth by the asserting which and the dying **for** which he became **the** King of our world—the truth of the FATHERHOOD OF GOD. No doubt this **truth was** suggested to him by the Old Testament scriptures, for it is really a

development and a widening of the truth that prevails
in them ; and possibly the name of " Father " for God
was given him from the sayings of some other Jewish
teacher, for we know it was not peculiar to him to use
it, though what he realised by it went far beyond what
it can have meant to any other.   Further, it is likely
that his father Joseph had died when he was young,
so that the use of the name " Father " for the Supreme
Father was left easy for him.   But these things had
but a small part in his attaining to the truth in
question.   Most to do with it had his own commanding
mind and his own royal heart—his mind, that was
able to discern the true nature of the Divine Presence,
and his heart, that had religion for its óne chief
interest ; his mind, that was able to discern the more
than creature nature in ordinary human beings, and
his heart, that in consequence loved all human beings,
especially the young, in whom he saw generosity,
trustfulness, and prevailing simplicity of character as
yet little corrupted, of whom he said that "of such "
was the "kingdom of God."   And next to his own
part to be reckoned as of importance in his attaining
to the truth was the goodness that lived in the lives of
his fellows around him.

That truth has every consequence for us, the
worshippers and disciples of Jesus ; it had, however, a
special consequence for Jesus's own earthly life.   One
more fact is to be added to what we can gather
regarding the private period of his life, and it is this,
that during that period he either continually possessed
or some time attained a notable Peace of Mind.   In
the midst of his public ministry he said to all, " Come
unto me, all ye that labour and are heavy laden,

Margin notes:

Taylor's sayings of the Jewish Fathers, p. 138, may be consulted. But cp. also Is. lxiii. 16, lxiv. 8, Deut. viii. 5. On point in regard to Joseph cp. Renan, c. 5.

Mk. x. 14. See above, p. 34, margin.

Mt. xi. 28.

and I will give you rest." And at the end of his
Jn. xiv. 27. ministry he said to his disciples, "Peace I leave with
you, my peace I give unto you." Rest and peace were
See, e.g.,
Lk. x. 58. his, it would thus appear. But during the time of the
ministry they were his only as a memory and as an
anticipation. It was in the hidden thirty years that
they had been to him an already experienced attainment. His peace was, to begin with, a repose on
the thought of that present heavenly Father who so
Mt. x. 30. cares for every one of His children that He may be
said to number the very hairs of their heads. It was,
however, further, an actual dwelling in the presence of
that Father. Everything around him spoke of the
Mt. vi.,
&c. Sacred Presence, and so in everything he read Promise.
The flowers, the birds, the life of man, all spoke to him
of a Fatherly Care, and in realising that he found a
calm joy which, we must say, was the nearest approach
possible for this world of struggle to what we picture
as Peace.

The veil that covers the life of Jesus for the time
previous to his ministry, lifts away not suddenly, like
a curtain artificially hung, but rather gradually, like a
mist clearing away in the physical world ; so that, just
before he plainly appears to us in history, we get a
view of him which is dim, but yet more than the indirect
view of reasoning and conjecture. When we keep
following the principle that has been before us, there
is an epoch in Jesus's life, still within the hidden period
but close to the end of it, in which we can more definitely describe what took place than we can describe
what took place in the earlier part of that period. This is
the epoch in which, his mind having become gradually
filled with treasures of thought, and his heart having

come to burn with sublime desire and emotion, he was
first conscious that he had a sacred Mission in the world,
and was on the eve of following it. The mist half
clears away from the life of the Master while he is still
the Carpenter, but soon to be such no longer. We can
without much use of the imagination picture to ourselves an event in the still private and unprofessing life.
What we see is a Figure, having laid aside work and
tools, buried in contemplation ; and as we look at this
figure with reverent interest, we see the face of a man
engaged in a struggle within himself, and we see his
lips moving, and we hear him express his thoughts in
words of unmistakable meaning. The words are
these : " Is a candle brought to be put under a bushel, Mk. iv. 21,
or under a bed? and not to be set on a candle- 22. Trace
stick ? For there is nothing hid, which shall not be Jesus's
manifested ; neither was anything kept secret, but that this
it should come abroad." Then the mist again closes in Jn. viii.
over the Sacred Figure—soon to roll away completely 12, xii. 35,
and leave Jesus clearly standing and moving amidst 46
summer brightness—that again, alas ! soon, in its
turn, to give place to a wild tempest shrieking
around him, and then carrying him finally away out
of our sight.

CHAPTER II.

THE FIRST MOVEMENT TOWARDS THE MINISTRY— A JOURNEY.

JESUS steps forward into clear historical reality as is described in these words of the evangelist Mark, " And it came to pass in those days, that Jesus came from Nazareth of Galilee, and was baptized of John in Jordan." By the "those days" is meant about the year 30 of our reckoning, and we can, with good probability, fix the time exactly to about the opening of the year 34. We can simply accept the statement of Luke, that Jesus was at this time "about thirty years of age."

All that may have prompted him to leave his home and work at Nazareth, we cannot tell. The natural growth of his personality is itself sufficient to account for his doing so. We may believe, however, that the fame of John the Baptist reaching his ears was the occasion of his self-consciousness coming to the decisive step.

John was—as can be learned from both the gospels and the historian Josephus—a man of intense moral enthusiasm combined with clear intelligence, who had become the leader of a religious movement. He

Mk. i. 9.

Keim, from Josephus.

Lk. iii. 23.

lived a hermit life, and, like the severer of the old prophets, like Amos, like Jeremiah, sternly called on the people of his nation and his time to show an actual life that would be in accordance with the high religious pretensions which as Israelites they made. Along with his preaching he administered the rite of Mt. iii.; baptism; that is, he bathed those who came to him with Lk. i.-iii. pure water, as a symbol of their making a fresh start and living a purer life. He also prophesied regarding the expected Messiah, saying that there would come after himself a greater "whose shoes he was not worthy to stoop down and unloose." He was surrounded Mk. i. 5. by a crowd of attentive hearers who came, it would Cp. Mt. xi. 7. seem, from all parts of Palestine. He seems to have lived at first in the midst of the Wilderness of Judæa ; Mk. i. 4. but he administered his baptism at the Jordan, and it seems as if he had come to frequent the side of the river that was opposite from Judæa, and under the rule Mk. vi. 14, of Herod the Tetrarch. &c.

Among others—though not, judging from what we have seen of his character, in close association with others—Jesus went from Galilee and joined John at the Jordan. He went, we must believe, to join one whose name was ringing throughout the land, with the purpose of making thus a first step towards the communication of his own ideas. This purpose— which is indicated by his own saying about the candle Mk. iv. 21. —is the only purpose that can be conceived of as having been before him, when we think of the com- manding character both of his personality and of his ideas. He went, we may say assuredly, with the purpose of making a communication to which his whole inner being had begun to drive him.

Mk. i. 9. Jesus underwent the baptism along with the others who surrounded John. And this event is a significant one for us and one that must be carefully explained. It must not be supposed for a moment, by way of explanation, that Jesus viewed himself as one in need of this baptism, with the change of life which it symbolised. The notion of some scholars that Jesus Conway, Essay on Christianity, p. 18. started as a disciple, or even a "convert," of John, is not a happy one, and cannot stand. It is destroyed completely by a thoughtful estimate of Jesus himself, either as we can see him directly or as we can see him through the impression which he made on others. For ourselves here now, it is enough to refer to what we have seen in the first chapter. With the Jesus in view that we have there learned of, we shall say, reverently, that Jesus needed neither any symbol of a change in his life nor the change itself. And with the glimpse of his thoughts and feelings which has thus already been afforded us, we shall see no suggestion of himself having supposed that he had such a need. Indeed we can go further than this, and notice that, while certainly Jesus did recognise baptism as a means of consecration for people in general, yet even in regard to people in general the idea of a necessary sweeping change, at first associated with baptism, cannot have been a favourite idea of Jesus. The religious consciousness which we have already in some way had before us as belonging to him, does not admit of the Mk. x. 39 is not an exception. See App. I. (2). prominence of that idea. And in what we shall further learn of him, we shall find nothing to indicate that either this general idea or the remembrance of his own baptism had any important place among his religious thoughts. We shall find him teaching that little

children are of the kingdom of God, and that the change
required of every one is the getting back of their simple Mk. x. 15.
nature.   We shall find him teaching that one of the Mk.xii.31
greatest virtues is to love one's neighbour as oneself, Lk. x. 25-
and that many who make no profession of religion are 37.
purer than those who make profession.   The notion,
therefore, of tracing Jesus's religious life to his baptism
by John is a mistake, and his undergoing the baptism
cannot even be looked at as having been the meeting
of what he felt as a want of his own nature.   Jesus's
receiving baptism from John is principally to be viewed
as an act having in it a spiritual quality, through which
it gives us the first important glimpse of Jesus's spiritual
character.   It was an act in which he who had himself
great ideas on the subject of religion and morality
submitted, for the time, to be a follower of another
whose worth and integrity as a teacher he believed in.
In undergoing the baptism, Jesus did two things: he
took a place beneath the Baptist, and he took a place
beside the humblest and the most erring that might
have, along with himself, obeyed the Baptist's call.
The act, therefore, was a modest act, in that by it he
took the most humble position that it was possible for
him to take.   It was a respectful act, in that by it
he gave unreserved obedience and honour to the other
teacher.   It was a prudent act, in that it showed the
knowledge of the true way for greatness to attain
ultimate supremacy.   And it was a beautiful and revealing act, in that it showed Greatness involving a
keen sense of greatness in others, and producing greatness of respect towards others.   Words, indeed, fail to
tell, but ordinary sympathy and experience will nevertheless understand, how it was that One who was about

to establish for himself a position in which he would gradually bring the world into a subjection to himself that would be established through inner influence, and would be declared by transfixing outward homage, began his public life by obeying the general invitation of another teacher, and receiving from him the cleansing water which was not so clear as the waters of thought and feeling that daily refreshed his own soul.

Mt. iii. 16, 17; Mk. i. 10, 11; Lk. iii. 22. Cp. also Jn. i.

All the three earlier gospels relate that at the baptism of Jesus by John there was seen a descent of the Spirit of God upon Jesus, and was heard a heavenly voice witnessing to Jesus being the Son of God. And as Mark relates this more simply than the others, allowing us to understand what he relates as just an experience of Jesus himself, it may be that the narrative was originally a narrative by Jesus himself of an inner experience attained by him at this time in relation to his position and his mission. If this is so, then we can see that the narrative got enhanced in outer impressiveness as it passed through the hands of the different evangelists. But it may be that the narrative is merely a particularising, on the part of the first Christian tradition, of the general fact recognised, that

Cp. Acts i. 2 and x. 37, 38.

the Spirit of God appeared plainly in him from the time in which he was with the Baptist; which was indeed the time of his first public appearance. At least, the narrative as it stands in the gospels has the significance of introducing the general fact that the Spirit of God dwelt in Jesus. And it is in the aspect of so signifying that the importance of it lies, rather than in the question of whether there may have been on the part of Jesus at this time a definite psychological experience.

We get no further information regarding the time in which Jesus remained among the followers of the Baptist from the Synoptic gospels. But we can get good probability, at least, of certain further facts by a careful reading of the later Fourth Gospel. In the Gospel of John there are some quite detailed notices of Jesus's life while he was with John. We are recognising, in this work, that the Gospel of John is in the main a doctrinal book, but that there runs through it a fragmentary historical account, independent of the accounts in the other gospels, though to be detected and verified by careful comparison with these accounts. This state of matters holds especially true in regard to the period at which we are now arrived. And we may find in the earlier chapters of John several historical materials intermingled with what is palpably doctrinal and from the evangelist himself.

Foremost of these materials is an account of intercourse between Jesus and some of John's disciples, Jn. i. 35- which can be simplified into the fact that Jesus had, 42. even at this beginning of his public life, a group who were surrounding himself, if not as disciples, at least as associates and respectful listeners to his conversation. The principles of investigation stated in the introduction to this book secure for us these facts to the extent of a probability which is almost a certainty. When we start with what we have seen of Jesus in the first chapter, and at the same time take an anticipatory glance into what is still to come before us, we do not indeed find it likely that he had any others accompanying him when he went to join the Baptist, for his going seems to have been a deliberated act of his own, arising out of his self-consciousness; but we do find there is every likelihood that when he did go and did meet others, he would both associate with them and See above, pp. 33-35. impress them. The first of these two points comes from our knowledge of his character; the second comes, by anticipation, from our knowledge of his general power to impress. Thus starting, then, we are on the outlook for anything that will tell in a natural way of his having met companions and impressed them, and this outlook is met by the account in the Fourth Gospel as abridged and simplified. Further, the earlier gospels give us no link between this time of Jesus's life and what they tell immediately Mt. iv. 13; Mk. i. 21. after, that he went and established himself as a teacher, not in the south, nor in his old home, but in a new place, Capernaum. We ask how it came about that Jesus took this course, as we get no information on the subject from the earlier gospels. And we shall find that the missing link is supplied when we receive, as simplified, the Fourth Gospel account.

Going then to the particulars of the account in the Fourth Gospel, so far as it can be accepted for history, we find they are to the following effect: That two of the others who surrounded John became interested in Jesus—being induced indeed by something that they Jn. i. 35-42. had heard John himself say of Jesus; that, as we may sum it up, they became quickly friends and associates of Jesus; that one of them was no other than Andrew, the brother of the famous Simon Peter; and that this was how Peter came to be a disciple of Jesus. At this point we are left to fill in the account ourselves; for the story, as it may be critically read, leaves it undetermined whether Peter was at the Jordan too, or only afterwards became acquainted with Jesus through

Andrew. What we must do is decide that the introduction took place immediately, from this consideration,
that if Andrew had become so intimate with Jesus as
to keep with him till they met Peter away in a different
part of the country, this would have meant that Peter
came to supersede Andrew in a very close intimacy,
which is unlikely. Receiving the story, then, we are
led on to believe that both brothers were at the Jordan,
that first Andrew met Jesus and heard John speak of
him, and that then Andrew introduced Peter to Jesus.
All that thus comes before us is most lifelike and, in
all respects, most probable. This falling in with
acquaintances and making friends of them—but yet
friends rendering homage—is in accordance both with
what we shall come to see and with what we have
already seen, in regard to Jesus's character, as, being
"about thirty years of age," he came "from Nazareth
of Galilee" to become known to the world.

Receiving this account from the Fourth Gospel, we
come into collision with advanced scholars, but not
seriously. The free and unprejudiced class of scholars
have so far been so much occupied with disproving the
Fourth Gospel's right to be called in general a source
of history, that they have both in some particulars too
greatly emphasised a distinction in the right of the
other gospels to be trusted as historical, and have
also been impatient rather than just to attempts to
extract from the Fourth Gospel historical elements;
but they have not denied that there may be historical elements in the Fourth Gospel, and many
such will come before us in this book which
are in agreement, not in disagreement, with the
advanced scholars' general conclusions. Regarding

4

the case before us, it must be said that what we
have taken from the Fourth Gospel here enriches,
rather than differs from, the account of the beginning
of Peter's discipleship which is given in the earlier
gospels. The earlier gospels, with their dramatic
account of a calling of disciples at the Sea of Galilee,
leave it to be imagined that Jesus must have become
known to his disciples previously. It is, in fact, to be
noted here that, while we recognise the superior
historical value of the Synoptic gospels, we must keep
also in mind that these gospels are in form very
dramatic. They are dramatic presentations of the
appearance of the Messiah. And thus, for historical
ends, we must deduce not only from such pictures as
the Annunciation and the Birth in the city of David,
but also from such as the Preaching from the Mount
and the Preaching from the Plain, certain facts thus
presented which must, in their reality, have happened
much more spontaneously and much less ceremoniously.
So here. The Synoptic account of the calling of disciples
must be said to be almost purely dramatic. It is most
unlikely that in reality the saying "Follow me" was
the occasion of the *very* beginning of the discipleship of
any, or that Jesus, having found in one place one pair
of disciples, found also another pair, equally willing,
near the same place, on just the same occasion.
Regarding Peter, judging from what we see of his
character, it is natural to believe that, as he was
attracted to Jesus, so he had been previously attracted
to the Baptist. And it is arbitrary to say that,
because he was a simple Galilean fisherman, he
cannot have travelled to Judæa and listened to the
Baptist. From all we learn of him it is plain that,

Mt. iv. 18-
22; Mk. i.
16-20.

See Mk.
i. 19.

besides being a fisherman, he was also a striking religious personality; and it is not likely that his religious life began with the influence of Jesus on him, or that before the preaching of Jesus he had listened to no other teacher. The story before us in its pruned form, therefore, is a most probable one. We may recognise it as a true reminiscence of the time of Jesus's intercourse with John, and we shall see that what it tells of had an important bearing on after-events.

When we go on to the notices which bring Jesus into connection with the Preacher of the Wilderness himself, our ground is not so certain; and yet we must incline to grasp at one or two passages as real reminiscences. The remarks ascribed to John in which he recognises Jesus as the Greater who, "coming after" himself, "is preferred before" himself, must be put aside, as the originals of them must certainly be considered as not having had special reference to Jesus, but having had reference just to the ideal Messiah of popular expectation. For this-- apart from the general unlikeliness of the supposition that John could have referred to Jesus at this time— there is strong argument in the consideration pointed out by scholars that, according to the Synoptic gospels, John later sent to ask Jesus if he was the Messiah. Even if that passage in the Synoptic gospels is not literally historical, it shows that at the time of these gospels being written it was not believed that John had recognised Jesus from the first. When, then, we go on to the saying of John with respect to Jesus, "Behold the Lamb of God, which taketh away the sin of the world," we shall first be inclined to reject it also,

Jn. i. 27. Cp. Mk. i. 7. 8.

Mt. xi. 2-6; Lk. vii 18-23.

Jn. i. 29.

4 *

as its whole language seems to allude to the death of
Jesus, which John could not possibly have foreseen, and
thus comes to suggest that what it really presents us with
is just a prediction put into the mouth of John from an
after time.   And yet **we need not** cast this saying of
John away altogether.   The evangelist makes reiterated
Jn. i. 7, iii. statements **of John having** "borne witness" to Jesus.
26, v. 33. **Now these statements have the** appearance of denoting
something that really happened.   **It is** going too far
to suppose that **the** assertion **they contain** would, if
Jn. v. 34. invented, be actually used to base **dogmatic** teaching
on, and not only used to base dogmatic teaching on,
but used **as** second-rate material for that **purpose,**
inferior to other material.   And such is the use made
of the assertion by the evangelist.   What comes to us,
therefore, is that **John** had indeed made some remark
upon Jesus's purity of character, though the words of
his remark **are** lost in their historical exactness, and
have taken instead a doctrinal form.   We have thus
spirit without body—a mere ghost of a fact.   But still,
what we have is valuable.   It is like some vague feeling
of remembrance in personal experience—which, while
it cannot tell definitely what happened, remembers a
something of which it retains a general impression.

Jn. i. 37.   "And **the** two disciples," says the evangelist,
referring to Andrew and the other, "heard him speak,
and they followed Jesus."   This statement we can now
accept as real history.   In other words, we may believe
that the **interest** in Jesus shown **by the** Preacher himself helped towards that forming of a group round
Jesus which **we have** recognised above.

Jn. iii. 23-   One more reminiscence asks our acceptance, though
36.   clearness has gone from **it.**   It is found in the third

chapter of John, where the evangelist, having already
run over the whole public appearance of Jesus to the
end, enters on new material and begins all over again.
In the third chapter of John it is related that once
when John was baptizing, some disciples spoke to him
about Jesus, and he said of him these words, " A man
can receive nothing except it be given him from
heaven," and again, " He that hath the bride is the
bridegroom : but the friend of the bridegroom, which
standeth and heareth him, rejoiceth greatly because of
the bridegroom's voice. This my joy therefore is
fulfilled." Now the passage in which these words
occur is just one of those having the phenomena which
have led scholars to a fixed conclusion recognising
free enlargements in the Fourth Evangelist's presentation—the contrarieties to the testimony of the other Cp. ver. 35
gospels, and the contrarieties to other statements 3, or cp.
within this same gospel itself. To particularise on these ver. 23 w.
phenomena does not belong to the work now before us. then
The truth really conveyed by the evangelist, as his w. iv. 2.
presentation stands, is that to be " the friend of
the bridegroom " was indeed the Baptist's historical
position, and that he had claimed no greater. But
besides reading this meaning in the passage, may we
not see something more in it both interesting and
instructive ? The view which we are looking for
establishment of as we proceed, is that the evangelist
by no means invented any narrative material to begin
with, but only worked up the material lying to his hand
into a doctrinal presentation. And the suggestions of
the passage before us give no disturbance of this view.
The passage, indeed, has such a form that plainness no
longer remains in regard to the scene at the Jordan

indicated by it. But with very great confidence we
may deduce from the passage these facts: That
among the followers of John there had arisen a discussion about "purifying"—a discussion, indeed, about
the new purity of life which seemed to come with the
administering of the rite of baptism; that the name of
Jesus was introduced into the discussion, as the name
of one who was already making himself known to be a
power both in pure living and in teaching the way to
pure living; and that all differences of view were in
the discussion brought under the rays of one benign
reality, a reality of which all were conscious, namely
this, that now God Himself was proving to be in
their midst in the way in which the prophet Isaiah
had foretold He one day would be, rejoicing over His
Is. lxii. 5. people "as the bridegroom rejoiceth over the bride,"
making the Baptist and every true worshipper care not
so much about the question of what Jesus would do or
into what further form the new awakening would be
led, as just simply about this, that they could "rejoice"
"because of the bridegroom's voice."

To estimate what may have been the influence which,
through this intercourse between Jesus and the Baptist,
the Baptist exercised on Jesus, is, if we go to details,
no easy task, and in every way requires considerable
thought.   We may confidently, however, set down the
general conclusion that, while Jesus certainly received
suggestions from the Baptist which supplied him with
both phrases for his teaching and hints for his action,
yet his real personality and his teaching in its real
substance owed very little to the Baptist. We may, in
fact, accept Jesus's own view that he and the Baptist
Lk. vii. 35. were two different men—two different "children" of

"wisdom"—whose characters were independently
formed, as against any hasty idea of criticism that
would incline to deduce much, from the fact of their
association for a short period. We can fearlessly lay
the full weight of this conclusion on our first chapter :
we have seen in our first chapter that Jesus went from From Mk.
his home in Nazareth already developed and already iv. 21, and much else.
equipped—a great unrevealed Power. We must be so
sure of this fact of his self-sufficiency at the time of his
leaving home that, if it were necessary, we should distrust any evidence of his having received his ideas from
the Baptist. There is, however, no evidence of his
having received more than supplementary ideas. The
particulars that the gospels give us support the general
conclusion which our first chapter supplies to us.
Looking at these particulars, there are four points in
Jesus's teaching that he may seem to have probably
learned from the Baptist—namely (1) his using the
phrase " the kingdom of heaven "; (2) his using certain Mt. iii. 2.
other less important phrases, principally his giving
good works the name of "fruits" and his calling the Vers. 7, 8.
Lk. iii. 7, 8
Pharisees a " generation of vipers "; (3) his instituting
baptism ; and (4) even his adopting for himself the title
of Messiah, or Christ. Now (1) the first of these may
be put out of consideration, as there is no mention of
John's having used the phrase in Mark or Luke, and
Matthew's adding it to the preaching of repentance can
most simply be explained as the adding by an uncritical
author of a phrase become familiar to him, which
seemed to bring out further what John was really
aiming at, and showed the union between him and
Jesus. (2) For the second point—having to do with
the smaller phrases—we can simply admit Jesus's

indebtedness to John for these phrases,—though it is
to be noticed that the most important of them, that of
the tree and its fruit, was applied by Jesus in quite a
different way from any in which John can have applied

Mt. xii. 25,
26, 35.

it. (3) For the third point—the instituting of baptism
—what meets us on consideration will first make us
incline to take the very contrary course to that which
we have taken with regard to the using of the phrase
" the kingdom of heaven "—that is, as we have not seen
ground for ascribing the one to John, not see ground
for ascribing the other to Jesus. It is a question which
thoughtful scholars find a difficult one to answer, when
Jesus really instituted baptism, if indeed he ever did it

Mt. xxviii.
19.

at all.   The gospels refer his instituting of baptism to
the period after the Resurrection. Whatever interpretation, however, may be given to what is thus
recorded, it is unlikely that baptism would have got
such a hold as it did without authority from the
Master in his lifetime. What is really likely to have
happened is that Jesus—beginning his public ministry,
as we can see he did, in intimate connection with that
of John—appropriated the rite without much criticism
of it. Recognising this, we can see at the same time
that he made little of it, and emphasised other things.
Baptism was not one of Jesus's own ideas, but an
adopted child of his dead friend and fellow-worker,
which he reverently brought up along with his own.
(4) A similar state of matters presents itself with regard
to the fourth point—the taking on himself by Jesus of
the name of the Messiah, or Christ. It is a question
greatly discussed by scholars, when Jesus really
adopted the Messiah character; and it is almost
probable enough to be called certain, both that the

time of his being with John was a time in which
he made important steps in relation to this, and
that the preaching of John had greatly to do
with these steps. So much, then, is to be allowed.
But, on the other hand, the Messiah-idea was itself
just a vessel for Jesus to put his own ideas into, or
a category to express that of which he himself was conscious. We have seen already that he was certainly From Mk.
conscious of a unique authority before he came away iv. 21, and
much else.
from his home. And it is further quite easy to see,
from reading the gospels, that even after the time of See Mk.
viii. Cp.
his being with John he avoided the name of the foregoing.
Messiah. He took indeed a name that had been given
to the ideal Messiah (" Son of man "); but this was a Dan. vii.
name which he carefully selected for himself out of the 13 ; Book
of Enoch
names that had been given to the Messiah, as if he c. xlvi.,
&c.
rejected the other associations with the whole character.
He had been and was HIMSELF—that alone really—
and the idea of the Christ was adopted by him to
express what he was conscious of as himself; but so
far from it presenting a character which he merely
lived up to, he was not altogether satisfied with it as
expressing what he himself was. It is thus that,
as we know, the idea of the Christ came to be an
altogether new idea after it had been associated with
Jesus. The Pauline Christ is .not the old-expected
Jewish Messiah, nor is the Johannine Christ, nor is
the now believed-in Christ. No ; all these are objects
of thought that are made up of many contributing
ideas, the principal one of which is not what the
Messiah-idea had in it when Jesus received it from
the old prophets or from John, but rather is what
came from Jesus's own self-consciousness, in which, as

a man, he was able to call himself Son to the Divine
Father. Just as with the baptism-idea, therefore, the
Messiah-idea, we can see, was adopted by Jesus from
John, but in such a way that his own original thoughts
far transcended what he adopted. Regarding all the
three points, it is to be maintained, as has been
already stated above, that Jesus received in them from
the Baptist supplementary ideas which helped him to
define his own thought and work, but that his thought
itself and his whole personality itself were what they
were with no debt of importance to John the Baptist.
We are to see here a *wisdom* in Jesus, such as he
displayed also in regard to other teachers than the
Baptist, which made him, while conscious of his
princely authority, not ashamed to receive leading
from others when it was good leading—in accordance
Mt. xx. 25- with his own words: "Ye know that the princes of
27.   the Gentiles exercise dominion over them, and they
that are great exercise authority upon them. But it
shall not be so among you: but whosoever will be
great among you, let him be your minister; and
whosoever will be chief among you, let him be your
servant."

The association with John was rudely put an end to
by a catastrophe which is described by the historian
Antiq. of Josephus in the following words: "Now when [many]
the Jews, others came to crowd about him [John], for they were
xviii. 5.
(Whis-   greatly moved [or pleased] by hearing his words, Herod,
ton's
Transla- who feared lest the great influence John had over the
tion.)   people might put it into his power and inclination to
raise a rebellion (for they seemed ready to do anything
he should advise), thought it best, by putting him to
death, to prevent any mischief he might cause, and

not bring himself into difficulties by sparing a man who might make him repent of it when it should be too late.   Accordingly he was sent a prisoner, out of Herod's suspicious temper, to Macherus, the castle I before mentioned, and was there put to death."

CHAPTER III.

WHAT could become of that band of earnest and
thoughtful Israelites that had eagerly listened to the
prophet, when he to whom they had listened was
violently removed from them? They could but be
scattered, as is the fate of earnest people along with
careless people universally when either the physical
world or barbarian power asserts itself. They could
but be scattered, dishonoured, and forced to escape to
save their lives. And that this is what really took
place is declared by the firm enough if vague indications that are in our possession. And what of that
One among them whose character, even at this stage
of our work, has begun to show a unique strength as
well as a unique beauty? Is it possible that it was
with him as with the rest? Is it to be conceived that
he was in danger, like any common man, of being
arrested by established powers at this very beginning
of his public appearance? and that, like a common
man, he joined in the general flight in order to escape
with his life? The facts tell us that it was so; and

that it was so is only in accordance with nature in
general. If an earthquake were to put in ruins a
house containing some priceless precious stone, the
precious stone would fall along with the meanest object
that the house contained—though afterwards it would
come about that care would be taken to recover the
stone. Or if a fire were to break out in a room where
was a safe containing important papers, not one inch
would the flames divert their wild leaps from the safe
and its valuable contents—though, when all was past,
it would be found that the papers remained unscathed
and only the outside of the safe was the worse. So it
evidently was when an assertion of brainless natural
force interfered with the benign life of Jesus.

There took place at this time of Jesus's life, we
must see, what was in accordance with nature.
Powerful as had been the impression he had made on
a few of the followers of John, he had had neither the
time nor the opportunities to get any special command
over them. He had no following to speak of, and he
was surrounded by strange country and people. What
was in accordance with nature was that he should
escape with the followers of John in general. And
this, we may conclude, was what did take place. If
with a purely arbitrary kind of worship we demand
marvel at every step we take, we are in this instance
simply refused by history our gratification. Marvel
enough we shall indeed meet with as we follow the
events of the year that from this point will be our
subject of consideration. But at this point there is no
marvel for us. What took place was in simple
accordance with nature.

Jesus escaped from the danger of being captured by

the wild creatures that obeyed a half-barbarian prince.
Mk. i. 12-14. Knowing that the Baptist had been arrested and conveyed to prison, but not knowing what further might
have befallen him, he joined the other followers in
avoiding a useless sharing of his fate. He found refuge
in a "wilderness," which was in all probability the
wilderness of Judæa. With a natural impulse the
scattered band crossed the Jordan, and got away from
the territory of the ruler who had laid hands on their
chief. And with them went Jesus, we must believe—
not thereby, as we shall see, to lose the majesty of his
personality, but to make that majesty appear in the
very midst of a seeming discomfiture.

Vers. 12, 13. &c. It is the gospel story of the "Temptation" which,
beyond the *a priori* likelihood, assures us of these
facts. The usual theory, indeed, of thoughtful scholars
regarding the Temptation story is, that what is directly
historical in it is to be referred to a voluntary with-
For this view see Keim. drawal by Jesus into the desert before the imprisonment
of the Baptist. But it is unlikely that Jesus would so
soon separate himself from the assembly that he had
travelled so far to join, especially as he was amidst
regions unfamiliar to him. He had left a life of thirty
years in a quiet spot to join a concourse of men, and,
believing in his fixedness of purpose, it is not easy
to see why he should just then have gone voluntarily
into a strange wilderness for any length of time that
would have made the event be so solemnly recorded as
it is recorded, or have led to its receiving the doctrinal
E.g., Mk. i. 35. application which the three gospels all give to it. It is
true that, as we shall find, he had the habit of retiring
to commune with the Divine Presence. But a retiring
for any lengthened period just at the time in which he

had emerged from retirement could only have occurred
as the result of some very deeply moving experience;
and the baptism by John, according to the view we
have been taking of it, cannot be supposed to have
been an experience of such a kind. Further, the
Gospel of Luke favours the idea that it was on his Lk. iv. 1.
returning to Galilee that the Temptation occurred; and
as for the other two gospels, this reading of them also
need not be considered any straining of their narrative
when there is taken into account their evident turning
of the story into a dramatic act in the Messiah's appearance. On the other hand, the explanation of
Jesus's withdrawal into the wilderness as being the
result of the break up of John the Baptist's following,
has every natural probability in its favour, and we
shall see that it is borne out by the details of the
Temptation story itself.

The gospel story of the Temptation both declares
the fact of Jesus's escape into the wilderness of Judæa
after John had been arrested, and also gives us a most
interesting view of what befell him there. We may
look at the pictorial account of the Temptation given
in Matthew and Luke as being almost exactly a narra- See App
tive which Jesus himself had related of the workings of I. (3).
his mind during this first reverse in the new undertaking on which he had entered. And we may read
through the narrative both the facts of Jesus's inner
experience and the outward events to which the inner
experience had reference. Jesus had been, as we
may suppose he himself told the story, "tempted of
the devil." As he suffered in the Wilderness, probably
for the first time in his life, the pangs of hunger, the
thought had come into his mind, Was this what was

led to by coming forth to assert man's sonship to the good kind God ? But he had remembered the lesson that God had meant the ancient Israelites to learn in *their* hunger in the Wilderness, " that man doth not live by bread only, but by every word that proceedeth out of the mouth of the Lord doth man live." And as he further meditated on the situation in which he was placed, the thought had occurred to him that it seemed as if to succeed in this world one must abandon such aims as those of John and himself, and devote one's powers to the service of the devil; but on this thought presenting itself, he had said, "Get thee hence, Satan," seeing in the very thought a calling in question of the sole and supreme rule of God. And then once more, thinking further of the truth he had come forward to assert, that of man's sonship to the good kind God, he had asked himself, Could not God be called upon to save good and great men from wild brute force such as had interfered with John and himself, as the words of the psalm expressed it which said, " He shall give his angels charge over thee, to keep thee in all thy ways. They shall bear thee up in their hands, lest thou dash thy foot against a stone "? But being in full possession of a religion that far transcended such questions, which could only lead to a negative answer, he had let his mind go for expression of a transcending faith again to the familiar ground of the history of the chosen people ; and remembering a case in which they had demanded an interference with nature for their sake, he recalled the lesson that was afterwards connected with that incident, " Ye shall not tempt the Lord your God, as ye tempted him in Massah." Out of such musings we may suppose he formed an imaginative

Margin references:
Deut. viii. 3.
Ps. xci. 11, 12.
Exod. xvii. 1-7.
Deut. vi. 16.

narrative which he afterwards told his disciples, according to his own tendency to convey thoughts in fanciful
presentation; and his narrative, we may believe, As an ex-
having been first passed from mouth to mouth and Jesus's
then written down, at last, retaining its substance, took habit of
the form in which it appears in the gospels of Matthew cating his
and Luke. Matthew and Mark give an ending to periences,
their accounts which, whether it was in Jesus's see Lk. x.
narrative or not, certainly represents what must have instances
taken place. "Behold angels," we read, "came and &c.; xii.
ministered unto him." Certainly the spirit of Jesus xxvi. 38.
was sustained during the trials of this time by many Mt. iv. 11.
cheering thoughts. Did his experiences, indeed, really
represent what our word *temptation* suggests? We can
confidently say, No. The tempting thoughts assuredly
only passed through the mind, and never really came
into touch with the true inclinations of Jesus. The
inner experiences that do come before us through the
account are these: A fixed hold on the idea of the
Fatherliness of God, a disappointment and an indignation at the rough handling of the barbarian authorities,
a keen sense of the hardships he had now to bear in a
world that had formerly seemed to him so beautiful,
and, last not least, an all-mastering religious consciousness, explaining every difficulty and the more firmly
holding to its knowledge of what is true and good.

In these experiences we see how personal his ideas
were—how, even when his thoughts were occasioned
by the failure of John's mission, they took their rise
from his own centre idea of the Fatherhood of God.

From the inner experiences thus narrated we can
also go to the outward course of events. The speaking
of hunger tells of endurance of hunger. And the being

5

"tempted" (too strong a word as we are supposing it) and the speaking of a temptation to think one must serve the devil to secure success, tell the general fact which we have already recognised, that a first repulse had been met by the Sacred Life in its coming forward to declare its benign messages.

At this point we have again to leave the comparatively easy paths cut out by the Synoptic gospels, to follow for a little the footprints which a very careful and critical reading of the later Fourth Gospel affords us. But before going on to this, we must pause for a moment to consider a little more particularly the position in which Jesus now was as regards companions or followers.

When the followers of John were scattered, the probability is that they would form into different bands, separated by influences of various kinds, but mostly having to do with the parts of the country from which they severally came. We should expect, therefore, to find Jesus—independently of considerations in regard to his character—keeping with some group of Galileans ; and our considerations drawn in the second chapter from the Fourth Gospel, will induce us to think that the group around him would consist of those few Galileans who had already come to be impressed by him. This group, however, might naturally now become larger, as the whole gathering was breaking up. And all that is thus suggested agrees so well with what, as we shall find, followed in Jesus's ministry, that it can with the greatest probability be held to have happened. Jesus, we may believe, had now around him a somewhat larger band of what we must call not yet followers, but rather admirers. And, in particular,

we may with great probability assign to this period the
beginning of the friendship between him and James
and John, the sons of Zebedee—having no evidence
of its having begun earlier. For this we have the
fact that all through the ministry James and John
appear, along with Peter, as in a confidential relation
to Jesus quite different from that of the other apostles,
which suggests that Jesus had known all three before
he began his ministry proper. Again, the intimacy
that existed between Jesus and these three is in
accordance with the supposition that they had passed ·
through special adversity together. Further still, the
Gospel of Mark relates the beginning of the disciple- Mk. i. 16-
ship of all three in a way that suggests this reading of ^{21.}
the matter, making Jesus dramatically call them to be
his disciples before he entered Capernaum, which, in
a thorough-going view of all the gospels, must be
set down unhesitatingly as the starting-point of his
ministry. And with these considerations before us, we
may add what is a thought by no means to be despised,
namely, that by this reading the ecclesiastical association of the Fourth Gospel with the Apostle John
becomes to a very important extent justified. If John
cannot have written the whole book, we can see he
may have easily supplied the material from which the
work of the book takes its beginnings, inasmuch as he
was indeed with Jesus sufficiently early to gather even
such of the material as is peculiar to the book. James
and John, then, were, it is most probable among the
little Galilean group that now kept with Jesus—as well
as Simon Peter, whose heart was already warming
towards the Presence, alike commanding and fascinat-
ing, that was afterwards to possess him body and

5 *

spirit. Thus Jesus had by this time found the friends who were to sustain him through the rest of his short life in this world.

The passage in the Fourth Gospel to which we now proceed, with the view of finding footprints to follow, is that which is formed by the fourth chapter. The fourth chapter of John, taken as a whole, is of course, like the rest of the gospel, a chapter of ecclesiastical doctrine—not strictly history. But also, like the rest of the gospel, it has the appearance of being made up from an original historical account which the evangelist —very likely finding it already historically incoherent— used for his ecclesiastical ends. The fourth chapter of John surely contains several pieces of real history which by careful reading may be separated from it. That this is so is urged upon us by the lifelikeness of the pieces. But it can be further established when we come to believe that the whole passage had an original form, before it was worked up by the evangelist, in which it was a narrative of real facts. And that this latter is so is borne out by the following three weighty considerations : (1) The passage begins with the words, " When therefore the Lord knew how the Pharisees had heard that Jesus made and baptized more disciples than John (though Jesus himself baptized not, but his disciples), he left Judæa, and departed again into Galilee." What recommends itself most strongly, by way of interpreting these words, is that they were originally the record of a real conviction on Jesus's part of his being likely to be involved in the movement by the authorities against John, and of his consequently determining to return to Galilee. And as the only time in which this could have happened was just after

Jn. iv. 1-3.

The parenthesis, written long after the event, must mean that the disciples baptized after Jesus's death.

John's arrest,—which was, as we can be quite sure from reading the earlier gospels, the only time in which Jesus did in his public life journey from Judæa to Galilee,—we have most probably here the beginning of an account of the journey to which the general consideration has now led us. When, further, we attend to the fact that the sentence thus before us, as only slightly changed, states the motive of the journey to be exactly one of the motives which we have detected independently through a careful reading of the earlier gospels, our position is made the more strong. (2) We find that the passage goes on to describe the journey as proceeding through Samaria, and then, catching up with the words "In the meanwhile" (that is to Jn. iv. 31. say, going *back*), actually represents Jesus as uttering words almost the same as some of those given in Mt. iv. 4. the "Temptation" story, along with other words very characteristic of Jesus as we otherwise know him. Jn. iv. 46. (3) The passage ends with an account which, though The condifficult to understand, suggests a more original form, fusion in ver. 46 telling of Jesus some time arriving at Capernaum. between All these three considerations, each one strong in Caper- naum and its way, suggest that the fourth chapter of John Cana to be ex- has been worked up out of a document that plained by the evan- originally told of this journey from the Jordan to gelist Galilee, of which the other gospels assure us; and as having already the three sections of the chapter on which the three substitut- ed Cana considerations are severally centred have each of them for Caper- naum in ii. something natural and lifelike not explicitly found in 1-11. the Synoptics, they suggest that the original document Jn. iv. 1, 35-44. has not been the Synoptics, but has been an independent account of the journey in the evangelist's possession.

With great confidence, therefore, we can proceed to read critically this passage of the Fourth Gospel;

and out of what is in its present form a chapter of theological teaching, we shall be able to bring to light at least two valuable reminiscences of what actually happened.

The first of these is presented by the part beginning Jn. iv. 31. " In the meanwhile." From it we come to believe that Jesus, while still in the desert along with his few friends, had even then uttered a saying conveying the same thought as one of those he afterwards introduced into his pictorial account of his experiences at this time—that pictorial account which we are supposing to have been the original of the story of the Temptation. Vers. 31-34. tation. The company may have been speaking of their want of food, or some among them may have asked him to eat—not in the causeless manner in which they appear to do so in the gospel, but likely by way of resisting his unwillingness to deprive some other. Whatever may have led up to his reply, the reply was, we may be pretty sure, as it is given, " I have meat to eat that ye know not of. . . . My meat is to do the will of him that sent me." The E.g., Mk. iii. 35. words are altogether like the other words of Jesus that remain to us. We have every reason to believe them authentic—though the clause added by the evangelist, Cp. Jn. v. 36. " and to finish his work," has likely originated out of the evangelist's own philosophy. We may contemplate Jesus, at the very time of his first reverse, having seen the. Baptist arrested in the midst of his good work, and having been "tempted" with the thought that only the devil succeeds in this world, calmly speaking of eternal ideas which no outward accidents can keep from nourishing him, and of a fixed purpose which no outward force can ever divert an inch from its straight path.

Joined to these words in the received gospel, are some other words which may have been spoken by Jesus (in Jn. iv. 35-38. their substance) at another time, but can well be believed to have been spoken at this time as an addition to those we have just considered. Scholars have indeed regarded them as the words of a later period regarding the history of the Church, put as a prophecy into the mouth of Jesus. But we may rather look at the reference to later history as having been in the mind of the mystical evangelist in inserting the words and unconsciously, perhaps, changing them a little, without going the length of believing they had their complete origin in that reference. The student of the life of Jesus will find in the character of the words themselves a sufficient claim to be recognised as belonging to Jesus and to this part of his life. There is in the character of the words themselves a something which is like a bold family likeness seen in the face of a person whom one has not hitherto met, whose relatives one knows well. The words as slightly pruned are as follows: " Say not ye, There are yet four months, and then cometh harvest? behold, I say unto you, Lift up your eyes, and look on the fields; for they are white already to harvest. And he that reapeth receiveth wages, and gathereth fruit; . . . that both he that soweth and he that reapeth may rejoice together." We see here, with almost a plain perception and almost no use of the imagination, a reference to the work of John the Baptist, who has begun the awakening of religious interest and faith. We see, too, a reference to Jesus's own intention to carry on a work that will not necessarily be the same as that work of John, but will follow it in a natural manner. We see an encouragement to the new friends whom Jesus would keep with him, to look at the hope there is for such a work. And we see, what is still more interesting,—we see what arrests and charms as it appears,—the same spirit of honouring the Baptist which in the second chapter has already come before us. Jesus, having first delicately honoured the Baptist by receiving his baptism, now, when circumstances have brought about that he is in some way to supersede the Baptist, still must give honour ; and so he employs the wealth of his fancy to provide, for the purpose of giving honour, a new picture, in which he suggests that he will be " he that reapeth," and mentions the end as being that the sower and the reaper will " rejoice together."

See above. pp. 45, 58.

Having with regard to that first reminiscence been travelling on firm ground, we must now leave the steady ground to walk very carefully as we approach the second reminiscence, which is to be found in the story of Jesus and the Woman of Samaria.

Jn. iv. 4 42.

The story of Jesus and the Woman of Samaria has been explained by various scholars as presenting a mere idealistic conception—the woman of Samaria standing for the religion of Samaria, and Jesus himself for the Christianity that was afterwards established. And certainly this explanation must not be rejected. We must, however, deal with this story as we have with the passage we have just considered, and see that here also, as indeed all through the Fourth Gospel, we have not idealistic invention entirely, but reminiscence worked up into idealistic story. Our task, in separating the historical element from the ideal element, is, in the case now before us, a specially difficult one, seeing almost all the detail of the story, as it reads, must be

See Pflei-derer, " Urchris-tenthum."

pronounced to have only that ideal trueness which scholars have found in it. For the historical truth we have to make a considerable use of the critical imagination. The following statement, however, probably presents very nearly what happened :—

Jesus and his friends had proceeded out of the desert on their journey northward, and had reached some point in Samaria. One day the friends had left Jesus for a little, and when they rejoined him, they found him at a well talking to a woman who had come to draw water there. He had asked the woman, evidently Jn. iv. 7. before they came up, for some water to drink; but as they came the woman was drawing the water, and Jesus was speaking to her on another subject, most Ver. 20. likely the religious differences between Jews and Samaritans, leading to a remark on his part about the Ver. 21: heavenly Father, who could be worshipped everywhere. cp. ver. 27. As the friends came up, the woman naturally hastened Vers. 27, to present the water to Jesus; and on his receiving it 28. from her, he took opportunity to say, "Whosoever drinketh of this water shall thirst again: but whosoever Vers. 13, drinketh of the water that I shall give him shall never 14. thirst;" to which the woman replied, "Sir, I perceive Jn. iv. 19. that thou art a prophet." The woman then went away, and though the friends, in the words of the gospel, "marvelled that he talked with the woman," "yet no Ver. 27. man said, What seekest thou? or, Why talkest thou with her?" Afterwards, however, they entered the town, or, more likely, village, in which the woman lived. The woman had told her friends of an impressive man speaking to her, evidently a "prophet"; and so it Vers. 39- came about that he was kindly received by the people 42. in the village or town, partly "for the saying of the woman " (which, we may believe, did not, as was afterwards told, refer to her " husbands " or to the things she had formerly done), but partly also from the impression which he made on themselves.

It need scarcely be added that a simple story such as we have thus before us has nothing to do with questions regarding Jesus's relation to Samaria in general. So that the objections of critics to the recognition of the story, on the ground of the history in the Synoptics and the Acts showing that Jesus had no hold on Samaria in his lifetime, do not apply to it as it is here curtailed. Here we have a simple occurrence, which need not have had any far-reaching consequences.

We are thus presented with a view of Jesus rising above all little prejudices, acting and speaking like himself, as we otherwise learn of him. And we are also presented with a saying of Jesus, very like others we possess, and also fitting in—with an exactness most persuasive of the authenticity of both—with another saying which we have found him to have uttered but shortly before. We know from the general study of Jesus's teaching, that it was his habit to turn all ordinary things into imagery to represent sacred things. And through the two reminiscences with which we are now dealing, we see that before he entered on his public preaching he began this kind of thought with two very simple examples. The examples had already been used by the older prophets ; but Jesus gave them a turn of his own. First, he said there was "meat" to eat, that consisted in doing God's will ; and then he said there was "water" to drink, which was such that any one who drank it would never thirst again. And

Is. lv. 1.

both that meat and that drink he professed to have
attained himself. Afterwards he would speak of trea- Mt. vi. 19.
sures to lay up, which would never be taken away from
one ; now he spoke of water to drink, which would
make one never thirst again. Afterwards he would
speak of a house to dwell in, which was doing God's Mt. vii. 24.
will ; now he spoke of meat to eat, which was doing
God's will. Afterwards he would profess himself to be
able to give people a yoke to bear that was compatible Mt. xi. 28,
with rest ; now, in speaking of the greater than temporal 29.
drink, he professed himself to be able to give it. In
each of those pairs of sayings the one confirms the
authenticity of the other.

"After two days," says the Fourth Evangelist, when
he has finished his account of these occurrences, Jesus
"departed thence, and went into Galilee." We may Jn. iv. 43.
believe that this is so far a true record, and that imme- Cp. Mk. i.
diately after the occurrences that have just been before 14.
us Jesus entered Galilee. But how did he enter it ?
Did he enter as one embarrassed and defeated in the
aim with which he had set out ? No ; the picture of
Jesus which history is to open up to us is of another
character than that would imply. Jesus entered Galilee
at this time not in the attitude of humiliation, as being
one of a scattered assembly, but in the dignity of a
purpose of his own initiating. For the consideration
of this purpose, however, and of the events directly
connected with it, we must enter on another chapter.

CHAPTER IV.

THE THIRD MOVEMENT TOWARDS THE MINISTRY—
A DEFINITE PURPOSE.

THE escape which Jesus had made from the danger of
sharing the fate of the Baptist, became the means of
his forming a special purpose. On leaving Nazareth for
the Jordan, he had had, as we have seen, the general
purpose of communicating his religious ideas, knowing
that they were great ideas, and believing that a
"candle" should not be hid, but placed where it would
give light. In the second chapter we have seen that
this general purpose became in all probability so far
defined that he began to think of himself as the One
who would realise the idea of the expected Messiah,
though he kept this meanwhile within himself, and even
within himself never thought of accommodating himself
and his ideas to the Messiah-character, but rather
thought of using the Messiah-character to give external
form to his own character, and be the means of spreading his own ideas. At the point to which we have
come, however, he was forced to form a quite definite
purpose. Having it still before him to communicate
his ideas, and being now cast adrift from the leading

to which he had chosen for the time to submit himself, he had to make some new plan towards the communication he had in view. What the definite purpose was, then, which he formed, we have now to consider.

There is no indication of his having at this time either made or thought of making open adoption of the Messiah-character. No doubt the influence of John's teaching still remained, and he still kept the Messiah-idea as a guide to his thoughts. And very possibly— though this is, of course, little more than mere conjecture—it may have been during his musings at this time that he chose for himself the name "Son of man," Dan. vii. a name which was indeed associated with the Messiah- 13. character that he was willing to adopt, but at the same time fittingly expressed his own consciousness and his own ideas, and besides retained for him the modesty which was congenial to him. But there is nothing to indicate and everything to deny that the Messiah-idea had yet to do directly with the definite purpose which he had before him. And, indeed, as he only knew of the imprisonment of the Baptist, and not of his death, the Messiah-character, involving as it did the " coming after" John, had not yet presented itself for practical consideration.

What the evidence tells us on the subject is, we may say, that he formed a plan not according to the *ideas* he had got from John, but rather according to the *opportunities* which the association with John had now left to him. That is to say, what seems to have been the case is that at this point he formed the purpose of carrying on a ministry similar to John's, beginning for his following with the few who accompanied him, teaching, however, not John's ideas, but his own. What meets

us on reading the gospels is, on the one hand, that he
appeared afterwards away in Galilee, quite removed
Mk. i. 14. from the scene of John's ministry, teaching in a very
Mt. v., &c. different way from the way in which John taught. On
the other hand, the intimate connection made by all
Mk. i. 1-3, the gospels between his ministry and that of John, his
&c.; Mt.xi.
7-19. own recorded way of speaking about John, and the very
fact of his ultimately being identified in the minds of all
his followers with the Greater who, "coming after"
John, was "preferred before" him, make us believe
that he in some way took up the threads of John's
work. These facts together lead us to the view just
stated regarding the definite purpose which he now
must have formed. We are believing that a few
Galileans who along with himself had listened to John
now adhered to him. In last chapter we found him
encouraging these few by telling them that while John
had done the sowing, there was still to be done the
reaping. We can believe these men were becoming
more and more impressed with his sayings and his
whole personality. And accordingly it is most likely
that Jesus now formed the purpose of making them the
nucleus of a body to receive his teaching—not in the
part of the country where they then were, but in the
northern regions to which all belonged.

His choosing Galilee as the place for carrying out his
purpose requires little explanation. He could not with
prudence return to the quarter about the Jordan from
which he had come. Going, again, to Jerusalem, to
which he was in every way strange, was as yet out of
the question. It was natural for him to go to the part
of the country where everything was familiar to him.
And his intention of doing so was made the more

necessary by the position of his new friends. Galilee was their country also, and doubtless in every way they found it convenient now to return to it.

Such, then, was the definite purpose which Jesus had formed. And this purpose he immediately began to carry out. He entered Galilee, we can perceive, not as one repelled and crushed, but with the eager intention to pursue now directly and unaided the Mission which had been given him.

At this point we come within the lines again of the narrative in the Synoptic gospels, and we find that Jesus, on entering Galilee, did not return to Nazareth, but went to a town called CAPERNAUM, situated on the banks of the Lake of Gennesaret, or Sea of Galilee, and only a few hours' journey to the east of Nazareth. *Mk. i. 21. Cp. Mt. iv 13.*

That CAPERNAUM was the starting-point of the ministry of Jesus may be set down as certain. The Gospel of Mark records this when it is rightly read ; for though it speaks of Jesus preaching in Galilee before it mentions Capernaum, this is not to be taken as meaning that first he went to other places in Galilee and then to Capernaum, but simply that Galilee was the scene of his activity in *general*, and then that Capernaum was the first place he came to in *particular*. The general is first stated, then the particular. The Gospel of Matthew, again, puts the matter in another way, but quite as decisively. "Now when Jesus," it says, "had heard that John was cast into prison, he departed into Galilee : And leaving Nazareth, he came and dwelt in Capernaum." This is evidently not to be taken as meaning that he actually, at the beginning of his ministry, was in Nazareth, and from it went straight to Capernaum, any more than the statement in Mark is *Mk. i 14-21.* *Mt. iv. 12 13.*

to be taken as meaning that he was first in some other part of Galilee and then in Capernaum, but is to be taken as meaning that Capernaum, at the beginning of his ministry, superseded Nazareth, his old home, as the place of his abode. The Gospel of Luke, once more, gives a strange account ; but its account points almost as clearly in the same direction. It speaks as if he first went to Nazareth ; but in giving the events which happened at Nazareth, it relates that Jesus said, "Ye will surely say unto me this proverb, Physician, heal thyself : whatsoever we have heard done in Capernaum, do also here in thy country," thus indicating that he had been at work in Capernaum before he was at Nazareth on that occasion, and also suggesting that Capernaum had come to be the place with which his ministry was specially associated. And finally, the Gospel of John points decidedly enough, if somewhat vaguely, to the same fact. To Capernaum, then, beyond doubt Jesus now went.

Lk. iv. 16-23.

Perhaps following Mt. iv. 13, and mis-understanding the statement there, but more led on by the contents of the narrative, which he places first for idealistic reasons.

Jn. iv. 46-50.

It is not difficult to see the reasons both why he did not go to Nazareth, and why he chose to go to Capernaum instead.

For the reason why he did not go to Nazareth on this occasion, we must turn again to the Fourth Gospel. In the Fourth Gospel account of the journey northward, which we had before us in the last chapter, these words occur, "Now after two days he departed thence, and went into Galilee. For Jesus himself testified, that a prophet hath no honour in his own country." Now in reading these words it seems at first sight as if the evangelist were maintaining that Galilee was not Jesus's country. But there is a better explanation of the words. It is too much to believe the evangelist

Jn. iv. 43, 44.

would convey a notion so contradictory of general belief as that Galilee was not Jesus's country, in so indirect and so uninterested a manner. And thus the most natural explanation of the occurrence of the words is that the evangelist had adopted them from a source in which either they had lost their connection or he had failed to notice it. Taking, then, the passage along with a general study of this stage of the ministry, it is a short step in thought to the conclusion that in the account which the evangelist followed these words were found, perhaps already obscured in meaning, but originally having been written to give the reason why Jesus did not go to Nazareth. This is confirmed by the fact that, immediately after, the evangelist speaks of Jesus as working at Capernaum, though, with his usual carelessness about matters of locality, his account suggests that Jesus did not take the trouble to enter Capernaum, but only worked a miracle there for the sake of a man who had come elsewhere to seek him out. Vers. 46-54.

The reason why he went to Capernaum in particular, having given up the thought of Nazareth, we can detect in the earliest gospel, if not with certainty, at least with what is almost certainty. It was, we may be practically certain, because his new friend Simon, and probably others of his new friends, belonged to that town. In all probability, indeed, he went to Capernaum invited by Simon, with whom it would seem he went to live. Mk. i. 21, 29.

On his way towards Capernaum his plan for the future was, it would seem, so far disclosed to his three special associates. They were probably speaking of their fishing business, to which naturally they would return. Jesus said to them, however, something like this: If

6

Mk. i. 16-20. you come with me, " I will make you to become fishers of men." How much they may have promised in response to this proposal we cannot tell. In a lengthened and popularised account of this incident which we find Lk. v. 3-11. in Luke, some words have been preserved that seem to indicate reluctance on the part of Simon Peter to associate himself with Jesus in a reforming undertaking, Ver. 8. on the ground of personal unfitness. We see, however, clearly enough the fact that they all three entered Vers. 10, 11. the town with Jesus at least in full friendship and , sympathy.

Regarding the *time* of this happening, in relation to our own reckoning of years, the abstruse calculations of Josephus, scholars contradict one another perplexingly. Dr. Keim Antiq. bk. and Wittichen—reasoning from the mention of John xviii. the Baptist in Josephus on the one side, and the time of the recall of Pilate from charge over Judaea, also mentioned there, on the other side—have fixed the death of Jesus to the spring of the year 35. Others So Renan, have arrived at earlier dates. The date 35 may be Weiss, and Weiz- adopted here, it being admitted that this bringing of säcker. the life into exact relationship with our own reckoning For cal- is, like certain other particulars in regard to the life, a culations Keim, probability not a certainty. The relations of time Caspari, &c., may within the life, however, can be more certainly defined. be con- And as the early gospels give only scope for a year's sulted. ministry or thereby, the event now before us must have happened in the year before Jesus's death—that is the year 34, if the other reckoning be right. It is Mk. ii. 23. further fixed to the *spring* of that year by the story of Jesus, evidently just a little time after the beginning of the ministry, walking among the ripe corn ; and this Jn. iv. 35. is confirmed by our own reading of the fourth chapter

of John, in which we have seen that in his journey
northward to begin the ministry, he spoke of it being
" four months" till harvest. *Hurry* marks all the
movements in the ministry of Jesus, as the gospels
clearly tell of them. It is according to this that the
time of his leaving Nazareth to join the Baptist has
been determined above as being about the beginning of
this same year 34 ; and according to this we can now
believe that the entry of Jesus and his associates into
Capernaum took place not more than three or four
months at the longest from the time he had left
Nazareth to go south.

About the *place* Capernaum little is known from contemporary history ; but from the gospels themselves it
has been concluded that it was a town of some size and
prosperity. It was situated on the Lake of Gennesareth,
which at that time, according to Josephus the historian, Jos., Wars
was a lake affording different kinds of fish and having of the
ships in it, surrounded by a beautiful and fruitful Jews, bk.
country. Into a prosperous oriental town, on the side iii., c. 10.
of a magnificent lake, in the spring-time of a year about
eighteen centuries and a half ago, very probably the
year 34 of our reckoning, we are to conceive Jesus and
his companions entering.

It is certainly both a solemn and a pathetic spectacle
that is presented to our reflection in this entry of Jesus
into Capernaum. When we remember that the return
journey to Galilee, although it did have an independent
purpose, was in some measure occasioned by the sight
of failure, and in a way by the participation in failure ;
when we remember that all Jesus had gained by his
journey to the south was the adherence of a few, perhaps
no more than three or four, men, along with some prac-

tical ideas which as yet he had not put to trial; and
when thus we discern that the return from Judæa, to
which he had gone with his great aim before him, must
have been accompanied by the disappointed feeling that
on coming back to Galilee he was no further forward
than when he left it—this entry into Capernaum must
appear to us something in most solemn contrast to the
superb triumph of Jesus's name and ministry in after-
years, as well as excite in us a reverent sympathy for
the august Subject of this study. We have before us a
beginning of a ministry in absolute littleness. We
have before us historical reality in accordance with the
bold figures of the infancy-story in the Gospel of Luke
—the being refused admission to the inn; the stable,
and the manger. The spectacle has, indeed, if not
quite a bright side, still a side with brightness shining
on it. Such is brought about by the fact of it having
been spring-time, through which Jesus must have felt
a sustaining and something of an inspiring from the
natural world around him, along with the fact of the
growing devotion of be it but three human beings,
which would combine with the spring to cheer and
speak of hope. But taking these things fully into
account, we still must have our wonder and awe
appealed to and our sympathies moved as we contemplate Jesus, with the little band of companions in whose
charge he has meanwhile placed himself, entering as an
unknown traveller the streets of a busy town, with the
aim of making its men and women his disciples.

PART II.

THE MINISTRY IN GALILEE.

CHAPTER V.

GOOD TIDINGS OF GREAT JOY TO ALL PEOPLE.

THE *supernaturalness*—in the proper sense of that word—
which truly is to be seen in the life of Jesus makes an
almost complete appearance in miniature in the events
of the beginning of the ministry at Capernaum. A
supernaturalness consisting in the power of Spirit, as
personified in Jesus, to command surrounding life, must
already, to any sympathetic reader of the foregoing
pages, be showing itself as having belonged to Jesus,
and will still further reveal itself as we proceed. This
supernaturalness may be said to have assumed a condensed or abridged form in the events which are now
to engage our attention. The more simply we now
run over these events the better. The passage in the Mk. i. 21-
Gospel of Mark which relates them is the most history- 45.

like of all parts of the gospels. We have but to reproduce it in modern language, filling up details from the other two early gospels. And if this be faithfully done, then there must appear to the reader a taking command by the spirit of Jesus of the life at Capernaum in the year 34, which is an epitome of the ascendancy soon after to be begun, in which the whole western world would come into subjection to him.

Jesus—as we may learn from thoughtfully reading the Gospel of Mark—on entering Capernaum became the guest of Simon Peter. In a very short time there was procured for him an opportunity to address the people of the town in a synagogue. He did address the people—once and probably more than once; and principally by means of his addresses, but partly also through accompanying actions, he became in a few days a popular centre of enthusiasm.

For us the first and most important question to answer is, What were the ideas which Jesus now communicated to the people at Capernaum?

There is no answer to this question to be found in the account in Mark—palpably for the very reason of its historical honesty. Of this first preaching no careful report would be made, because there were none who yet knew the importance of the preacher. The gospel account, accordingly, shows its trustworthiness in its very refraining from supplying us with anything like a report. And thus, indeed, we must expect for our question no answer which will give us particular details. We get, however, an indication which will enable us to learn what must have been the drift of this first preaching of Jesus, and what, in brief, were those ideas which Jesus had come forth to communi-

Side notes: Mk. i. 29. Cp. Mk. ii. 1. Mk. i. 21.

cate, and now did communicate, from sayings that
have been preserved from his utterances in general.
The Gospel of Mark gives us a sentence which pro- Mk. i. 14.
fesses to sum up the first preaching of Jesus ; and the [15.]
gospels of Matthew and Luke give each of them a Mt. v.-
sample discourse from his general preaching. When vii. ; Lk. vi. 17-49.
we consider the solidity of thought and the power of
enthusiasm which appear in Jesus, we shall believe
that all the outpourings of his mind must have
contained essentially the same ideas, and that one
or a few samples will tell us of all his addresses, and
especially of the first that he spoke after long years
of silence. And we can hold to this even though it is
to be admitted that much of the teaching to be found
in the sample discourses was in all likelihood given,
as we find it, not in public discourses, but in private
conversation with the disciples. The ideas themselves
are of such a nature that we cannot believe he would
express them only to a limited audience. So that those
sample discourses which the gospels of Matthew and
Luke put into our possession—along with the sentence
in the Gospel of Mark—are as valuable for the purpose
of telling us what were the ideas which Jesus communicated in his first preaching at Capernaum, or what
was the drift of his first addresses, as a report of the
addresses themselves would have been.

The summing-up sentence of the Gospel of Mark is
in these words : "Now after that John was put in prison, Mk. i. 14.
Jesus came into Galilee, preaching the gospel of the [15.]
kingdom of God, And saying, The time is fulfilled, and
the kingdom of God is at hand: repent ye, and
believe the gospel." As to the call to "repent," or *metanoeite.*
change, it need hardly be taken into account for our

purpose. It is the same call as is attributed also to the Baptist, and, in the case of Jesus at least, we may set down as certain that there is nothing dogmatic conveyed in the mere idea of the changing. Then as regards the words "believe the gospel," these must be put aside also for the meantime—though we shall return to them afterwards—as a survey of the whole records of teaching does not bear out the opinion that Jesus ever dwelt much on the "gospel" (*euangelion* = good news) as an *expression*. What remains to us of the sentence is that Jesus preached the *kingdom of God*, and that he said that it was *at hand*.

Cp. above, p. 44.

Cp. Mk. iv. 26-34; Mt. xiii. 24-52, &c.

The records of the teaching of Jesus thoroughly bear out his having put forth this last conception. The kingdom of God undoubtedly Jesus preached, and he said that it was at hand.

And yet we cannot even now claim to have arrived at the essence of Jesus's teaching. No, we shall find that his ideas were vastly further-reaching than this summing-up sentence of the Gospel of Mark would indicate.

The Gospel of Mark in this sentence has presented the outward form without portraying the life. That is to say, the conception of the *kingdom of God* is to be looked at as a setting for the ideas of Jesus, or a category through which he helped to make them clear to his own mind and to convey them to the minds of his countrymen. It had the same use for him as we have seen the Messiah-idea had. Only he fixed his thoughts and sayings more to it than to that other, as it kept his own personality more in the background. That God would one day set up a kingdom had been a popular religious notion among the Israelite people for centuries before the time of Jesus. It had had its origin in the strength of the religious consciousness of the old prophets. It had been provided by the prophets as a new hope to take the place of the disappointed expectation of the Israelite nation being maintained as a chosen people under the Divine government. Thus in a way the hope of a *kingdom of God* was a mere commonplace of Israelite religious faith. And further, it had been stated expressly in the Book of Daniel, which was evidently a book with which Jesus was familiar. All that Jesus did in regard to the conception was to adopt it to serve his own ideas. He said it would soon be realised—in the same free and inexact way in which he said the expectation that "Elias must first come" had been realised, namely, by the life of John the Baptist, who had not literally been Elias at all.

More particularly, the relation to Jesus's ideas of this conception or this phrase, "the kingdom of God," was that it expressed a consequence for which the free course of his ideas was to be the moving power. It was the conception which, in the common way of looking at things of his people and time, represented the general conception of an establishment of religion, or of the Divine Presence becoming a real centre of attention. Jesus, in the strength of his own religious consciousness, was proclaiming an establishment of religion which would take place through his own means. He accordingly laid hold of this conception, which, for himself and others, was equivalent to or at least included an establishment of religion, and by saying that it was about to be realised, made his solemn proclamation in a way both natural to himself and intelligible to his

Dan. ii. 37, 44.

Mk. ix. 13.

Cp. Jn. ii. 19. Mk. xiv. 58.

hearers. The means, however, by which he promised
that the object of his proclamation would come about,
were the receiving and adopting of **certain ideas of his
own.** These ideas of his own **were not what was
expressed** in the phrase or conception of the "kingdom
of God." The kingdom **of God** was the establishment
of religion, to which **the** making **known of his** ideas
would lead.

It must be stated here with some emphasis **that the**
conception of the *kingdom of God* had **no more to do**
with the teaching of Jesus than that it thus helped him
to express and enforce his own ideas. In other words,
it must be maintained that Jesus's own special ideas
were distinct from this conception. The importance of
taking up such a position emphatically lies in this, that
the true centre of religious knowledge and interest
cannot be in any mere object **of** hope in the future as
distinct from the past, but **must be** an eternal overruling, to be conceived of as **prevailing** in all ages.
Religion is largely deprived of **its place** as a rational
interest, let alone the place which **is due to** it of the
supreme rational interest—when its object of attention
is narrowed down to the future as opposed to the past.
All the great sciences—and religious knowledge at the
head of them—have to do with the eternal. So that if
it were to be found that Jesus's teaching had concerned itself only with a future establishment of religion
or future time of human welfare in general, such as the
conception of the *kingdom of God* naturally implied, we
should be confronted with something very perplexing.
That supreme prophetic attitude, which, with all Christendom, we are here ascribing to Jesus only among all
teachers, could not concern itself with the future alone.

Cp. w.
this Kings-
ley's *Hy-
patia*, p.
381.

Perfection, in this matter, implies insight into the present as well as the future. In a broad and scientific view, what must be truly called the kingdom of God—giving respect to the conception of God which the thought of the world has attained—is the eternal rule of God, the rule of God of yesterday, to-day, to-morrow, and always. The "kingdom" which is confined to the establishment of religion is properly man's response to a rule which has ever been exercised. And if Jesus's prophetic insight was unique, was ideal, it cannot have been taken up with the response apart from the rule which precedes the response. But it is possible to show beyond question that Jesus's ideas far transcended the conception of the kingdom of God in its narrower application. Sayings with other ideas far greater have been preserved and ascribed to him—sayings indicating, among other things, that the reign of God, which he believed in and taught, was the eternal overruling. These latter sayings are of such a kind that they could have no other source than in genius. Setting them, therefore, opposite to the conception now before us, there is no question as to which side shows us what was working in the mind of Jesus and forcing itself into expression. On the one side we have what we recognise at once as a popular conception; on the other side we have what is the evident outcome of an individual mind. In the sayings on this other side, and not in that sentence from the Gospel of Mark which we set opposite to them, we are to find the ideas that were the outcome of Jesus's individual self and formed the essential part of his teaching. To antici- pate what these sayings were, we may run over such sayings as those regarding little children, those re-

Mk. ix. 37,
x. 14;
Mt. x. 30; garding the valuing of man by God, those regarding life above and beyond this world, and those regarding
Lk. vi. 35;
Mt. vi. 19, the experience of heathens and outcasts showing often
20; Lk. x. greater goodness than the professedly religious. **These**
30-37. are enough to assure us that the ideas of Jesus, the enthusiasm of Jesus, and the whole interest of Jesus, are not to be looked for in any conception or phrase that would suggest him to have been a revolutionary or utopian.

There is greater importance to be attributed to Jesus's proclaiming that the kingdom of God was " at hand "; that is to say, as we are interpreting that proclamation, that he himself would bring about a new establishment of religion. That proclamation was a prediction made on the strength of his self-consciousness, and it has been fulfilled. Many as have been the misunderstandings of Jesus and his teaching, there is no doubt that from his time religion has become, broadly speaking, established as a new power in the world. But even when we recognise this, our chief interest will not be so much in the mere proclamation of this triumph of religion through Jesus, as in the particular ideas of Jesus and the particular enthusiasms of Jesus which made him able to give the power to religion in which it did triumph. To his real ideas, therefore, which have so far eluded our search, we must still press on. We have learned from the Gospel of Mark what was the setting which Jesus's ideas had assumed; for what the ideas were in themselves we have to proceed to the gospels of Matthew and Luke.

There is provided to our hands a reliable statement
Mt. v.-vii. of the IDEAS OF JESUS in the famous SERMON ON THE

MOUNT. And our grasp of them is made the more complete when we compare with the Sermon on the Mount other sayings reported throughout the first three gospels, and especially the collection given in the sixth chapter of Luke, which we can appropriately call the SERMON ON THE PLAIN. ^{Lk. vi. 17-49.}

The notion that the Sermon on the Mount, as we have it, is one complete discourse of Jesus, preached by him from a mountain, vanishes at the first thoughtful consideration of the matter. The question as to what historical reality there is at the back of the words in verse 1 of the fifth chapter of Matthew, will be considered in a later chapter. It is now, however, to be said that the origin of connecting the whole discourse as it reads in Matthew with a mountain, is principally to be traced to the doctrinal imagination of the first Christians. The Israelites had long lived in the belief that their ancient law had been given to earth by God ^{Exod. xix. 3.} from a mountain. When, therefore, the Christian faith superseded the ancient faith in the minds of many Israelites, the belief grew that God had come to earth again, and, again standing above men on a mountain, had given them a new law. This course of doctrinal thought can be seen quite plainly in these words in the Epistle to the Hebrews: "For ye are ^{Heb. xii. 18-24.} not come unto the mount that might be touched, and that burned with fire, nor unto blackness, and darkness, and tempest, And the sound of a trumpet, and the voice of words; which voice they that heard entreated that the word should not be spoken to them any more: . . . But ye are come unto Mount Sion, and unto the city of the living God, the heavenly Jerusalem, and to an innumerable company of angels,

To the general assembly and church of the **first-born**,
which are written **in** heaven, and to God the Judge **of**
all, and to the spirits **of just men made perfect, and to**
Jesus the **mediator of** the new covenant, **and to the**
blood **of** sprinkling, that speaketh better things than
that of Abel." It is **just a** step further in the mystical
thought to be seen in this passage, that is to be detected
in the First Gospel, when, in giving a sample collection
of the teachings of Jesus, it **declares they were delivered**

The origi-
nal is
to oros
and so in
corre-
sponding
passages
in the
other gos-
pels. The
force of
the article
is a ques-
tion for
scholars ;
but it is
by no
means
certain
that it
has not
here a
definite
significa-
tion. See
the com-
mentary
of Meyer.

from a mountain—or *the* mountain. **And so we** can
understand how we find in the Third **Gospel a collection**
of sayings almost the same—even in the order **of** their
occurrence—but having a different setting **of time and**
place. **The** third evangelist gives his sample discourse
as having **been** delivered, **not** at the beginning of
Jesus's ministry, but **at the time of** sending out the
disciples. And certainly **if the** discourses of the two
evangelists had been taken **from any** one speech of
Jesus, that one speech would more likely have belonged
to the later time than the earlier, seeing that at the
earlier time Jesus's hearers would not yet be the
length of carefully noting his sayings. The historical
truth of the matter is likely, as we shall see, that parts
of the collections were taken down from some speeches
of Jesus delivered about **the** time to which Luke
ascribes **the** whole. **But what** is important at this
point to notice is that **the** third evangelist brings
his representation of Jesus, **as** uttering the discourse,

Ver. 17.

down from **the** mountain to the *plain*. " He came
down **with them,** and stood in the plain," we read.
What **we are to understand by** this is principally that
the evangelist Luke, with **a** keen perception of the
spirit **of Jesus's** teaching, felt there was something

wrong in placing it, like the old Jewish law, away above
men as a thing merely given them to obey, and saw
that it was teaching which, in its tone of sympathy and
encouragement, suggested God coming down to help
men themselves to live pure and generous lives. For us
both the settings have a value—an idealistic value.
We must recognise that the teaching of Jesus stands
still high up above us in its unique purity and power;
and we must also recognise that it comes down into
the hearts of the humblest of us in its perfect sympathy
and care. But looking at the historical detail of the
matter, the collections must be believed to have been
gathered from several speeches of Jesus, and for us
now they are to be accepted as informing us on the
question of what must have been the general thoughts
of those first addresses delivered by him in the synagogue at Capernaum.

The sample discourses ring with two words. The
one is FATHER; the other is BROTHER, or, as the case
may be, SISTER. They are full of two eternal truths.
The one is the Fatherly relation of God to men; the
other is the purpose, in men's receiving life, that they
should be brothers and sisters to each other. The
one is the truth of the *infinite care of God for man;* the
other is the truth of the *infinite responsibility of man to
man.* With those two truths or those two words in
our minds—or with the passages which tell of the one,
and the passages which tell of the other, before us—
we can, with a sufficient exactness for our purpose,
bring before us what Jesus preached to the people at
Capernaum.

He told them, we can gather, of a Care extended
over them which had begun with their lives and would

[margin: Cp. Mk. v. 7.]

[margin: Mt. vi. 19-34 and x. 29-31 w. similar passages in Lk. Lk. vi. 27-38 and Mt. v. 21-48.]

Mt. vi. 26, **never end.** This care was—according **to** his mind,
28-30, x.
29-31, vi. and most likely according to his definite utterances at
34. this **time—so wide that** the birds and the flowers
might be said to be included in it, though, as they
were of limited **value, it** was for **them of** limited
duration, whereas for men and women, who were of
indefinitely greater value, it knew no limits at all. It
was so complete, **too, that if they** would but think of

Mt. vi. 34. **it they could put away all anxiety for the future, and**
let the morrow ever "take thought **for the things of**
itself." And as for the depth and the intensity of this
Care, to describe this his fancy went—most likely in
these first addresses, but certainly in some **of his**
utterances—further **than that of** any poet describing a
mother's affection for **her child or** a maiden's adoration
of her lover; for what has come down to us of **his**
sayings with respect to this **is that** it was such as to

Mt. x. 30. number the very hairs of **the head.** But also, while
the Care **was thus like** human **love** made ever so much
greater, it had at the same time one characteristic in
which it soared away completely from human parallels

Lk. vi. 21- **as** ordinarily seen and judged, and this was that it
23, 35. chose **always as its** special objects the souls most
abandoned **for the** time by what makes life happy. It
was a Care most of **all for** the mourner, the poor, and
the hungry, and even for **the** unthankful and the evil.

This teaching, we can see, **had** its origin in the fact
that Jesus himself both had a keen sense that perceived
the Divine **Presence** and also **was** conscious of a relation of perfect oneness with that Presence. God ever
and **everywhere** present **had been** the object of his
knowledge. **That God was** he perceived, and what
God **was he perceived.** And he had learned, through

thus perceiving what was there beside him, that God
was all care and consideration—for himself certainly,
but also for all beings that breathe and think.
And evidently there was nothing in Jesus that could
disturb the assurance that came with this perception.
He had no habit of minute analysing to prompt him to
explain away the glory of what he perceived. Nor
had he, on the other side, such a sense of the moral
abasement of man as might have made him hold man to
be shut out from expecting the blessings which that glory
promised. Plainly his own heart was pure as are not So also in-
those of other men. Plainly his own remembrance was testimony
not as those of others are, touched with shame. But of Paul
there was more than this that prevented him, as a man, säcker).
from having a despairing feeling of the moral abasement
of men in general. There was his consciousness that
all thinking beings were outcomes of the very life of
the Divine Presence, and that the Care over them was
perfect because it was the care of God for His own.

He told the people also, we can say, of a purpose in
their existence which was no less than this, that as
God cared for them, they were to come to care for Lk. vi. 35.
others. The motive of their every thought, he brought 36; Mt. v.
out, if they lived as they ought to live, was to be care, Lk. vi. 35.
pure care, uninfluenced by any other feeling or notion.
As God loved, forgave, and was kind, they were to
love, forgive, and be kind. Adopting an ancient saying
in the name of God, " Ye shall be holy: for I the Lord Lev. xix 2.
your God am holy," he enriched this from his own
fresh knowledge of God into, " Be ye . . . merciful, as Lk. vi. 36;
your Father also is merciful," and he gave this as what cp. Mt. v.
properly would be the sole motive-power in a human 48.
life. He pointed out that men should cease to need

7

detailed prohibitions of this and that. They should change, he pointed out, from slaves of the Sovereign Power to children of the Sovereign Power, and substitute for every "Thou shalt not" the responsible feeling of a brother or a sister.

This teaching also, we can see, had its source in the fact that Jesus perceived the Divine Presence and was conscious of a relation of perfect oneness with it. His perception of God and his consciousness of relationship to God told not only of the care of God for man, but also of what is indeed just the development of that same truth, the care being so great that it would make man live the life of God. And every indication gives the lie to the notion afterwards to be entertained by his followers, that he claimed this relationship for himself but denied it to others. The thought is quite the other way both in the Sermon on the Mount and in the Sermon on the Plain. All, he quite plainly thought and said, had the calling of brothers and sisters and the duty of brothers and sisters. He did, indeed, claim a special relation to God. He did claim special greatness, and perhaps special purity. But the specialness, *as he claimed it*, was of a kind that time and the awakening of man's true nature would ever be breaking down. For Jesus, evidently, the world contained God and His children—nothing more, except those evil powers which were to fall before the power of these two.

The two circles of ideas thus indicated, which, as already suggested, can be summed up in the two words *Father* and *brother*, were united both in Jesus's own mind and in his teaching into ONE IDEA for the explaining of human life—namely, that every thinking being born into this world is born a unit, never again to lose

Marginal note: Mt. v. 21-48. Most valuable also as examples of his teaching in this line are Lk. xvi. 1-13, and xvii. 7-10, of which both it is difficult to determine the historical connection.

individuality, in the Eternal Life of God. To Jesus Mt. xxv.
each new individual stepped at the moment of birth $\substack{14-30.\ \text{Cp.}\\ \text{Mk. ix. 49}}$
within not one but two worlds—the one this most $\substack{\text{Lk. vi. 20-}\\23.}$
easily seen world, from which each soon must vanish, Mt. vii. 11;
but the other a less easily seen world, in which each $\substack{\text{Jn. xii. 24.}\\25.}$
will for ever live and grow. And his practical exhorta-
tion, which was the outcome of this central idea, we
may conceive as very likely to have taken form in this
first preaching at Capernaum, in words almost the
same as those grand words in our possession, " Lay Mt. vi. 19,
not up for yourselves treasures upon earth, where moth $^{20.}$
and rust doth corrupt, and where thieves break through
and steal: But lay up for yourselves treasures in
heaven, where neither moth nor rust doth corrupt,
and where thieves do not break through nor steal."

These were the ideas which, as surely as almost
anything in the past is sure, were the ideas expressed
by him who has shown himself to have been the
greatest power in the world of mankind. These were
the ideas which formed the essential part of Jesus's
thought and teaching. These were the ideas which,
burning within his mind, had made him conscious of
his princely calling in Nazareth. And these are the
ideas which for us are now to tell what Jesus was and
what he taught.

And now we can return to the summing-up sentence
of the Gospel of Mark, and take from it what, for the
time, we left behind. Now we can see that, whether
or not our Lord Jesus literally began his teaching with
a mention of the " gospel," the evangelist was justified
in introducing the word. For the teaching was indeed
the gospel. It was the Good Tidings which the world
had been waiting for. No threatening prediction of

7 *

new horrors, as his groping followers have too often
interpreted it and expounded it, it was the Message
come in a more than human face, and in a word glowing with more than human authority, assuring those
bound by the horrors which nature itself has brought,
that God is greater than nature, and that for the
deepest dismay there is still deeper love.

It is indeed to be added that there was a less ethereal
element in his preaching, necessitated by the fact of
there being old doctrine around him which his masterly
understanding of religious matters made him hate and
demand to have cleared away.   There was a polemical
element in his teaching.   He began what was to grow
into a war between him and the scribes and the
Pharisees.   The self-assertive disputations indeed in
the Fourth Gospel are not to be ascribed to the personality of Jesus, or to the period of his earthly life.
They are the answers put forward to later objections by
the Church in his name.   Otherwise they would be in
contradiction to everything about Jesus in the other
gospels.   Also all indications point to the fact that it
was only at the end of his ministry that he took up a
directly aggressive position in relation to the " scribes
and Pharisees."   But that even in his early preaching
he in some way attacked the accepted religious teachers
of his time is certain, if it were for nothing more than
the way in which they turned against him.   He did not,
we may say certainly, at this earlier time go the length
of making direct charges against them ; but he struck,
in a way that could not be mistaken, at their system.
Jesus, most likely at this very time in Capernaum, as
he preached to the people the kingdom of God, and
told them the truths that needed to be recognised in

Jn. v.-ix.

Mt. xv. 14,
not in Mk.
might
seem to be
an excep-
tion in
testimony,
but it can
be viewed
as infusion
of report
of later
sayings
into
narrative.
Cp. ver. 13
with Jn.
xv. 2.

order to bring the kingdom of God, also said they
would not be worthy to enter the kingdom of God
unless their righteousness would " exceed the righteous- Mt. v. 20.
ness of the scribes and Pharisees."

The *manner* of his preaching we can only in part be
certain of. Whether in these first addresses he employed, as commonly afterwards, the simple stories
which have come to be called *parables*, or stated the great Cp. Justin
truths in the terse form in which we find them in the Martyr,
Apol.i. 14.
sample discourses, we cannot tell. One thing, however,
is clear. He taught in a tone of authority, as one who had Mk. i. 22,
himself become master of his subject, and with an enthus- 27.
iasm which was capable of carrying conviction with it.

To all this teaching Jesus began at once to show
corresponding actions. He began himself to do actions
in relation to the people around that were kind as the
heavenly Father is kind. And these actions proceeded
on a faith that God would fill up, in His care, what Mk. x. 27.
human limitations left yet imperfect. Of the detail of
what he did in this way we are given these facts : That Mk. i. 29-
he in some way cured of a fever the mother of Simon's 31.
wife ; that when he was preaching, a man " with an Vers. 23-
unclean spirit " interrupted him, and that he called out 26.
to the man, and through his " authority " silenced the
interruption ; and that, following up these two actions,
he healed others of diseases, and exercised his authority Ver. 34.
in calming other troubled minds.

The task of determining with any accuracy what kind
of power Jesus exercised on the man who interrupted
him in the synagogue and other similar persons spoken
of in the gospels, is one which, in this study, may not
unwisely be left unaccomplished. For the aim before
us it is enough to notice that these persons were in

some way of unstrung if not unsound mind, and that the **power** exercised **over them** by Jesus **cannot be** doubted.   And it may **be** added that the certainty **of** this general state of matters is the more emphasised by **the way** in which the evangelists describe what occurred from the point of view of **the patients as well as of the**

Mk. i. 34, iii. 11, v. 6.

onlooker.   The demons *knew* **Jesus as their master, we** are repeatedly informed by Mark. **This, surely, is no** mere doctrinal commentary.   **It is rather as much as** to assure **us of what we** may accept **as indubitable, that** before the presence of Jesus **those** persons **of** troubled mind became at once conscious of a command over them.

Looking, **however, now at both** the silencing **of the** man and **the curing of Simon's** mother-in-law, it **is of** great importance **for us to notice, in the** interests both **of truth and** of religion, that **these** and other similar

Cp. Justin Martyr, Apol. i. 30, and Origen, ag. Celsus i., 38.

good **actions of** Jesus are capable of **being** regarded as essentially human actions. That is to say, the "miraculous" element in them need not be **supposed to have** been any kind of magic, or recondite interference with ordinary laws and processes. It can be seen by thought-

Mk. i. 44, iii. 12 ; Mt. xii. 39, xvii. 20.

ful reading of the gospels that Jesus himself disliked the **popular** notion of his actions that called them miraculous in the sense of magical ; and had they been miraculous in this sense, they would have been without **the real importance they** possess for us. What we are fortunate in being able to see in them is that they were simple outcomes of his own teaching regarding the son-

The early Church was at one with modern study in this. See

ship **of man to God and the** duty of man to act like **God ; and this they** could **not** have been had they **made** use **of means essentially** different from those **granted to ordinary** human **beings. We are** to be

thankful, then, that scholars have been able to show
that these actions of Jesus were not necessarily
miraculous in a sense that would place a barrier
between Jesus and those whom he called to share his
way of life with him. The first chapter of Mark tells,
in the language of Jesus's people and time, of actions
in the best sense human. As for the silencing the
hysterical man, and the other actions similar to that,
which in the language of the time are described as
casting out demons—it can be seen from the gospels
that in general belief the casting out of demons was a
power possessed by various people, and not confined to
Jesus; and the historian Josephus tells of the power
having been possessed by some as confidently as the
evangelists tell of it in regard to Jesus. And as for the
curing Simon's mother-in-law and the other actions
similar to that, there is nothing in the simple account
of Mark to take them out of the sphere of human
actions. Jesus evidently had a power of healing which
arrested the people among whom he moved, and combined with his teaching to draw them around him ; and
in his later acts of healing, a *faith* in this power was
assuredly a most important factor in the cure. Nothing
will be further from the results, as nothing is further
from the aim, of this and every reverent study, than to
minimise or even too inquisitively to rationalise this
special power of Jesus. But that the power was in
him become a human power, and that it is possible for
man to participate in his power and do actions kindred
to his actions, accords with his own teaching, and must
be believed to accord with the facts. Also that Jesus
may have used specific remedies to a small extent, is
neither itself improbable nor inadmissible from the

Margin notes:
Origen for ex. ag. Celsus i. 67, and Iren. Haer. iii 18 (5). It is the view of the world that is different between the older and the newer.

Mt. xii. 27 ; Mk. ix. 38.

Jos., Ant. viii. 2. 5.

Mk. vi. 7, ix. 18-19. xi. 22-33.

gospel accounts; and in this first act, the curing of
Simon's mother-in-law, there was, it is most likely,
some particular remedy employed as well as some good
practical advice given, which would both work along
with the faith aroused by the commanding stranger
that had entered the house. Jesus's good acts, then,
we may believe, made use of human means; and, it
may be added, they were performed within human conditions. They brought no clean sweep of suffering and
death; they only had relation to some few human
beings with whom his ordinary life brought him into
contact, and even for them had only a temporary and
relative effect.

Cp. the
excellent
account of
the truth
regarding
his sub-
ject in
Clodd's
'Jesus of
Nazareth.'

And now, having cleared away the mischievous notion
of miracle in the sense of magic, we can go on to see
what was really special in these actions of Jesus. They
had two very important special characteristics, which
can be described as miraculous if that word be only
given its derivative meaning of *wonderful*. First, Jesus
showed in these actions a unique and worshipful
personal power. This is described to us in the Gospel
of Mark in the words that tell of the impression he
made on the people; and the words convey the facts to

Mk. i. 22.

us through their very simplicity. "He taught them,"
we read, "as one that had authority, and not as the

Ver. 27.

scribes;" and again, "And they were all amazed,
insomuch that they questioned among themselves,
saying, What thing is this? what new doctrine is this?
for *with authority* commandeth he even the unclean
spirits, and they do obey him." The good actions of
Jesus in general, and these first actions now before us
in particular, proceeded from a soul of unique power in
both intelligence, enthusiasm, and will; and this was

the secret of their success.   This was what urged Jesus
to take known means to ensure success.   This, too,
was what made him have a command over the so-
called possessed by demons by his very manner.   And
this was what aroused on the part of the sufferers
a faith in Jesus, so as to cause an assertion of the
spirits of the sufferers themselves against their own
weaknesses.   The other special quality of these actions
was that they were done *in the name of religion*.   They
were done, in Jesus's confident tone of authority, as
instances of that kindness which, according to Jesus's
teaching, is the Ruling Force in the universe.

In a few days we learn there was an immense popular   Mk. i. 28,
movement of recognition of Jesus.   This was simply ³³·
brought about by the facts which we have been following.   Jesus endowed with a unique power and a unique
purity of nature, and having acquired a true knowledge
of the most important of all realities, had had opportunity of becoming known to a number of ordinary
human beings through teaching and through action ;
and the result was that they rose up in enthusiasm and
admiration of him.

We notice, indeed, in critically looking at this
response of the people of Capernaum, the working of
the common laws according to which the less essential
powers seem to make more impression than the more
essential.   No doubt what first arrested these people
was not so much Jesus's teaching as his seeming to be
able to cast out the demons.   No doubt, also, in his
teaching, what first arrested them was not the *matter* so   Ver. 22.
much as the *manner*, as the account plainly tells.   No
doubt, also, even in the *matter* the real creations of his
genius did not carry them away so much as the repeti-

tion of the familiar-sounding phrase "**the** kingdom of God," and the proclaiming with force and fire that it was "at hand." But **also** a great part of the way **he** made with them—and almost all of the lasting position he held with them—was **attained** through those sweet simple truths which no human being can ever fail to be affected **by**. And even allowing that the less important elements helped forward the **movement**, we must take human nature **as it** is, and we **can see here** God over-ruling human nature and making it respond **to what is** good, where it does not itself fully know the character of that to which it is responding.

Mk. i. 35.   Such sudden success profoundly affected the sensitive **spirit of** Jesus, **and he** withdrew out of notice, to commune with the **Divine** Presence that had inspired him. **He was not allowed** to remain long alone. **Simon,** joyful at the great position attained by him whom he had begun to love, went after **him with** the others, and said

Ver. 37.   to him, "**All** men seek for thee." He did not, however, need **to** be urged to what he knew was his mission.

Ver. 38.   **He** answered Simon and the others that he must go round some of the other towns and preach in them

Ver. 39.   also.   **He** did go accordingly, followed in all likelihood not **only** by Peter, Andrew, James, and John, but by

Vers. 40-45.   others **who had** become interested in him at Capernaum; and the most notable event that seems to have happened in the little journey was that he showed the greatness of his soul by touching and showing kindness to a man afflicted with leprosy.   The journey seems to **have been** otherwise little marked; and altogether it is to be looked at as **a** tentative rather than a missionary

Mk. ii. 1.   movement.   Jesus soon returned to Capernaum, where he had still his initiatory work to build up.

The mission was begun. Jesus's "candle" was set on a "candlestick." And though it has been subjected to many a rough handling on the part of awkward friends as well as of enemies, it still burns, through the mercy of God, for our guidance and our delight, as we have learned it burned for the people of Capernaum.

CHAPTER VI.

THE CONTINUED MINISTRY OF JESUS, AND THE RESISTANCE OF THE ESTABLISHED TEACHERS.

Mk. ii. SOON after the return of Jesus to Capernaum he seems to have entered on something of a regular ministry, which lasted a number of weeks—from the spring of Ver. 23. the year 34 till the late summer. It was a ministry continuing as his ministry had hitherto been, made up of kind actions on the one side, and teaching regarding Ver. 2. the kind God on the other side. At first it was attended by popular excitement, and had its chief importance, in the eyes of the public, in that it was accompanied Vers. 2, 3. by the healing of diseases. But later it settled into being a quiet ministry of instruction, through improving conversation and public addresses. And we can see plainly enough Jesus's wish to have his ministry assume this quieter and, at the same time, more widely valuable character. As it is suggestively told in the Vers. 13. Gospel of Mark, he withdrew from the turmoil of the town and the crowd of believers in his healing powers, and taught "by the seaside." His wish, we can perceive, was not to have his work too much associated with healings from his own person, which were but temporary at the best, but rather to have it known as a work of teaching regarding that everlasting healing which, according to his mind, was being accomplished, through time, for all by the Heavenly Care that cared for all. The open air was the surrounding in best agreement with such teaching : the murmur of the sea sounded in harmony with it ; and the summer sunshine in quietness looked approval of it. Jesus withdrew as soon as he could to the shore of the Lake of Gennesaret, and there enforced the truths of a free and rational religion, standing on the beach or sitting in some boat, amidst the congenial surroundings of clear sky and rippling water.

We are compelled to ask, from more than mere curiosity, what were the outer conditions of Jesus's life during this ministry—when we think how this ministry comes the nearest of all Jesus's action to that quiet and settled kind of ministry which is required of most of those who among ourselves wish to be special ministers of Jesus. But we get only a very partial answer to this question. From various indications, Mk. ii. 1 ; it seems more than likely that Jesus had a fixed Mt. iv. 13 ; Jn. ii. 12. dwelling in Capernaum at this time. This may have been still the house of Peter, or it may have been, as some scholars think, a house he had secured for Reasoning himself. Beyond the fact of his having had this fixed from Mk. ii. 15 ; but abode, we can find out little about his outer life at this on that time. Conjecture may suppose that he had come from see App. I. Nazareth with means sufficient to maintain himself in (4). comfort for a time. Fancy may add that no doubt the Mk. ii. 15 ; entertaining by those who became interested in him Lk. vii. 36, viii. 3 ; would make his supporting himself the easier. And Mk. xv. 41. our faith, well grounded on the sure indications of his

character, will assure us that, in any way of the matter,
he was living in the dignity of independence. But what
exactly were the circumstances of his life we cannot
tell. The state of the evidence, indeed, seems to
preach to us the lesson of his own life and words, that
the important thing in all cases is not what are the
circumstances in which one is placed, but how does
one live in the circumstances? The circumstances of
Jesus's short settled ministry are only vaguely to be
descried; how he lived in them is to be read by us
quite plainly.

One accompaniment of his ministry which is to
engage our attention in this chapter, began soon and
never left it. That was the resistance to him of
established teachers, who believed they knew better
about the subjects of God and goodness than he did.
The ordinary religious authorities of the time—the
scribes, or expounders of the Law, and the Pharisees,
or party of enthusiasts for the traditional religious
faith—rose in opposition to Jesus. They had been
stung, no doubt, by his attacks on their system in his
first addresses. They had been waiting to learn more
of him in no friendly attitude. And now in his life
and conduct they began to find points on which to
attack him, with the view of undermining his influence
on the people. The points they thus laid hold of
deserve our careful attention, as, both in themselves
and in the way Jesus defended them, they are capable
of arousing an initiatory appreciation of his personality.

For the facts of what took place we are, as mostly
hitherto, in the main dependent on the Gospel of
Mark. This gospel presents us with four special
narratives—the last a double one, containing two

Mk. ii.

incidents bringing out the same point—evidently strung together with an intelligent purpose, but at the same time carrying with them all the signs of historical truth. The other two early gospels only confirm the narratives, through giving the same materials more loosely joined together. The Fourth Gospel, however—through that more reserved acceptance of its statements which alone we have been allowing ourselves—gives us an important filling up of our historical picture.

As the fourth chapter of John has evidently been built up from a lost narrative of the journey from Jordan to Galilee, so the main part of the fifth chapter has evidently been built up from a lost narrative of the same events as are related in the second chapter of Mark. Important points of similarity between the two accounts have been, one and another, recognised by advanced scholars. These are not to be under-estimated. An original identity in the materials of the two passages is hardly to be disputed. And as, according to the view with which we are proceeding, this state of matters arises not from the use of Mark by the Fourth Evangelist, but from the Fourth Evangelist having had an independent source, the one account must enrich the other. The Fourth Evangelist, we must recognise, has had before him material containing a record of the contents of two out of Mark's four narratives. And though he has used his material for the pupose of setting fourth his metaphysical doctrine on the relation of Father and Son, yet a careful and critical reading must also find in what he presents a valuable historical element. Also, the second chapter of John, where the evangelist has anticipated this stage, in his first range over the whole ministry, presents a

[margin notes:] Along with some of the 2d chapter. See below, section 3 of this chapter. Cp. Jn. v. 8 w. Mk. ii. 9; Jn. v. 14 w. Mk. ii. 5; perh. Jn. v. 4 w. Mk. ii. 4: also the common subjects them-selves, and espec. cp. Jn. vi. 1 w. Mk. iii. 9. See espec. Oscar Holtz-mann for emphasis-ing of likenesses. Jn. ii.1-11.

short, materialised account, having the contents of
one of Mark's other two narratives. The remaining
one of Mark's four narratives has been left uncon-
firmed, though in no way contradicted, by the Fourth
Evangelist.

In the four special narratives in Mark there are
separately brought out four points in Jesus's conduct
on which his opponents laid hold. These are as
follows :—

Mk. ii. 7 ;   1. That he called God his Father.
Jn v. 18.
              2. That while professing to be religious he associated
Mk. ii. 16.   with " publicans " and other people held to be
                  not respectable.
Mk. ii. 18.   3. That while professing to be religious he did not
                  fast.
Ver. 24, iii. 4. That he followed his own courses, instead of what
2 ; Jn. v.   was believed to be the course required by God,
18.
                  regarding behaviour on the Sabbath-day.

While each of the narratives, however, brings out one
of these points separately along with Jesus's defence of
his action having to do with it, they all together are
such as to enable us to form some idea of his continuous
life at this time.

As this chapter is necessarily a long one, it may be
divided from this place on according to the four points
in Jesus's conduct with which his opponents found
fault.

1. *His calling God his Father.*

Mk. ii. 1.   Shortly, then, it would seem, after Jesus's return to
Capernaum from his visit to the other towns and
villages, it was once known that he was teaching in
the house in which he resided. The friends of a

certain man afflicted with palsy heard of where he
was; and his fame for healing being at its height, they
brought their patient to let him see him. The crowd
was so great that they could not carry him in by the
door, and getting him up to some opening in the roof,
" they let down the bed wherein the sick of the palsy Ver 4.
lay." The " faith " exhibited in the action touched Ver. 5.
Jesus acutely. But nevertheless his attention did not
remain centred on such an abstract object as either
the faith or the suggestion which it brought of his own
success. There was before Jesus's eyes a living man
who was suffering; and what Jesus did was to stop
his teaching for a moment, and exclaim, " Son, thy sins Mk. ii. 5.
be forgiven thee." This saying, certainly authentic,
was just a simple kindly saying. It meant that God
would surely relieve the poor suffering man. Jesus
evidently gave some adherence to the common belief
that illnesses were the punishments of special sins Lk. xiii.
(though there is good reason to believe that he soon 1-5; Jn.
ix. 3. See
quite threw off all such adherence, and though, indeed, account
below of
this very incident may have formed one of the steps the teaching in Je-
towards his doing so—his own exclamation of kindness rusalem.
leading to after-reflection in which he went further).
This belief thus still gave a turn to his way of expressing
himself; and so he spoke the words of tender promise
to the sick man, which meant in his lips, So sure am
I of the presence of One who is all kindness that I can
promise the sin is forgiven, and the punishment will be
succeeded by new health and joy. The saying was a
spontaneous, unpremeditated outcome of his own consciousness of the heavenly Father—that consciousness
which was also the source of his teaching that we had
before us in the fifth chapter. We shall have a special

8

interest, however, in the saying in that it is the first
expression of his consciousness which we have met
that must be called a pure outburst of feeling.   It
was an outburst of that kind of feeling which we call
Compassion, and of that quality in which compassion
was Jesus's own peculiar attainment, and when we
contemplate it in him makes us in the one act
worship him and love him, call him divine and call
him human.

The Pharisees, however, took a very different view
from this of Jesus's great-hearted saying.   They were
prejudiced against him, and they had been watching
him for something over which to quarrel with him.
And so the meaning of the saying struck on their ears
without effect.   Its meaning was of no interest to
them.   They only cared for the saying in as far as it
might be an occasion through which to find a quarrel.
Its mere words made it capable of a turn through
which it served this purpose.   It was the very thing
they had been waiting for.   Their conduct comes
before us with certainty, and in most unlovely reality.
Ah (they said to themselves, no doubt), here is our
chance!   Ah (they said, no doubt, aloud), he forgives
sins, does he?   Looks of intelligence—unpleasant looks
of an intelligence badly employed—passed between
them.   A word formed itself in their different small
minds, and they knew they had got what they wanted.
Blasphemy was the word.   Yes, they said; for " who
can forgive sins but God only ?"   *Blasphemy*, they
expressed to one another with satisfaction, was what
they would join with the name of this troublesome
teacher, and then would be found whose side would
prevail with priest and with people.

Mk. ii. 7.

Jesus "perceived in his spirit," Mark says, "that they so reasoned within themselves." And Matthew, putting it even more simply, speaks of him as "knowing their thoughts." So far the accounts in the earlier gospels take us as uncritical followers. But from this point a critical freedom must be permitted, which, in a proper understanding of the first three gospels, by no means undervalues the accounts. Without doubt, it is history that Jesus knew their thoughts, and that he proceeded to meet their attack. Also, it must be said to be history that the man in some way recovered— whether the recovery began immediately or not, is of little moment—and that that was what, for Jesus's disciples, proved the most effectual answer. But still, there must have been in the facts a filling up which the Synoptic narrative has leapt over. Whether the recovery really began at once or took place gradually, one cannot escape the impression that in the making Jesus's answer centre on the recovery we have one of those dramatic treatings of fact from the later point of view of disciples, in which what at the later time seemed the important element is brought alone into notice. This impression is strengthened and, indeed, placed virtually on secure ground by a comparison of the Fourth Gospel account.

The Fourth Gospel account both induces us to believe that the facts were more drawn out into detail than the dramatic picture of the earlier gospels gives knowledge of, and also conveys to us most convincingly the filling up which the earlier gospels have left wanting. The fifth chapter of John gives us at least one thing in which the second chapter of Mark fails us: and that is an indication which, by renewed com-

Marginal notes: Ver. 8: Mt. ix. 4

Cp. above, p. 50.

8 *

parison of his account with that of Mark, informs us how really Jesus *answered* his opponents at this time.

Mk. ii. 11;
Jn. v. 8.
Both evangelists relate that Jesus said, Rise, take up thy bed, and walk. But the Fourth Evangelist does not present this as having been an answer to

Jn. v. 18.
opponents. He gives the charge of the opponents in a place quite disconnected from this command and its consequence. And he supplies for it a very different kind of answer. The answer which he gives is one of justification in *word*.

That what the evangelist thus supplies is largely his own, must be asserted. Here, however, as elsewhere throughout the book, the state of matters most strongly suggests that the evangelist's work is no free invention, but an elaborating into form of reminiscences from the Master's own sayings. How are we to separate the elements? In no way, perhaps, so as to give much detail. But at least one fact is virtually assured us by the methods which we had before us in the introduction.

The one fact of which we may become assured is indicated by the opening words of the discourse which

Jn. v. 19-
20.
the evangelist gives, namely these, " Verily, verily, I say unto you, The Son can do nothing of himself, but what he seeth the Father do: for what things soever he doeth, these also doeth the Son likewise. For the Father loveth the Son, and sheweth him all things that himself doeth." The historical fact which these words indicate is that Jesus had given an answer of which these words are partly a report and partly an adaptation. Can we dare to guess at the original? The scene of the Synoptic account itself suggests that the original words were *almost* as they are reported, the

" almost " merely requiring the elimination of the peculiarly Johannine mode of expression and the substitution
of that which the early gospels attribute to Jesus. Thus
we shall have it that, upon knowing their thoughts, Jesus
first, in all probability, considered for a little, and then
spoke these significant words, " The *Son of man* can do Jn. v. 19,
nothing of himself, but what he seeth *God* do. . . . *God* [20.]
loveth the *Son of man*, and showeth him all things that
himself doeth." The words thus adopted and slightly
changed fit so exactly to the exclamation recorded by
the Synoptists as a thoughtful justification to a spontaneous outburst of what one has long been conscious
of, and at the same time describe so exactly what
Jesus's consciousness can be seen to have been from
his teaching, that they force us to accept them at this
place in our narrative. And we shall be the more
induced to do so if we notice that, by stripping them
of their philosophical dressing, they come to form a
missing link leading naturally up to the words which,
according to the Synoptic account, Jesus uttered as he
healed the man—these words, in their turn, stripped of Mk. ii. 11.
what makes them rest chiefly on the success of the Ver. 10.
healing. We may suppose Jesus to have said, " The See App.
Son of man can do nothing of himself, but what he I. (5).
seeth *God* do. . . . *God* loveth the *Son of man*, and
showeth him all things that himself doeth. *Therefore*
the Son of man hath power on earth to forgive sins."
The meaning of the word is easily read. Jesus would
have had them see how he had spoken directly out of
his consciousness of the Divine Presence, and his
consequent knowledge that God was forgiving such
sufferers as the man before him. He would have had
them see he had spoken to the man the words of

kindness and promise because of the Presence that is
all kindness and promise,

Espec.
probably
in vers.
25, 29 (see
App. VI),
and in ver.
30.
The rest of the Johannine discourse may present
something more of what Jesus said. We must suppose
that Jesus's inspired words made some impression on
these by no means irreligious "scribes and Pharisees."
And it is more than likely that, as the discourse
indicates, he spoke further to them, developing his
thoughts. The disjoining, however, of the original
from the representation is too delicate a work to be
advisable.

One thing more only we may conjecture regarding
this scene, and that is that the speech and action of
Jesus at this time brought about that the Pharisees and
scribes began to take up seriously his claims, not, alas!
in any open-minded way, but in prejudice and spiteful-
ness. There is a notice, evidently spontaneous, further
Mk. iii. 22.
See also
Mk. vii. 1.
on in the Gospel of Mark which speaks of "scribes
which came down from Jerusalem." We may believe
that it was most likely at the point we have now reached
that the teachers in the north sent for some more
influential of their colleagues to come and help them
to meet the claims and refute the doctrines of the new
teacher.

2. *His associating with publicans and suchlike.*

It was after the event having to do with the sick
man that, according to Mark, Jesus withdrew to teach
at the seaside. During the course of this teaching, we
next may learn, he made the acquaintance of one LEVI,
Mk. ii. 14.
a member of the class of "publicans" or tax-gatherers
a class hated by the Jews. This Levi was most likely
an interested hearer, and in this way became acquainted

with Jesus. Through him Jesus got an opportunity,
which he boldly embraced, of becoming acquainted
with various members of this class. The facts present
themselves, if not in so many written sentences, yet
plainly enough to any thoughtful person. Jesus got
opportunity to meet these people, and was received
with interest by them; and his whole character and
mind—knowing, as they did, no exclusiveness—were
such as not to prevent his associating with them, but
rather to make him feel impelled to it.   He accordingly Ver. 15:
even, as is probable, accepted an invitation to the house Lk. v. 29.
of Levi; and there he met people who, if not really as See App.
great "sinners" as the national prejudice called them, I. (4).
were certainly people who did not possess a very
religious character.

It is important to notice that Jesus here acted on
opportunity presenting itself. The associating with these
people was brought about by his teaching leading him
among them, and by their susceptibility to his influence.
That Jesus met in free companionship people who bore
the name of "sinners," who really were people careless
about religion, and, it also may be, careless even about
morality, is a certain historical fact; but at the same
time that he did not do so in the way of making a
plunge out of the surroundings in which he lived,
but rather welcomed in sublime beauty of character
surroundings that had themselves, as it were, made
the movement and come to him, is also certain
for those that will thoughtfully read over our
materials. Opportunity brought about the assertion
of a part of Jesus's character. Likeness to his conduct in the matter would be found not so exactly in
any who might turn their back upon their own class

to go and live in a less respectable class, as in those, who within the class they find themselves placed in, choose the less fortunate and the less eminently respectable as the objects of their kindness and their reverence.

This conduct of Jesus came to the knowledge of his Mk. ii. 16. enemies, and they said to his disciples, " How is it that he eateth and drinketh with publicans and sinners ? " They only, it would seem, addressed themselves to his disciples at this time. Perhaps they were a little awed by Jesus, and did not care to come into close quarters with him ; and perhaps also they wished, by pointing out supposed faults in Jesus's conduct, to disaffect the disciples one by one towards him, and so weaken his following. The disciples told Jesus what they had said to them, and Jesus said Mk. ii. 17. something like this, " They that are whole have no On Mt. ix. 13, see need of the physician, but they that are sick : I came App. I.(6). not to call the righteous, but sinners to repentance." These words were, we may feel certain, uttered in the presence of his disciples and friends, and not in public. As we shall see, his manner in the actual presence of See, e.g., people called " sinners " was one more delicate than Lk. xix. 5, 9, and Jn. would have been shown had these words been said in viii. 11,&c. their hearing. The words were a justification of his conduct quite expressing a view he had of the situation, but only intended for the consideration of religious enthusiasts.

3. *His not Fasting.*

Mk. ii. 18.   " And " (we can at this point best quote, word for word, from Mark) "the disciples of John and of the Pharisees used to fast : and they come and say unto him, Why do the disciples of John and of the Pharisees fast, but thy disciples fast not ? " The enemies of

Jesus now interfered with him because his disciples did not *fast ;* and this time they addressed not the disciples but Jesus himself.

The answer of Jesus to this objection was, as Mark presents it, as follows, " Can the children of the bridechamber fast while the bridegroom is with them ? as long as they have the bridegroom with them, they Mk. ii. 19-cannot fast. But the days will come, when the bride- ²² groom shall be taken away from them, and then shall they fast in those days. No man also seweth a piece of new cloth on an old garment : else the new piece that filled it up taketh away from the old, and the rent is made worse. And no man putteth new wine into old bottles : else the new wine doth burst the bottles, and the wine is spilled, and the bottles will be marred : but new wine must be put into new bottles." Of the first of these two sayings—the "bridegroom " saying and the "wine " saying—the second half may be commentary, in accordance with a liberty taken by the earlier evangelists ; but in any case, the substance of the answer is in these words, " Can the children of the bridechamber fast while the bridegroom is with them ? " The second saying is reported by Luke in a slightly Lk. v. 36-different form ; but the difference is not such as to ³⁹ leave the point doubtful. The meaning of the complete answer is partly on the surface, and easily read. This was no time for fasting, Jesus claimed, it being a time of special visitation—the bridegroom was with them ; but also, he claimed that a new religious movement was beginning, and that that would require its own ceremonious practices—new wine must be put into new bottles.

The first of the two sayings, however, when further

considered, raises a difficulty.   The difficulty comes

Is. lxii. 5. from the " bridegroom " imagery.   This same imagery
had been used by the **writer** of the sixty-second chapter
of Isaiah **to** figure the relationship of God Himself
towards His people.   And that at once suggests the
question, If Jesus was remembering the use of **the**
imagery in Isaiah, was it not a visitation of God Him-
self which he was claiming **to have taken** place ?   And
the question is **of** the greater urgency **in that,** beyond

See Mt.
xxv. 6 ;
Rev. xix.
7, xxi. 9. all doubt, the explanation of Jesus's words adopted **by**
the early Church referred them to that idea in Isaiah.
The importance of the question for our present consideration lies in this, that if it be concluded that
Jesus here did involve the idea of Isaiah, he seems to
have, even at this stage, **been** claiming a superhuman
life—a thing of which otherwise **we** find no trace in
what the earlier gospels record.

To help in deciding the question, we may turn to

Jn. ii.1-11. the Fourth Gospel.   The story in **the** second chapter
of John **of** the " first miracle," or first sign, cannot
long remain unrecognised by any thoughtful reader as
being another account of the same occurrence as that
to which we have come.   In rich profusion of symbol,
the whole situation of Jesus **at** the outset of his

Ver. 2. ministry is set forth in it.   Jesus and his disciples had
been called away from common life to a marriage—
what marriage but the marriage of the superhuman

Ver. 4, cp.
Mk. iii. 21,
31-35. and the human that was about to be celebrated ?   This
was to cause misunderstanding and disagreement
between Jesus and his own family.   At the marriage

Ver. 9. Jesus made of water wine—what wine but the teaching
which he himself metaphorically called wine ?   and,
though it was commonly thought that old wine was

better than new, yet in this case the bridegroom had Ver. 10,
given new wine which was better than the old. The elucidated
by Lk. v.
dispensing of this " new wine," along with an arresting 39.
of attention by sayings in which the imagery of the
wine, the water, and the bridegroom, was introduced,
was at least one " beginning of signs" in Jesus's Ver. 11.
ministry, according to the early and reliable Gospel of Mk. ii. 22,
cp. iii. 6.
Mark as well as according to the Gospel of John.

The existence of this richly imaginative account in
the Fourth Gospel, having all the substance of what
the earlier gospels relate more simply, is decisive
confirmation of the historicity of the words under
review ; and the tenor of it—the comparing of the old
and the new in teaching—is as decisive confirmation
of the suggestion that the bridegroom alluded to was
the bridegroom of the passage in Isaiah, still loving
his bride, and now celebrating the marriage. Also,
however, the story in the Fourth Gospel helps to get
over the difficulty in regard to the self-profession of
Jesus. Against acceptance of the belief that Jesus
at this stage professed, in his own utterances, to represent God Himself, the teaching of the Sermon on the
Mount, along with the plain development in his self-
assertion and the waiting for recognition on the
Messiah question, both indicated by Mark, are too
strong to yield to the disturbance by one piece of
imagery. But this Fourth Gospel story gives to the
imagery an explanation which removes its perplexity.
In the Fourth Gospel story Jesus himself is not
identified with the bridegroom. The bridegroom is In Mark
only introduced as being *appealed to*. And thus, surely, the bride-
groom
opens up the historical fact :—Jesus, in his answer to *imagery* is
the objections of the scribes, indicated that the Eternal appealed
to.

Cp. above, p. 54. Lord was plainly visiting His people, arousing anew their devotion, about to begin among them a new way of living, which, having been expressed as a new reign or "kingdom," was also to be expressed as a new union between Himself and them. It was for the followers of Jesus, in the Divine government, to develop further this thought, and see that the Lord who was the bridegroom had dwelt in him who spoke and worked himself—that it was through a human nature made pure, driven by duty, and melting into compassion, that the Lord had visited His people.

4. *His free conduct on the Sabbath.*

The last point on which the teachers attacked the conduct of Jesus had to do with his conduct in relation to the Sabbath-day. Jesus was found, during this Mk ii. 23. summer which he spent at Capernaum, walking with his disciples in the corn-fields on the Sabbath-day, and Deut. xxiii. 25. plucking the ears of corn—a thing allowed on other days, but not considered right on the Sabbath. The teachers spoke on the subject, not as in the case of the kindly saying to the sick man, to each other merely, nor as in the case of the sitting at meat with "publicans and sinners," to the disciples, but as in the case of the fasting, directly to Jesus. Their interference had been becoming bolder, perhaps through the growing familiarity of his appearance among them. Mk. ii. 24. They said to him, "Behold, why do they on the Sabbath-day that which is not lawful?"

The nature of the action to which Jesus thus lent himself, as well as the nature of the objection which the teachers raised against it, would be difficult to estimate accurately, if it had not been the case that

the whole state of matters regarding Sabbath-keeping
is very much the same with ourselves in Britain in the
nineteenth Christian century as it was in Palestine in
this year in which Jesus was only laying the founda-
tions of Christianity. But we can understand the
whole state of the case, because our Christian Sunday
has, both in popular acceptance of its obligations and
in the ways of fulfilling the obligations, come to be
in exactly the same position in Protestant countries as
the Sabbath was among the Jews. The commandment
in the Decalogue regarding the Sabbath is of a rather
more arbitrary character than any of the other nine.
It is not, indeed, in its essence arbitrary. It is in
accordance, like all the rest, with the Israelite genius,
and is based, like all the rest, on the religious consciousness of the Israelite people, which demanded a
sovereignty for God over all other life. To have held
that God never demanded a worship that was apart
from ordinary conduct might have seemed to encourage
the pantheistic opinion that God was Himself in no
way apart from the ordinary course of nature. Israelite
thought recognised a separateness between God and
nature; and the Sabbath-command, or command to
rest from ordinary life on one day in the week, was a
reminder that one should show in conduct a recognition of God such as could in no way be confused with
merely following nature. While, however, the Sabbath-
command is thus based on religious principle, as
apprehended by the Israelite consciousness, just as is
the case with the other nine commandments in the
Decalogue, it certainly leaves to those who would
obey it more freedom in regard to particulars. Not
to speak of the number 7 being chosen for the time

between Sabbath and Sabbath, which is certainly
arbitrary, there is a world of variety possible in the
ways of resting from ordinary life.   Now to fill up
this defect in regard to the Sabbath-command, there
had stepped in among the Jews two new factors that
had come to be reverenced like the command itself—
these were *custom* and the *opinion* of the Jewish rabbis.
The case is the same with ourselves.   The Sabbath-
command has been wisely accepted from the Israelites
by all Christian communities.   It has for us all the
value it had for the Israelites, of reminding us of a Life
that is above any established system of things around
us ; and it has, further, like all truly religious injunc-
tions, not only the value of making us worship God,
but at the same time the value of making us minister
to the good of man, in that it provides rest for many
classes of men who are not in a position to choose
themselves their times of rest and of labour.   With us
also, however, the particulars of obedience are left
undetermined by the command itself ; and so with us
also there have grown up to determine these particulars
the same two powers—custom and learned opinion.
Thus we can understand what Jesus now really did,
and also how it was that his action offended the
Pharisees and scribes.   He, without in the least
implying any criticism of the Sabbath-command itself,
disregarded those particular lines of action which
custom and opinion had supplied for the obedience to
it, and went on a line of his own.   We can illustrate
his action by means of many actions that may have
been done in England and Scotland.   Playing games
on Sunday, while that is not in accordance with what
custom and opinion prescribe ; walking on Sunday

during the time not so long ago in which that was, in
Scotland at least, not in accordance with what custom
and opinion prescribed—such are, in relation to the
Sabbath-command, viewed as bringing an obligation on
all, exact parallels to the conduct of Jesus (whether
they could be as well justified is a different question),
as with his disciples he plucked the corn on the Sabbath-
day, in defiance of all around, who he knew would
look upon his action as a breaking of the laws of God.

Jesus gave to his objectors an answer such as might
appeal to their slavishly Scripture-led minds. " Have Mk ii. 25.
ye never read," he said, "what David did, when he had xxi. 6.
need, and was an hungered, he, and they that were
with him ? How he went into the house of God in the
days of Abiathar the high priest, and did eat the showbread, which is not lawful to eat but for the priests,
and gave also to them that were with him." But, as in
other cases, he did not stop short at what might appeal
at the moment, but went on to rest his actions boldly
on principle. " The Sabbath," he said, " was made for Mk. ii. 27.
man, and not man for the Sabbath." These important
words, though scholars have discovered two other
sayings—the one in the Second Book of Maccabees, Holtz-
and the other in the Talmud or collection of Rabbinical mann.
teachings—with something of the same ring, were none
the less words of genius and of power. They expressed
in a simple way the attitude of the religion which Jesus
taught towards such an institution as the Sabbath.
His religion was one having as its first principle the
care of God for man, and its second the sonship of
man to God. He would continue, accordingly, to
respect the Sabbath where it could be shown to
minister to the welfare of man ; but where, as in the

case before them, its obligation, as popularly understood, inanely interfered with the welfare of man, he
would without hesitation set it aside.

In the accounts of Matthew and of Luke, Jesus's
answer is said to have been first, as in Mark, the
saying about David and the showbread, and then the
words, " The Son of man is Lord even of the Sabbath-
day." (Matthew inserts also a saying appealing to the
authority of the Old Testament regarding mercy being
better than sacrifice; but this is more likely to be
a kind of commentary on the part of the writer, or
writers, of the First Gospel in their usual tendency to
make everything start from the authority of the Old
Testament.) These words, indeed, are also in Mark,
but are unnaturally tacked on to the words above
quoted with a "therefore," suggesting that they have
been added to the Gospel of Mark afterwards from
the other two. They are, however, likely to have
been also uttered by Jesus at this time, seeing they
are characteristic of Jesus as well as sufficiently
attested, through their appearance in Matthew and
Luke. Most likely Jesus added them in the hearing of
all as a contemplative expression of his own relation to
the Sabbath-obligation—as it were bringing the subject
back from the more general aspect to its particular
aspect, in which it was related specially to himself.
The meaning of the words was the same as that of the
above-quoted words, except that they introduced a
claim on the part of himself to be able to decide, as a
man, what was best for man, without any direction
being imposed for his guidance.

As Jesus's use of the name "Son of man" to
designate himself has first come prominently before us

See
above,
Intr.,
p. 12.

in this chapter, we may here pause for the considera- Dan. vii. 13. Enoch
tion of the question what in general he meant by it.
The name is found in the Book of Daniel as applied to cc. xlvi.
an ideal deliverer, and in the Book of Enoch it is and xlviii.
found definitely as a title of the expected Messiah.
Now scholars are not agreed as to whether the notices
in the Book of Enoch regarding the "Son of man" Pfleide-
may not belong to the period after Jesus lived. But rer's view, e.g., Chris-
even if it were otherwise, and Jesus learned this tian inter-
name as a definite name for the Messiah from acquain- polations, probably.
tance with the Book of Enoch, it must be maintained
that he chose it as a simple title, conveying the
assurance that what he claimed to be was a man and
a brother-man. We must rely on the general presentation that is given here of the teaching of Jesus to
support this contention. It may be enough, by way of
argument, to say that the applications of the name Mk. ii. 10,
which are attributed to Jesus are nearly all in agreement 28, viii. 31, 38, ix. 9,
with this use of it. There are a very few, indeed, that 12, 31, &c.; Lk.
would make him out to have used the expression in a ix. 58.
transcendental sense; but in these, as we shall see The
when we come to the consideration of them in ordinary "apoca- lyptic"
course, it can be shown either that the words of Jesus passages in Mk. xiii.
have been not quite accurately quoted, or that he and Mt. xxiv.,xxv.;
spoke in a figurative way. also, per-
When, therefore, Jesus said, as we have seen he haps, Mk. viii. 38.
said, that he could forgive sins because the *Son of man
sees what the heavenly Father does* or *what God does*, and
said also that he could have a freedom of conduct on
the Sabbath because *the Son of man was lord of the
Sabbath*, he meant, we must say, that he was a Man
among men, who was conscious of the Divine Presence,

9

and knew that it was man's nature and calling to grow into the very life of God.

Shortly after the interference with the plucking the corn on the Sabbath-day, the same trouble, it would seem, arose again over Jesus's performing one of his acts of healing on the Sabbath-day. This time, as Mark relates, and as was most natural at the rising up of an objection which had already been so forcibly repelled, Jesus "looked round about on them with anger, being grieved for the hardness of their hearts." The words attributed to him by all the three gospels as answer on this occasion, " Is it lawful to do good on the Sabbath days, or to do evil ? to save life, or to kill ?" (Mark's form of them), may be accepted without criticism, as also the grand words given only in Matthew, "What man shall there be among you that shall have one sheep, and if it fall into a pit on the Sabbath-day, will he not lay hold on it, and lift it out ? How much then is a man better than a sheep ?"

When we go beyond the mere record of these events, and try to fix our gaze on the Figure that is disclosed through them, what do we see ?

Attending first to the answers with which Jesus met his opponents, they are all in accordance with the teaching which was before us in the fourth chapter, and bring before us an authoritative mind able to perceive the Divine Presence, and out of its own intellectual power to choose its conduct and explain its conduct with no other leading than the Divine Presence itself. As the Divine Presence was seen by Jesus to be *heavenly Father*, and as every human being was perceived by him to be in real nature and calling

Mk. iii. 1-5.

Mk. iii. 5.

Ver. 4.

Mt. xii. 11. 12.

son, sonship to God was to him the sole guide for conduct, and he was able both to see what conduct it guided to and to explain in words how he found the conduct. He promised the goodwill and the help of God to a suffering man because he "saw" God himself doing the same. He justified his entering into the company of people of evil repute, on the ground that their having anything wrong with them showed they were all the more in need of a "physician." He refused to follow the custom of habitual fasting, because fasting was not of a piece with his religion, which was based on the consciousness of sonship to the Divine Father. He justified a free use of the Sabbath-day, on the ground that such was required for the good of man, which was the purpose of having a Sabbath at all. In all this we see One whose nature was altogether fixed on the true God—having first the power to perceive God in such a way as to need no other guide for his conduct, and then also having the power to declare to others what he perceived.

All this meets us with even greater impressiveness when we turn from the justifications of the conduct to the conduct itself.

The very novelty of Jesus's conduct, viewed as religious conduct, disclosed his original power. For a careless person it would not have been a remarkable thing to associate with people of bad name, nor to break the Sabbath, nor to care nothing about the efficacy of formal fasting, though this was made much of not only by the established authorities about religion, but also by the great independent preacher to whom Jesus had in some way given allegiance. But that all these things were done by a person who at the

9 *

same time professed to be a teacher of the most strict
morality and a prophet of God Himself—by a person
who was, moreover, as we can discern Jesus to have
been, really most sensitive about being recognised for
what he was—has left for us the sight of a moral
courage, a self-confidence, and a determination to
make the reasonably good and true the only guide, in
utter disregard of the ordinary fashions of thought and
action that all of us feel we need the help of,—which
all entitle us to say of Jesus that he was a spirit not
only possessing an unstained devotion to the Divine
Presence, so as to need no ordinary discipline, but
also possessing an intellectual grasp of the subject of
morality which made him perfectly confident in his
power to select the essential and leave the accidental,
to disregard the merely proper and hold to the good.

And if the novelty of his conduct arrests us and
tells us we have to do with a superior being, the *detail*
of the conduct will clearly bring before us an Authority
on religion that stands above all criticism. The whole
conduct of Jesus which we have seen in this chapter
shows that his action was simply in perfect harmony
with his consciousness of sonship to God. He would
go among "publicans and sinners," because that was
like a son of God and a sacred brother; he would not
subject himself or his friends to formal fasting, because
that was not like a son of God and a sacred brother.
What was in agreement with sacred sonship he did
and wished others to do; what was not in agreement
with it he left alone. And especially when we look at
the most notable part of the conduct, the associating
with people whose names were "cast out" "as evil,"
we see the strength of character, the individuality, and

the attractiveness which his conduct displayed. To understand what was involved in Jesus's action in relation to those people of bad name, we must divest ourselves altogether of the idea that Jesus was, to the view of onlookers, acting in condescension. Condescending his conduct may be called by us who are · able to see his nature; but at the time of his action it would not be apparent to the ordinary observer that he was in a position to condescend. Nor indeed did he himself approach the people with any condescending manner. He approached them as a man—as a brother-man. He first met them through himself receiving hospitality from one of them. And all our later indications show that his attitude towards them was not dictatorial, but courteous, and indeed respectful. It must be said, therefore, that he went to be with them simply because he was drawn by a common nature which he perceived to be a sacred nature. In our own experience we see young children associating with each other without shame on either side, even if it be that one has a good name while the other has been found out in a grave misdemeanour. We see in our own experience grown people, when in danger, forgetting for the moment differences of character and of name, and for the moment facing together as human beings the enemies of human welfare. But Jesus as a grown man, and in times of no special distinction from other times, deliberately associated with men who got the name of caring nothing for religion, if indeed even caring anything for morality, though he himself had his whole mind filled with religion; he deliberately associated with them because he saw in them men, and knew that of men God was the Supreme Father.

See Lk. xix. 1-10; and cp. vii. 36-50, Jn. viii. 11, &c.

In doing so, Jesus, it can be quite clearly seen, had a master-insight into the meaning of life, a master-enthusiasm to act in accordance with truth, and a master-will to go, if need be, against a whole nation obstructing him, simply where his own insight and his own enthusiasm led him.

And if the novelty of his action and the detail of his action thus disclose him, the *results* of his action will enable us to complete the picture of him. We cannot imagine a man of ordinary good character associating with those who care little about religion in a purely companionable way without his incurring a certain risk of being influenced by the prevailing lower tone, so as to lose some of his own purity of thought and action. If this result be averted in any case, it must be through decided strength of character. Jesus, however, we find, not only remained himself as pure and high-toned as before, but raised the others towards his level—and did so through no other means than simple courteous companionship. There can be no doubt of this to a careful reader of the gospels. If it were nothing else, the speedy application to him by so many of the Messiah character in the special aspect of Healer of diseases cannot have been based on mere bodily healings, but must have rested greatly on the fact that the characters of his associates were in almost all cases visibly improved by their intercourse with him. Through the results, then, that followed from his conduct he is himself reflected to us, and we see that there was in him a personality that carried a charm with it. Part, indeed, of the charm can be explained as referable to that very respectfulness with which, as we have seen, he approached all. We can picture him with those

See Mt.
xi. 2-6.
Cp. Lk. v.
8; Acts x.
38; Jn. i.
45, 46.

commonly unrespected companions on some day on
which the Eastern sun had risen in all its splendour
to shine, as his words expressed it, " on the evil and Mt. v. 45
on the good "; and as we look at the company, we can
see that like the sun was himself, asking no questions,
but just shining in kindness, with the result that all
began to be purer in thought and in feeling. But
there was more than can be explained in a personality
that, surrounded as his was, could remain itself intact
and influence others. Jesus, indeed, through his power
over others, is a witness of the truth in general that
in a human being as such there is more than can be
explained, and that beyond the whole body, which can
be analysed and measured, there is the Soul, which
can only be reverenced. But also as regards himself
in particular, the power that he exercised on others
has left us a knowledge. It enables us to know that
he had a magical personality, caring for aims the
highest, the broadest, and the best, and having the
strength both of character and of spiritual perception
in which he could assert that those aims would be
reached.

CHAPTER VII.

THE MOUNTAIN SCENE.

WHAT next followed in Jesus's life and ministry can easily be traced through the gospel accounts, and can be seen to have been in perfect agreement with a natural development of events. Oppositions continued on the one side. On the other side popular enthusiasm continued, and indeed increased. Jesus began to think of extending his ministry beyond the neighbourhood in which he had met with so great success; and at the same time he began to think of putting some system into his work by delegating part of it to others. More careful reports of his speeches began to be made. And, finally, the rapid growth of his success and fame, as was to be expected, was not without his having to experience various small annoyances. He had, for example, this to bear, that some persons who at first had joined in the popular movement in his favour began to take umbrage at some of his sayings, and so left him.

Going to particulars: there first comes before us of what took place one scene which is at least alluded to

Mk. iii.,
iv.

Jn. vi. 66.

in all the four gospels. It is a scene on a mountain or hill. Matthew tells of it in this way, " And seeing the multitudes, he went up into a mountain: and when he was set, his disciples came unto him." Mark says, "And he goeth up into a mountain, and calleth unto him whom he would: and they came unto him. And he ordained twelve, that they should be with him, and that he might send them forth to preach." Luke says, "And it came to pass in those days, that he went out into a mountain to pray, and continued all night in prayer to God. And when it was day, he called unto him his disciples: and of them he chose twelve, whom also he named apostles." And even John brings the scene before us in these words, " And Jesus went up into a mountain, and there he sat with his disciples." _{Mt. v. 1.} _{Mk iii. 13. 14.} _{Lk. vi. 12, 13.} _{Jn. vi. 3.}

It is not difficult to discern the meaning of this scene and the course of events that led to it. Jesus, we learn from Mark, was at this time followed by a great multitude. It was a multitude, says Mark, made up of people "from Jerusalem, and from Idumea, and from beyond Jordan," and also from Tyre and Sidon. Jesus's fame had spread. In a few short months he had realised his majestic supremacy of nature among his fellows. Now what we can further see is that, in the full torrent of his success, just as had been at the first rush of it, he became so deeply moved that one time he felt constrained to go apart from the world for a little while in order to engage in contemplation and in communion with the Unseen Presence. He felt, we may believe, that he must engage in quiet contemplation over the significance of what had come about, and must decide, with prayer, on the question of his future action.

Mt. v. 1.

Mk iii. 13. 14.

Lk. vi. 12, 13.

Jn. vi. 3. Or *the* mountain; in all four cases *To Oros.* But cp. Mt. xiv 23, xv. 29 (Meyer).

Mk. iii. 7, 8.

He withdrew, accordingly, to a hill—an eminence
Ps. cxxi. away above the bustle of the world—in the spirit of the
psalmist, seeking to be alone with the Creator. All
Lk. vi. 12. night, we learn, he "continued in prayer to God." **In**
the morning, as in the case of the earlier retirement, he
was followed by **the faithful** Simon and other devoted
followers. He was ready to receive them with a new
Mk. iii. and practical **idea. During the night he had been**
forming a plan—a practical plan, and yet a fanciful plan
—a plan of universal importance, and yet of Jewish
colouring ; he had decided to choose from his disciples
some special ministers, and there were to be Twelve of
them, according to the number of the tribes of Israel.

The notion of the *Apostoloi*—that is, *Sent-men*—as it
comes down to us from the institution of Jesus, is an
interesting **one.** There **is probably** nothing having to
do with Jesus that can be determined with less doubt
than the question what it was that this notion meant
for him. It meant that he looked upon himself as one
sent by God to accomplish a Mission, and that, **carry-**
ing out this idea in his own mind, he took upon him, in
the name of the Unseen One who was sending himself,
to send others. As all **the** gospels speak of Jesus
E.g., Mk. *sending*, there can be no doubt that Jesus had this idea
vi. 7. of sending as he himself was sent. The idea is summed
Mt. x. 40. up in these words reported in Matthew, " He that
receiveth you, receiveth me ; and he that receiveth me,
receiveth him that sent me." And it is also summed
Jn.xvii.18. up in these words of prayer reported in John, " As thou
hast sent me into the world, even so have I also sent
them into the world." The idea, we can say, reached
its maturity in the mind of Jesus one night during
his short ministry in Capernaum in the summer of

a year that was probably the year 34, while he was com-
muning with the Unseen on a hill away from the town.

Of the individual apostles, the most striking, certainly,
was that Simon to whom Jesus himself gave the name
by which we best know him, PETER. He was a fisher- Mk. i. 16.
man by trade, but was also a religious enthusiast. He
was not an excessively poor man; for, as we have seen,
he had left his business for a time to go and hear John See above,
the Baptist at the Jordan, and had also, most likely, as pp. 50-51.
we have also seen, invited Jesus to his house in Caper- Above,
naum. The striking good point in his character was p. 86.
an overflowing enthusiasm that was capable of being
aroused when he came under the power of good
influences. He was a man most susceptible to good Mk. viii.
teaching. And it must have been on account of this xxii. 33.
that Jesus called him Peter, meaning a rock, and said Mt.xvi.18;
that on that rock he would build his Church. Com- Jn. i. 42.
bined, however, with this good point of character, he
had one very bad one. He was, like many of similar
temperament, apt to waver when under the power of
two or more authorities that for the time were opposed
to each other. He was like a rock in being one that
could be built upon; but it was the receptivity of a
rock, not the force or the hardness of a rock, that gave
the likeness. His wavering was exemplified in his
famous conduct at the trial of Jesus, and also in certain
later action of his, of which the Apostle Paul tells, in Gal. ii. 11-
relation to the questions between Jewish and Gentile 14.
Christians. As for the position that this apostle had in
relation to the early Church, the Catholic tradition
which would make him have been the first representative of Jesus in Rome, has truth underlying it, in that
Peter had evidently a very great deal to do with the

rallying Jesus's followers after Jesus's death. And especially it is evident that he had greatly to do with the earliest experiences in regard to Jesus's resurrection. In this way Jesus's prediction about building his Church Jn. xxi. 19. on Peter was verified. It may be said of him in general both that he had himself a religious perception keener than that of the other apostles, and that he had a greater receptivity than the others to the impression made by Jesus's personality. It may be held certain that he showed his devotion to Jesus and to religion to the extent of suffering martyrdom for the cause of Christianity.

JAMES was probably a more important apostle than Mk. i. 19. one is at first apt to suppose. Like Peter, he was a fisherman ; and we have seen how in all likelihood he fell in with Jesus during the scattering of those who had listened to John the Baptist. But we have an indication which tells us pretty clearly that, with his brother, he gave up good business prospects to keep with Jesus. The indication is in the words by which Ver. 20. Mark narrates the beginning of his discipleship, "They left their father Zebedee in the ship with the hired servants, and went after him." The leaving the father Zebedee might be taken for mere imaginative colouring of the narrative if it were not that we must compare it Mk. x. 29. with Jesus's saying to his disciples, " There is no man 30. that hath left house, or brethren, or sisters, or father, or mother, [or wife,] or children, or lands, for my sake, and the gospel's, but he shall receive an hundred-fold," &c. From comparing this saying of Jesus with Mark's statement just quoted, and reflecting that there must have been something leading Jesus to utter it more than the mere question of Peter, which introduces

it in the gospels, we may suppose the statement of
Mark regarding the beginning of James's discipleship
to be a condensed statement of the fact that James and
John—no doubt facing thereby keen displeasure—left See App. I. (7).
Zebedee himself to carry on, with the assistance of his
hired servants, the business in which formerly they had,
as was natural, assisted him. James and John were
called by Jesus, Boanerges, or Sons of Thunder. And Mk. iii. 17.
the trueness of the name as regards James was shown
by his so early meeting his death at the hands of Herod. Acts xii.
James was evidently a man of profound religious feel- 1, 2.
ing, but at the same time, unlike the Master, impatient Name
of all opposition to what his own religious feeling taught. Boanerges and Lk.
Also it is likely that he failed to enter into the inner ix. 54.
circle of Jesus's ideas. Jesus's personality and his proclaiming the kingdom of God were probably what most
bound him to Jesus. Accordingly, after the death of
Jesus, he began to preach in a style that led to his being
apprehended and put to death—very likely because it Acts xii.
was a style that gave ground for the belief that he was 1, 2.
a revolutionary. At the same time the very fact of
Herod's considering him a dangerous man, and therefore removing him, itself points to his having been a
man of considerable power. He evidently, under the
influence of Jesus, became something of a real prophet,
and met the fate which in these barbarous times was
that of prophets as a rule.

Regarding JOHN, our conclusion depends on what
authority we are to recognise in the indications regarding him in the Fourth Gospel. While these indications
have been followed for centuries in such a way as to
make out of John a saintly person, not far removed in
beauty of character from the Master himself, modern

criticism has largely taken the other extreme, and refused to recognise them as of any historical value. It
may be said that, after all discovered by criticism in
relation to the subject, the old belief in general, in John
having been Jesus's most beloved disciple, will hold **its**
ground. **No one** can dispute the general fact that this
disciple was one of Jesus's **three** intimate associates.
Nor can his being **James's brother account for this, as
Andrew had** not the same close intimacy, though he was
Peter's brother. There must have been, therefore, some
special attachment between Jesus and this disciple.
Jn. xiii. 23. And it is most likely that, as the notices in the Fourth
xix. 26, xxi. Gospel seem to indicate, he had endeared himself to
20. Jesus even more **than had been** the case with the
earnest Peter and the zealous **James.** Error, however,
is to be detected in the traditional belief where it goes
the length of ascribing to **this** disciple grandeur of
Mk. x. 35- character. **In** the evidences that have come down
41; Lk. ix. **to** us there is no foundation for the belief that he
49, 54. possessed this, but indeed considerable suggestion of the
contrary. And Jesus, we may say, was not such as to
single out only those of authoritative character for the
objects of his esteem. **It is** likely that John was a
generous-natured, but perhaps by no means learned or
even clever, young man, who had given to Jesus kind-
Cp. Mk. x. ness and sympathy. Jesus's affection for him would
17-21, and **thus be** greatly connected with sensibility to kindness
xiv. 6. and sympathy; and the fact that we are finding such a
touch of human nature **in** Jesus through that gospel
which is the most ecclesiastical of all the gospels, is
interesting, but is sufficiently reasonable to be accepted
simply as a fact. As for John's relation to the Church
of Jesus, it is hard to decide what amount of truth there

may be in the traditions attaching to this and in the
suggestions afforded by the notices in the Book of
Revelation. We have seen, however, that at least it is See above,
to be believed that he conveyed some reminiscences of p. 67.
him who had loved him to those who preserved them,
till they were worked up into the extraordinary book
which now goes by his name. And to this it may be
added that, according to the Acts of the Apostles, Acts iii.
supported by the Epistle to the Galatians, he evidently Gal. ii. 9.
continued with Peter maintaining the Christian faith
for a considerable time after the Master's death, not,
however, showing therein any special genius or breadth
of view.

ANDREW, in the light that real history gives us, is little Jn. i. 40, 41.
more than a lay-figure. Having introduced his brother
Peter to Jesus, he evidently fell into the background.
Still it is likely that he continued after Jesus's death
faithful to Jesus's cause, and perished in one of the early
persecutions. Tradition at least ascribes to him martyr- Apocry-
dom; and a most extravagant story was in the early pels, &c.,
ages worked up out of this, of how he continued three tr. by
days discoursing from a cross, and finally refused to be Walker.
released, preferring to die.

Of PHILIP there are some notices in the Fourth Jn. xiv. 8, 9.
Gospel, which have probably a historical background.
One of them brings him before us as causing pain to
Jesus by failing to understand him. Another tells of
how he brought to Jesus a person called Nathanael. Jn. i. 44, 45.
We shall come back to the story of Nathanael later on;
it is more interesting regarding Nathanael than regarding Philip. Another notice still represents him as having
been approached in Jerusalem by certain "Greeks" Jn. xii. 21.
who happened to be there, with the request that they

might see Jesus. This notice and the notice of him introducing Nathanael together suggest that he had a certain outward prominence in relation to the cause of Jesus. He would seem to have been a vehement, but not very intellectual, follower, who kept himself in the foreground, and expected to see under Jesus a speedy establishment of "the kingdom of God."

BARTHOLOMEW was an apostle of whom little can be said with any confidence. The traditions, however, regarding him, though hardly to be taken very seriously, *Apocr.* have an interest. One is to the effect that he knew *Gosp., &c.* Jesus as a boy; another to the effect that he was ultimately martyred by being thrown into the sea.

MATTHEW was beyond doubt a very important apostle. In the first place, taking all things together, it may be *See App.* concluded that the First Gospel is correct when it iden- *I. (8).* tifies him with *Levi*, the publican whose acquaintance with Jesus was the occasion of action so important on Jesus's part. Levi seems to have been so influenced by Jesus that he left a comfortable settled position and followed Jesus during the remaining months of his *Above, p.* ministry. This Levi, then, or Matthew, had already *118.* taken a very important place in relation to Jesus. But further, this Matthew, or Levi, no doubt possessing, though a member of a class morally despised, certain abilities of mind which the fishermen-disciples did not possess, did an important work which the fishermen- *See above,* disciples could not do so well—namely, no less than *Introduc-* make a record of the divine sayings of Jesus, which *tion, p. 7.* under God saved them from oblivion, and preserved them for us who now love and treasure them. It is as certain as need be that to Matthew we are greatly indebted for our knowledge of what the historical Jesus was, and especially, it may be said, for our knowledge of his sayings. Thus Matthew became, as we must look at things, a disciple whose importance is not second even to that of the more intimate Peter and James and John.

Of THOMAS, all that need be said is that what is related of him in the Fourth Gospel is likely to have a historical background. It would seem that after Jesus's death he was slower than the others in falling in with the belief in Jesus's resurrection. This must have been, we can simply conclude, because he had a more matter-of-fact mind than the rest. At the same time the Fourth Gospel tells in the pictorial way that Thomas gave assent to the idea that Jesus was risen, and exclaimed regarding him, "My Lord and my God." These words may have really been uttered by Thomas in some conversation in which he was charged by the others with want of faith in Jesus, because he hardly looked at the matter in the same way as they did. The character of doubting that has been ascribed to him was thus very likely in reality a character more empirical, less mystical, than was the case with the others. There is nothing, further, to make us question, but everything to make us believe, that he remained a faithful disciple of Jesus till his own death.

Jn. xx. 24-28.

Cp. also Jn. xi. 14. 16.

Of JAMES THE SON OF ALPHEUS nothing is known. We may suppose he met Jesus at the house of his brother Levi, and quietly entered into his following.

JUDAS, THADDEUS, or LEBBEUS was an apostle of Jesus who has become for history nothing more than a name—or rather, the three names that indicate him to us. The little epistle in the New Testament, professing to come from "Jude, the servant of Jesus Christ, and

See vers. 3, 17, 18 of Jude. In the gospels he is

connected
with
James;
but the
word
"brother"
is supplied
in transl.

Josephus,
Wars, iv.
3, &c.
brother of James," cannot have been by this apostle. This apostle may, however, have been a brother of James, and of Levi, and thus another son of Alpheus.

SIMON ZELOTES is chiefly interesting from this, that his name indicates his having belonged to a certain fanatical political party known as the Zealots. His becoming a disciple of Jesus helps to show the power of Jesus to bring under his influence men of all sorts of pronounced views.

Mk. xiv.
10, 11.
JUDAS ISCARIOT was evidently, unlike the others, of southern origin, belonging to the village of *Kerioth*, in Judæa. While at this time a disciple of sufficient prominence to be chosen as an apostle, he afterwards betrayed Jesus to his enemies. Many attempts have been made to explain the character that could bring one into the unenviable position which this man occupied. Here it may be enough to say that Judas Iscariot was evidently a man of susceptibility to good teaching, but without having himself the simple qualities of faithfulness and honesty.

Of the apostles in general it is to be said that, while it is not reasonable to hold they were great men, as ecclesiastical tradition soon came to make them out to have been, they were, nevertheless, suitable for the purpose for which Jesus chose them. They seem to have been all men of very decided religious temperament ; and all, there is good reason to believe, with the one unhappy exception of Judas, heroically continued Jesus's mission after his death, most of them meeting a similar fate to that of their Lord.

General
testimony
of tradi-
tion which
is valu-
able,
though
particular
legends
are not.
See also
Rev. xviii.
20.
The First and the Third Gospels both give discourses of Jesus as having been uttered by him on this occasion. We have already seen how the Sermon on the Mount

and the Sermon on the Plain have, each of them, Mt. v.-vii.; Lk. vi.
idealistic significance. It is to be said now, however,
that we must accept from the gospel narrative for the
history of the matter this much, that Jesus evidently, at
the time to which we have come, gave utterance to
some of the words which go to make up the two discourses, and that it was about this time that these
words were reported and preserved. For the exact
detail of time and place in the matter, Mark must, as
usual, be followed rather than the other two. And we
find he gives some of the words found in the two discourses as having been spoken neither when Jesus was
still up on the hill nor immediately on his coming down Mk. iv. 21-25.
to the plain, but a little later, at the seaside. We may
make out the whole state of the case to have been
something like the following :—

The words in which Jesus told his apostles that they
were the " salt of the earth " and the "light of the Mt. v. 13, 14.
world," given in Matthew, may most likely have been
uttered as he chose the apostles on the mountain. And
along with the latter very likely there was spoken the
"candle" saying, reported by Mark as well as by Mk. iv. 21; Mt. v. 15.
Matthew. This saying was no doubt originally applied
by Jesus in his own mind to himself, in allusion to his
special enlightenment ; and now it was only applied by
him to the apostles in that he was regarding them as
emissaries of himself. So that we are justified in Above, p. 41.
taking this saying, as we have done, as supplying a clue
to Jesus's earlier action. But evidently the time of
sending the apostles was a time in which Jesus uttered
this saying, and the time in which a record was made
of it.
Mk. iii. 20; Lk. vi. 17.
When Jesus came down from the hill along with the

newly chosen apostles, he found, we learn, the large
multitude that had been following him still gathered in
expectation of seeing and hearing him.   It was as he
looked at them, we may believe, that he gave utterance

Lk. vi. 20-
22. Ver.23,
probably
inter-
woven
from Mt.
v. 12.
to the words recorded in Luke, " Blessed be ye poor :
for yours is the kingdom of God.   Blessed are ye that
hunger now : for ye shall be filled.   Blessed are ye that
weep now : for ye shall laugh.   Blessed are ye when
men . . . shall reproach you, and cast out your name
as evil."   The words following in the text—containing

Lk. vi. 24-
26.
the " woes "—we may take as being just a set-off on
the part of the evangelist, who is inclined to overstate the opposition between rich and poor all through.

Mt.v. 1-12.
The " beatitudes " of Matthew we may take as equally
historical with the above-quoted words from Luke.
Jesus would doubtless repeat and vary his sayings, and
thus allow of varied reports.   And it is exceedingly lifelike that he should have first given utterance to a burst
of promise, in the name of God, to all poor and needy
souls, and that he should have, some time very soon
after, applied this in a didactic way, conveying, as in
Matthew, the general thought that those who are
themselves *ready* to be poor and humble for the time, or
are "in spirit " poor and humble, are to be commended
and assured of their reward.

Lk. vi. 27-
38 : Mt.vii.
The beautiful verses in Luke—given slightly differently in Matthew—about the Divine love and forgiveness and mercifulness, are likely to have been taken
from sayings uttered about this time, a little after the
coming down from the mountain.   While thus their
historical position can be found to have been very
nearly at the sending of the apostles, it may be further
said that they represent what ought to be read at the

start by all real apostles and disciples of Jesus. So that Luke would seem to have first related them, following Mark, in their proper connection, speaking broadly, Mk. iv. 24. and to have then given them the more exact connection of the very time of sending the apostles, from well-judged idealistic considerations.

Regarding the rest of the Sermon on the Mount, we need not determine when it was delivered. It is evidently all, in substance, faithfully reported from Jesus. The part that opposes Jesus's teaching to what was said " by them of old time," may have been put in the pointed form by the evangelist. The passage about the care of God would likely be delivered in various forms, at different times throughout Jesus's ministry, in and around Capernaum.

Jesus came down again with his "apostles " among Mt. viii. 1; Lk. vi. 17. the multitude from whom he had withdrawn—as we must believe, with the intention of soon entering, with his newly made " apostles," on an extension of the field of his ministry and teaching. He did not begin this at once, however, but made a pause, in which he continued for a little his teaching about Capernaum. This pause and its meaning, with the teaching and other circumstances which accompanied it, we must leave for another chapter.

CHAPTER VIII.

SOME FURTHER TEACHING.

WHAT made Jesus pause before actually sending away his newly chosen "apostles" can be set down as having been partly that the enthusiasm and interest centering on himself among the people were now at their height and prevented him from making any new start, and partly that he considered it wise to let his apostles hear a little further of his teaching, so that in their efforts to spread it they might be saved from merely repeating phrases which he might have used, with meanings different from his own.

An instance of the interest in him now reigning, which seems to have considerably affected both Jesus himself and his followers, is recorded by both Matthew and Luke, and referred to the time at which our account has arrived. It is also recorded in the Fourth Gospel; and it is there put earlier, probably from its having assumed such an importance in the eyes of the first followers, that the narrator who had supplied it had given it a first place among the occurrences at Capernaum. An officer of the Roman Government—

Mk. iii. 2c.

Mk. iv. 1.

Mt. viii 5-13.

Jn. iv. 46-54

Holtz-mann says rather of Herod.

one who already had gained the reputation of "loving" Lk. vii. 5
the nation or people among whom his duty had placed
him—came to him on behalf of a servant he had that
was ill. Being, he seems to have said, "a man under Mt. viii. 9.
authority," and at the same time a man exercising
authority, he believed in Jesus's authority over the
unseen powers of evil. The followers of Jesus would,
no doubt, be most moved by the social importance
of the man; but Jesus himself, we see, was greatly
affected at finding himself believed in by one who was
not an Israelite. These words in the Gospel of
Matthew — spoken, it is likely, in reference to the
wish of the man to see Jesus, along with his words
about the "authority"—bring simply before us the Vers. 10-
historical truth, "Verily I say unto you, I have not 11.
found so great faith, no, not in Israel. And I say
unto you, That many shall come from the east and
west, and shall sit down with Abraham, and Isaac, and
Jacob, in the kingdom of heaven."

The interest and the enthusiasm of the people in
general seem at this time to have been overpowering.
In the words of Mark, "And the multitude cometh Mk. iii. 20.
together again, so that they could not so much as eat
bread." Such enthusiasm and interest Jesus seems to
have taken advantage of to give some further teaching
to multitude and disciples alike before going further
in regard to the extending of his ministry.

For a moment, however, he was interrupted in this
action by an occurrence probably not unlooked for.
As he met the worshipping crowd, he also met his Vers. 22-
enemies coming to renew their opposition. Their 30.
attack this time was of a more thorough-going
character than their previous attacks had been. They

could not now disregard the fact that he had taken a command amongst the people, and that, indeed, he really seemed to have some power over those "devils" whom all believed to be the causers of trouble in human lives. They had, accordingly, men of their own orders from Jerusalem to assist them in meeting his claims ; and these latter brought against him the charge, evil as it was stupid, that he cast out devils through the help of the chief devil himself. Jesus met this charge by pointing out the absurdity of reasoning that sought to prove what was conquering evil to be itself an evil power. At the same time he gave utterance to some expressions in which we can follow the course of his thought as he contemplated the virulent attack which they were making on him. Everything, he said, would be forgiven men except "the blasphemy against the Holy Ghost," by which, we may say, he meant calling by evil names what is proved to be the work of the Divine Spirit, by its being pure and true. And this was just what his opponents were doing. But yet—to follow Matthew's account—he went on to say, speaking against himself would be forgiven, though blaspheming the Holy Ghost could not be passed over. This we must interpret as meaning that, as he was perplexed by the unreasonableness of their attack and tried to explain it, he, with his own magnanimity, sought to excuse them by suggesting it was something about himself they opposed themselves to, and saying that that was not so bad as if they were resisting what was good independently of its connection with a particular man. He called upon them, however, to recognise a "good tree " through its bearing good fruit, and maintained

Mk. iii. 22-30; Mt. xii, 24-42.

Cp. above, pp. 45. 72.

that even those who speak what is good have good
within them. They next asked a "sign" from him.
He replied in the same course of thought as he had been
following, saying that it showed something wrong about
the whole "generation" to be asking for a sign, and
that all the sign they would get would be the sign which
the prophet Jonah, for example, had shown when
he managed to appeal to people through the truth of
what he said. He unfavourably compared their conduct both with that of the men of Nineveh, who had
listened to Jonah, and with that of the queen of Sheba,
who had listened to Solomon. These former great
men, he brought out, who had not been so great as
himself, had been received on their own merits. His
words, telling of bitter disappointment with his countrymen, but also telling of a consciousness on his own
part of greatness before which we will bow, ring down
the ages, "Behold a greater than Jonas is here."—
"Behold a greater than Solomon is here."

In the course also of his arguments with these
opponents, he gave expression to some quaint reflections
about the subject of casting out devils in general, in
which, it has been pointed out, he showed his own
belief in the merely partial character of these victories
over evil. Also while he was speaking, it would seem,
a woman in the company called out, "Blessed is the
womb that bare thee, and the paps which thou hast
sucked"; to which he replied, "Yea rather, blessed
are they that hear the word of God, and keep it."

A more painful opposition had at this same time to
be faced by him. The news of what had been taking
place had reached the ears of his own relatives in
Nazareth. And they, seeing the danger in which he

Margin notes:

Trace of this in Jn. v. 36. It is even possible that "John" there is a mistake for "Jonah." Note "greater"; cp. Mt. xii. 41. See also Jn. vi. 30.

Mt. xii. 41, 42.

Vers. 43-45. Wittichen.

Lk. xi. 27, 28.

Mk. iii. 21.

was placing himself, came to Capernaum and tried to
dissuade him, even going the length, according to the
Evangelist Mark, of trying to force him away, saying
that he was "beside himself." Jesus in his pain at
their not understanding him turned away, and said
bitterly that his disciples were (now) the only real
mother and sisters and brothers that he had. It has
surely been an egregious blunder to deduce from this
incident the notion that Jesus and his family did not
incline to one another. The indications of the incident
are really quite the other way. The remark of Jesus
was an impulsive one, having to do with the occasion
only. And the whole incident was a simple and natural
one, disclosing relations of the warmest affection on
both sides.

Being rid of his opponents, and having turned with
pain from his misunderstanding mother and brothers,
Jesus went with the people to the seaside; and there,
amid the surroundings that he loved, he taught his
disciples and the multitude. He addressed them sitting
in a boat. He "entered into a ship, and sat in the
sea; and the whole multitude was by the sea on the
land." He spoke to them about the "kingdom of
God," or rule of religion, which all were expecting to
come: and he illustrated it by "parables" or stories.
The parables which he told can be read in the fourth
chapter of Mark and the thirteenth chapter of Matthew.
They are parables about *seeds* in various aspects, about
leaven, about a fish-net, and about pearls. They mostly
bring out this idea, that it would be not sweepingly,
but by *growth*, that the "kingdom of God" would
come.

There is, however, to be carefully noticed a difference

[margin note:] Vers. 31-35. This incident roughly confirmed by Jn. ii. 12

[margin note:] Mk. iv.

between the two reports of Matthew and of Mark.
Mark's report speaks always of the kingdom of *God*,
Matthew's of the kingdom of *heaven*. And the difference
is not merely one of words. Mark's report seems to
make the teaching refer to something coming on earth;
Matthew's seems to make it in great measure refer to
something to be experienced beyond earth. We have
now, therefore, to ask, (1) Which expression did Jesus
really use? and (2) what did he mean by the expression
that he used?

The question as to which of the two expressions was
really used by Jesus can be answered with a good deal
of confidence. The "kingdom of God" was the
natural name of the idea long believed in; and from
its frequency in Mark and Luke we may conclude that
it was a name popularly used and generally understood.
It is natural to believe, therefore, that this phrase
would at least sometimes be used by Jesus. We might,
then, be inclined to go further. Seeing this is the
phrase always reported as that of Jesus in Mark and
Luke, the other being peculiar to Matthew, and seeing
Mark is the earlier and more generally trustworthy
gospel, we might be inclined to conclude that the
expression "kingdom of heaven" is very weakly attested
as having been used by Jesus. But that would be a
hasty conclusion. The question arises, Why has the
change been made in Matthew? The "kingdom of
heaven," not being found in Mark or Luke, does not
seem to have been a common expression. The "kingdom
of God," on the other hand, being found in all three,
though in Matthew not so much as in the others,
seems to have been the generally recognised phrase for
expressing the idea believed in. The peculiarity of

"the kingdom of heaven," therefore, to Matthew would seem to have had some special cause. Now it might be said that this expression agrees with a tendency in the Gospel of Matthew to dwell on the future beyond earth. But the tendency is not sufficiently marked in distinction to the state of matters in the other gospels, to make us believe that the ascribing of the expression to Jesus was without historical evidence to support it. Rather we must believe that in the independent material possessed by the author or authors of the First Gospel, this expression was found as that of Jesus, and thus that the author or authors introduced it in correction of what they found in the earlier gospel. We must therefore conclude that Jesus used the common expression "kingdom of God," but often substituted for it the phrase "kingdom of heaven"; and what he meant by so doing we shall presently see.

See App. I. (9).

We have, secondly, to ask, What did Jesus mean by the expression "kingdom of God" or "kingdom of heaven" at this time, seeing there appears the uncertainty between the future of earth and the future beyond earth? In a previous chapter we have found Jesus using the phrase "kingdom of God" as meaning a future establishment of religion. Did he now mean to refer this "kingdom of God" to the future of earth, or was he meaning to direct the thoughts of his hearers to the regions beyond the earthly life into which as individuals they would one and all soon vanish?

Above, p. 89.

What we have just come to—namely, that he often substituted the phrase "the kingdom of heaven" for the popular phrase—helps us to answer this question. There is needed, however, for the clear understanding

of Jesus's thought, a further key; and that key must
be looked for in the religious books written about the
time of Jesus. It is simplest to suppose that Jesus's
thoughts on the subject first followed what was taught
and generally believed in his time; let it be that we
find he himself made an advance on that. And what
was taught and generally believed in his time must be
looked for in the literature which emanated from his
time and shortly before it. Now, especially valuable
for this use is a group of books that have come down
to us, called by scholars *Apocalyptic* books, or books of
Revelation, comprising the following: The Book of
Daniel, the Book of Enoch, the Fourth (in the collection of the "Apocrypha" called Second) Book of Esra
(Esdras), the Sybilline Oracles, and the Revelation, or
Apocalypse, to be found at the end of the New Testa-
ment. With these there has been classed part of the ^{Pfleiderer.}
"Second Epistle to the Thessalonians" of our New
Testament; and indeed many of the books of the New
Testament contain more or less of the same kind of
thought. We find, then, that in the books just men- *E.g.*, 2
tioned, in the same way as in the reports of Jesus's Esdr. c.
xiii. Cp.
teaching, there is a wavering of the object of religious xiv. 35.
hope between the future of the earth and the future of
individuals beyond earth. The state of the case can be
determined by concluding that the hope for individuals Also
beyond the grave had been gradually coming to possess Enoch,
c. lxi., tr.
the minds of the thoughtful, and that it was only by Laur-
ence.
gradually that it came to fit in exactly with the hope
for the future of the world, which had formerly had a
greater hold on the minds of the thoughtful Israelites.
Thus in Daniel the hope seems to be that the individual Dan. vii.
27, xii. 2,
saints will in heaven join with the Supreme Ruler in 3.

establishing the rule of what is good on earth. This
hope, we may say, prevails more or less through **all**
these books ; but also **in** the later ones there appears a
new thought, to the effect that the world is coming to
an end altogether, so that the whole ideal becomes
transferred from earth to heaven. This latter thought,
which **is in some way a retrograde** one, shows **how**
the relation between the two objects **of** hope was **very**
undefined.

2 Esdr. xii.
34 ; Rev.
xxi. 1.
See also
1 Thess.
iv. 16, 17.

Jesus, then, we may say, received from contemporary
thought these two objects of religious hope which **were**
cast about disconnectedly in people's minds. We may
conclude, **from** a thoughtful survey of the reports before
us, that he gave recognition **to** both of them. And now
we can say that he gave **to them a** rational—we may
almost say scientific—welding together. This is found
in the *Seed-idea*. From thinking a little over Jesus's use
of the seed-idea, and noticing that he made **it** apply to
the life of individuals beyond the grave, as well **as** to
the prevalence of religion in the future of the world, we
can read in his teaching this grand thought—That he
expected individual spirits to spring **to** new life and
consciousness in the arms of nature after death, like
seeds after being sown ; and that in their new life, which
would be a life of improved knowledge and feeling,
they would enter into the happiness of seeing the im-
provement which by a similar process was also meanwhile coming about **in** the world generally. Thus,
starting **at** this **time** with the conception of the
"kingdom **of** God," or future rule of religion in the
world, he agreed with **the** belief that was held by those
who wrote the apocalyptic books and by many others,
that this would be a kingdom of *heaven*—that is, a

Mt. xiii. :
cp. Jn. xii.
23-25.

Cp. Jn.
xii. 23, 24.

kingdom in which the revived spirits of men and
women would reign along with God ; but he showed
his hearers how this would all come about gradually
through the growth in the whole world of nature.

While, however, we must recognise that, as Matthew
indicates, Jesus taught that the object of hope was to
be beyond earth for individuals as well as on earth for
future generations, we must not go with Matthew when
he ascribes to Jesus in these teachings a *dualistic* view of
human beings, or view according to which only some
human spirits are to attain the object of hope and the
rest are to be " severed " from them for ever. That
this was not the view of Jesus we can assert fearlessly,
on the grounds that, first, such an idea is quite
opposed to what is found in regard to the subject in
the Gospel of Mark, which is generally the more trustworthy of the two ; and that, second, the whole spirit
of Jesus's teaching excludes it. Especially, we may
say, it is excluded by that very seed-idea which comes
before us in the parables now under our consideration.
The mind that could produce those parables, in which
the prevailing ideas are unity and development, could
not have been a mind entertaining the notion of an
everlasting dualism. We must, then, hold that, as
Matthew relates, Jesus at this time used the phrase
" kingdom of heaven " as well as the phrase " kingdom
of God," thereby showing his belief that human spirits
were to reign with God as His children ; but we must
not believe that Jesus took Matthew's dualistic view
regarding human spirits. We must also hold that
Matthew has greatly enriched our knowledge of Jesus's
teaching at this time by adding to what Mark reports
the parables of the Tares and the Fish-net, which

Marginal notes:

For this meaning of *ouranos* (heaven) see Mk. x. 21, xii. 25; Mt. vi. 20, xviii. 10; Lk. xxiv. 51. Cp use of the word in " Revelation."

Mt. xiii. 49.

Cp. Mk. ix. 49.

See Mk. ix. 43-50.

centre the object of hope in the life of individuals
beyond the grave, as well as in the general life of the
world in the future ; but we must believe he has gone
astray in his explanations of these two parables.   The
Gospel of Matthew is emphatically a book having to do
with morals ; and all moral enthusiasts, both men and
books, if they be not at the same time religious enthusiasts in the higher way, overstate the differences
between man and man.   The "tares" assuredly, in
Jesus's mind, were not living and thinking beings,—
for of such had not God numbered the very hairs of
the heads ?—but the evil elements in the composition
of one and all, which, through growth and through
the power of good influences, would be cast "into a
furnace of fire" and become as if they had never been.

Jesus, then, at this time addressed his newly-made
apostles along with the whole multitude, taking as his
subject that coming "kingdom of God" in which all
believed.   He had at the start of his preaching
announced that that "kingdom of God" was "at
hand," and he had recently taken steps towards its
realisation.   It remained for him to make clear what
he held to be the true nature of the ideal which was
named by that phrase.   And this he did now as he
sat in the boat, with the sea in its beauty, the sun in
its warmth and brightness, and the sky in its majesty,
all bearing witness to a kingdom of what is good, that
transcended the limited range of time to which the
popular phrase applied—a kingdom which the combined powers of evil had never really removed.   He
gave it to be understood, through one striking parable
Mk. iv.   after another, that the ideal which was meant by that
phrase with which he had started, was to be realised

not in a future that would rudely break with the past,
but in a future that would silently grow out of the past
and present. And gently altering the phrase in a Mt. xiii.
direction which led to the thought that human souls
themselves would help to reign with God as that ideal
became more and more established, he diverted their
minds from looking for the ideal in embodiments that met
their present vision—to look for it in a region where its
more complete realisation would be found, namely, among
embodiments yet to be attained by their own spirits,
but not distinguished as such by their earthly senses.
And then he gave parables that illustrated this secondary thought. His discourse on the subject, probably
only in part reported to us, began to concern itself with
the movements of spirit-life that go beyond the time of
earthly existence. In the yet unperceived region, he
taught, into which those movements would lead human
souls, there would still be growing up that prevailing
of God and that prevailing of the children of God Vers. 30.
of which prophets had vaguely dreamed, as those [48]
children of God had what was evil in them cast away
like the refuse of a fish-net or like tares among the
wheat, and had what was good in them gathered and
secured for their everlasting possession.

CHAPTER IX.

THE EXTENDING OF JESUS'S MINISTRY.

HAVING given, by the seaside, his great teaching which

Mk. iv. 35-41. Cp. Jn. vi. 1.

we considered in last chapter, Jesus applied himself directly to that extending of the field of his ministry and teaching for which the choosing of "apostles" had been the introduction. He and his apostles crossed the lake in the evening. And as they crossed, in the excited condition of mind to which they had been aroused, something happened which came to be told as a story of how there had been a great storm, and how

Ver. 39.

Jesus had ended it by saying simply, "Peace, be still." What the original of this story had really been we can-

See especially ver. 40. Ver. 41 probably means he had made "wind and sea" become illustrations, as he did with all nature.

not tell now. It may have been nothing more than this, that the apostles were noisy, argumentative, and full of wild projects, that Jesus alone was calm and silent, and that in dignified reproof he restored peace and patience among them, calling their attention to the beauty of the evening calm in the lake around them. Be this, however, as it may, a fine historical picture comes down to us with practical certainty, in spite of the uncertainty of the details. It is the picture of

Jesus in the midst of those roughly nurtured men, as they all sail across the lake in a rude fishing-boat, holding one and all bound in reverence by his mere presence, so that even when, after the great fatigues to which he has been subjected, he has fallen asleep in the stern of the boat, and when he has spoken some words that have changed to them the whole situation around them, they, perhaps as he sleeps, regard him with a mingling of awe and affection, saying to each other, "What manner of man is this, that even the wind and the sea" serve him!

The little voyage, however, is interesting from another point of view. It is interesting as having been the first Christian missionary journey. Jesus was by nature, we may say, no missionary. His habit of mind was too introspective and contemplative for him to apply himself to the organisation required for a missionary enterprise. And we can see that this little journey to the other side of the lake was a mere loosely conceived venture, of short duration. Still we cannot but pause a moment to fix our attention on the little event, as we notice how it may be looked at as having been indeed the first step towards spreading the religion of Jesus over the world. When Jesus and his disciples entered their boats and pushed out on the lake, the religion of Jesus, we may say, entered a boat unseen by the natural eyes, in which it was to be carried over every ocean that separates land from land.

In the time in which the little company was on the other side of the lake, only one event seems to have happened that was considered worth remembering. It was Jesus's helping some poor man of troubled or unsound mind. The record given of this event, Mk. v. 1-20.

coloured as it is by the imagination of the time, is
evidently faithful in preserving both some interesting
words of Jesus himself, and also some words of the
poor troubled man, that have an importance to us.
The poor man is made out to have said, by way of
resistance of his "unclean spirit" to be interfered with
Mk. v. 7. by Jesus, "What have I to do with thee, Jesus, thou
Son of the most high God? I adjure thee by God that
thou torment me not." There is no need to doubt the
report of the words. We may believe that the man
really said almost exactly what is conveyed in at least
the first half of the report, and that, as best recommends itself on looking back from our modern stand-
point, he said it by way of personal comment on Jesus's
teaching. The words thus meant, we must suppose,
that the man, believing he had a "devil" in him,
asked how he could have anything "to do" with one
who asserted that men were the children of God. The
words are interesting and important, in that they confirm the fact of Jesus having very specially taught the
truth of the Fatherhood of God in his early ministry.
And they are further important in that they bear out
its having been a general Fatherhood that he taught.
They do this, we may say, inasmuch as the point in
them is that the man felt his own nature to be different
from that which, according to Jesus's teaching, it
ought to have been. Jesus exercised over this man
an extraordinary power, and restored the calm of his
Vers. 8, mind; and then the man, it seems, wished to join his
15, 17. followers. But Jesus replied, "Go home to thy friends,
Ver. 19. and tell them how great things the Lord hath done for
thee, and hath had compassion on thee." These
words are even more interesting to us than the words

of the troubled man that have just been before us. They show that Jesus had a prudence which could make him reject apostles as well as choose apostles. But they also help to destroy some of the prevalent errors regarding his whole character and views. They help to show that he was no revolutionary, seeking to rouse the community into an uproar. And they also give one more blow to that most injurious error P. 154. which we have just above been considering, to the effect that he cared not for family life, and sought earnest men to leave their natural relationships to become attached to himself.

Jesus soon returned to Capernaum, and stayed a Mk. v. 21; short time, before leaving for another little journey. Mt. ix. 1.

At this time several events happened which have been recorded. One of them was that Jesus was called to see the daughter of a certain Jairus, " one of the Mk. v. 22- rulers of the synagogue "—that is, the chief minister 43. of some synagogue—let us suppose, the chief minister of the synagogue in which Jesus had delivered his first wonderful discourses. What exactly happened in regard to Jairus's daughter it is difficult for sober modern thought to decide. Word seems to have come to Jesus, before he reached the house, that the girl was dead ; and Jesus spoke these lovely words of universal application, " The damsel is not dead, but sleepeth." Ver. 39. The gospel narrative declares that Jesus *raised* her from the dead. The fact on which this declaration is based might be that it was found her having died had been a false report. But it is much more likely—as we shall see was the case with regard to Lazarus—that Jesus raised her only through the words just quoted—that is, See App. raised her in promise only. He promised authoritatively I. (10).

her resurrection in the eternal rule of the heavenly
Father.

Another event of this short time in which Jesus was
Mk. v.
25-34. back in Capernaum, was that a certain sick woman
had so great faith in Jesus that, as he was passing, she
Mk. v. 29. touched his clothes behind, and at the very touch " felt
in her body that she was healed of that plague."

Lk. vii.
36-50. There is still another event of importance which we
may fix to this short time in Capernaum, as we have
no clue to the time of its having happened except that
it is related by Luke shortly after his narrative of the
choosing of apostles. Jesus was partaking the hos-
Vers. 37,
38. pitality of a certain Pharisee. "A woman in the city,
which was a sinner, when she knew that Jesus sat at
meat in the Pharisee's house," came "and stood at his
feet behind him weeping, and began to wash his feet
with tears." The Pharisee objected, and Jesus told
one of the most benign of his parables to meet the
objection of the Pharisee. The account of this occurrence, indeed, which is only given in Luke, has evidently
got mixed up a little with the record of another
This spe-
cially fol-
ows the
criticism
of Witti-
chen. occurrence, to which we shall come later on. But as
far as it has just been related, it is likely to have
happened. The parable, which may be read in the
seventh chapter of Luke, recommends itself strongly,
and the event related as having led to it may be accepted
also.

Impelled still, doubtless, by the feeling that the time
had come in which his message ought to be extended,
and still, no doubt, being himself without any very
complete scheme for the accomplishment of this, Jesus,
after only a few days' stay in Capernaum, resolved, as
Mk. vi. 1. we may gather, on a visit to his own town.

The apostles accompanied him. And we can believe
the intention from the start to have been that in some
way they were to separate from him during the journey, Mk. vi. 1.
to spread his teaching.

It may have been also at this time that there began
to accompany him a number of earnest women. Jesus
was, beyond doubt, during much of his public ministry, Mk. xv.
accompanied by women, who were very likely the first 41; Lk.
viii. 1-3.
to regard him with that kind of devotion which is to be
called no ordinary devotion, but worship. They were,
several of them, women who had felt themselves
delivered from spiritual diseases or troubles by his
presence and power. The most notable of the class
was Mary of Magdala—a village near Capernaum—for Mt. xv. 39.
so her name, "Magdalene," seems best interpreted.
Out of her, the record tells, "went seven devils."
This by no means implies that she had been an evil-
living woman. Her trouble may not have been moral
trouble, but may have been merely nervous. All these See above,
women helped to supply the material wants of Jesus. pp. 109-
110.
This may have begun during the settled ministry in
Capernaum.

Regarding Jesus's visit to Nazareth, several main
facts are practically certain. One is found related in
all the first three gospels. And a few others are found
through careful reading of two notices, both demanding
recognition, the one in Luke and the other in John.

The fact which is related by all of the Synoptic Mk. vi. 1-
gospels is simply that Jesus was not well received by 5; Lk. iv.
16-29; Mt.
the people of his own town. As it is told in Mark, xiii. 54-58.
they said, " Is not this the carpenter, the son of Mary,
the brother of James, and Joses, and of Juda, and
Simon ? and are not his sisters here with us ? " And

Mark adds, " And they were offended at him." Jesus at this time **repeated** the saying which, **as we have** gathered, he had uttered already about the prophet in his **own** country—perhaps enlarging on **it as Mark** reports it : " A prophet **is not** without honour, but in his own country, and among **his own kin, and in his** own house." Mark closes the **account** with this most lifelike statement : " **And he could there** do no mighty **work,** save that he laid his **hands upon a few sick** folk, **and healed them. And** he marvelled **because of their** unbelief."

Next, we get a reminiscence of this visit from Luke. Luke has **palpably** misplaced the incident altogether— likely for reasons quite intelligible, as we have seen above. But **on the other hand, in the first place, Luke** **is surely to be trusted when he tells us that Jesus,** in his address to the people **of his own town,** took a **passage** from the Book of Isaiah **containing** a Divine message of **good** news for all the unfortunate of the **earth,** and then added that he himself was not merely repeating that message in the name of **God, but was** bringing about the beginning of its fulfilment in this **world.** Had it been the case that Luke of himself put **this** into **the** mouth **of Jesus,** just by way of making **plain** to the readers of the gospel the spirit of Jesus's teaching, it would not have been easy to see why he should have **connected** it **with** the Nazareth visit, especially as he so transparently misplaces the Nazareth visit to bring this quotation and addition into the foreground. Rather the state of matters points to the fact that the Evangelist had found the words of Jesus **in an** account **of the** Nazareth visit, and discerning **their** suitableness to his purpose of bringing out the

Above, p. 80.

Mk. vi. 4.

Lk. iv. 16-29. Cp. above, p. 80, with marginal note there.

Is. lxi. 1, 2.

spirit of Jesus's teaching, put the whole thing in the foreground, careless of his thereby letting it be easily seen that he had departed from the historical order of events. Besides this, Luke records certain words as having been spoken by Jesus at Nazareth at this time, having a ring that cannot be mistaken for anything short of indicating that they were in substance uttered by Jesus. They are these: " But I tell you of a truth, many widows were in Israel in the days of Elias, when the heaven was shut up three years and six months, when great famine was throughout all the land ; but unto none of them was Elias sent, save unto Sarepta, a city of Sidon, unto a woman that was a widow. And many lepers were in Israel in the time of Eliseus the prophet ; and none of them was cleansed, saving Naaman the Syrian." These words would likely be said not to the people generally, but to the disciples; and they are very interesting in that they present one of the links in a chain of thought in which Jesus *explained*, to others and to himself, the unreasonable oppositions which he encountered. We have seen above that, in thinking over the opposition from the scribes and Pharisees, he went just the length, in explanation, of suggesting that what they were doing was perhaps occasioned by their taking some offence at his own personality, and that that was not so bad as if they were directly resisting the Divine Spirit. In the words now before us we see a new thought that he had come to by way of explaining oppositions. It was to this effect, that every mission had limitations; in other words, that to one was given one region to benefit, and to another another, and that to none was given the whole world at once. We shall see that

Marginal notes:

Perhaps also justifying himself from Mt. iv. 13. See above. p. 80. Lk. iv. 25-27.

Cp. 1 Kings xvii. 9, xviii. 1 ; also 2 Kings v. 14. See App. I. (11).

P. 152.

See independent and most completely confirming record in Jn. vi. 43. 44, intermingled there

with the
Evange-
list's own
doctrine
in ver. 45.
Jesus carried out this thought further when he met
the more terrible oppositions that awaited him in
Jerusalem. The modesty which thus beautifully shines
in those recorded words of our Master, was not opposed
to, but rather was the historic prelude to, the worship
on the part of his disciples, which no longer views his
case as having had parallels in that of any Elias or
Eliseus, and knows that his name and his spirit were to
take captive not Capernaum merely, not Nazareth, not
Galilee merely, not the land of Israel, but the world.

And lastly, to learn about this visit to Nazareth, we
go back to the guidance of our Fourth Gospel, which
for a time we have been neglecting. After the point at
which we last received information from the Fourth
c.vi.
Gospel, it becomes very doctrinal and unhistorical;
but still it contains several notices which, critically
viewed, so tally with what the other gospels relate, and
yet so exhibit freedom, that we must recognise they
come from an independent record which has been
worked up into the doctrinal whole. We find recorded
the crossing the lake, the multitude following, the
vi. 1, 2,
3, v. 36,
vi. 30, ii.
12,
vii. 3, vi.
44, 65, 42.
"mountain" incident, the seeking a sign, (the visit of
the mother and brothers to Capernaum,) the visit of
Jesus and the disciples to Nazareth, and the words
of the people of Nazareth—all these things in confused
connections, and mixed up with them several other
events recorded by the earlier gospels, which we have
not yet come to. About Nazareth, then, first, the
Jn. vi. 42. words of the people there are given in the sixth chapter,
Ver. 41. interlaced with doctrinal matter, and are referred
Jn. vii. 1-
9. vaguely to "the Jews"; then a little way on there is
an independent story which is so natural that we must
accept it, and accept it as a gem from the historical

reality of the Nazareth visit.   It is to this effect, that
Jesus had an interview while at Nazareth with his
brothers, that they, becoming, as we may gather, by
this time impressed with him, but still remaining in a
state of fear and distrust at his bold opposing of people
in authority, suggested, if he was indeed a great man,
he ought to go up to Jerusalem and get properly known
there, and that Jesus gave as his answer that his time
"was not yet come."   This incident is most lifelike.
Jesus's brothers, we see, did not understand him ; and
yet their family affection asserted itself, and they
showed they were quite willing to believe he was the
Prophet he held himself to be.   They gave him the
advice, however, to go to Jerusalem, no doubt having
the opinion that if he was what he thought himself,
his proper course was to get recognised by people who
knew better than they about the subjects which he
handled.   We have here an example of the common
attitude towards an out-of-the-way character, which is
an attitude of timidity until the authorities in one's
own little world have given a decision.   We have also Cp. above,
here one more hard blow for the—let us hope already pp. 32, 33,
extinguished—fancy that Jesus and his family were not 154, 165.
united by affection.

   This little notice of the Fourth Gospel is also important in that it helps us in our chronology.   It may
seem arbitrary to accept information on this subject
from the Fourth Gospel in one case and reject its
testimony regarding the subject in other cases ; and in
general, as we have seen, it must be said the Fourth
Gospel has—and probably professes to have—no claims
to be taken as trustworthy regarding time and place.
But the little notice now before us contains a state-

ment which is so spontaneous and so bound up with
the lifelike story itself, that we need not relegate it
to the Evangelist's unhistorical treatment of days and
years, but accept it as a statement of fact.   It is this :
Jn. vii. 2. "Now the Jews' feast of tabernacles was at hand."
Ex. xxiii. The feast of Tabernacles, or feast of Ingathering, was
16 ; Lev.
xxiii. 39 ; held in the autumn—about September.   Jesus thus
Deut. xvi. had spent the whole summer about Capernaum ; the
13-15.
events on the other side of the lake had lasted
just a few days ; and now in the autumn he was at
Nazareth, which probably he had left less than a
year before.

After this Jesus sent out his apostles to extend his
Mk. vi. 7. message.   He sent them, says Mark, "by two and
two."   A number of instructions are recorded in the
Vers. 8-11. Gospel of Mark as having been given by him to them
as he sent them.   These are probably in substance
authentic ; but we need not notice them, as they must
be viewed as having had to do merely with immediate
circumstances, and as having no very great general signi-
Mt. x. ficance.   The Gospel of Matthew gives a much longer
list of instructions to the apostles.   Taken as a whole,
this list of Matthew's is in the same position as the
Sermon on the Mount.   It is compiled from various
sayings of Jesus uttered at different times ; and as
these sayings are presented in it, they have been
changed, if not added to, through the idealistic purpose
of showing the instructions of the Messiah to his messengers, for the later time in which the gospel was
written, as well as for the time in Jesus's life to which we
have come.   Some of the sayings were originally uttered
most probably, as we shall see, at a later time than
this, at Capernaum.   Some of them, again, were

originally uttered in Jerusalem, just before Jesus's death, as we shall also see. There are likely, however, to have been some of them uttered at this time, thus forming a background. And such may have been these, certainly authentic, sayings of Jesus: " Are not *Mt. x. 29-* two sparrows sold for a farthing ? and one of them *31.* shall not fall on the ground without your Father. . . . Fear ye not, therefore, ye are of more value than many sparrows," and again, " The very hairs of your head *Ver. 30.* are all numbered."

After the sending out of the apostles, there comes an obvious gap in the gospel narrative. We may gather, *Mk vi. 6,* however, with great probability, that Jesus agreed to *30, 45.* meet them all again at Capernaum, that he kept two *From Mt.* or three by himself, and that several weeks elapsed *xi., &c.* before all met again, bringing the time on towards the end of the year.

Three recorded events which, from their harmony with the other events, may be accepted as historical, happened, we may say, just about this time—very probably in these intervening weeks—and may be mentioned as providing a fitting close for this chapter.

First, certain persons who had listened to John the *Mt. xi. 2-6.* Baptist began to be so impressed by Jesus as to go the length of bringing forward the question whether he might not be the Great Coming One of whom John *Cp. Lk.* had spoken. In the gospels it is represented that John *vii.* himself asked the question, sending messengers from his prison to ask it of Jesus himself. It is difficult to conceive this to have been literally possible, and it is not to show any disrespect to the accounts to suppose that the name of John may have come in them to stand for himself and his following, and that it was followers, not himself, who asked the question. This point may be left undecided, however; the importance of the narrative centres on Jesus's answer. Jesus, hearing of the question, said something like this, "Go

Mt. xi. 4-5. and show John again those things which ye do hear

Cp. Is. xxxv. 5-6, xlii. 7, &c. and see: the blind receive their sight, and the lame walk, the lepers are cleansed, and the deaf hear, the dead are raised up, and the poor have the Gospel preached to them." Jesus still, we must gather, was making no outward claim to be the Jewish Messiah, and yet, when the question of whether he could be called so was brought before him, he did not refuse to have the question entertained, but referred it to his favourite, unimpeachable canon of letting works or

Vers. 7-19. "fruits" be the test. He then went on to pay a high tribute to the character of the Baptist, at the same time showing his own independence of the Baptist, both in his personality and in the ideal he had before him. The words of his eulogy were probably almost exactly as they are reported in the eleventh chapter of Matthew and in the seventh chapter of Luke.

Vers. 20-24. The second event was that at this time he bitterly reproached the towns in which he had laboured for their meeting him with so much annoyance, opposition, and coldness.

Vers. 25-30. The third event was the counterpart of the second. While Jesus had met with oppositions which perplexed and grieved him, he had also met with much recognition which uplifted him. The uplifting from without intensified his own joy, which was occasioned by the consciousness of a religion like a "pearl of great price." And so we learn that at this time he once let his joyful emotion at what he knew he had inwardly attained rise up and express itself in these jubilant words : " I thank thee, O Father, Lord of heaven and earth, because thou hast hid these things from the wise and prudent, and hast revealed them unto babes. Even so, Father ; for so it seemed good in thy sight." And then, as his religious consciousness was ever such that after centering itself on God it spread itself out towards his fellow men, his thankfulness was succeeded by a feeling of power to impart, his feeling of power to impart was succeeded by a desire to impart, and he gave utterance to this exclamation, as grand as it is famous : " Come unto me, all ye that labour and are heavy laden, and I will give you rest. Take my yoke upon you, and learn of me : for I am meek and lowly in heart : and ye shall find rest unto your souls. For my yoke is easy, and my burden is light."

Cp. the book in Apocrypha, Ecclesiasticus, li. 23-27.

CHAPTER X.

THE SECOND RETREAT.

Mt. ix. 37, 38. Cp. Lk. x. 2. IT is recorded in the First Gospel that before Jesus sent out his apostles he said to them these words, " The harvest truly is plenteous, but the labourers are few; pray ye therefore the Lord of the harvest, that he will send forth labourers unto his harvest." These words, certainly authentic, must either have been uttered some time before the sending out of the apostles, or else have had a restricted signification. In the work of spreading the name and message of Jesus, in the latter part of the year in which most of his public ministry took place, the labourers were in a Mk. vi., vii. way, at least, no longer few. This is seen from the result that followed, which was no less than this, that the people of the whole surrounding country came to talk and discuss about him. They said, we learn, that a prophet had appeared, some comparing him to Mk. vi. 15. Elijah, others comparing him to John the Baptist. And so we can believe that the extensiveness of the number of preachers is pointed out by Luke when he Lk. x. 1. relates that after Jesus had sent out the twelve he also sent out seventy. That Jesus repeated the formal action of sending apostles forth, choosing the number 70 instead of the number 12, is hardly to be taken literally as a fact ; but we may believe that what Luke relates is a dramatic account of the fact that far more than twelve took up at this time Jesus's mission, and may indeed have been in some way definitely commissioned by himself. The name of Jesus was sent resounding all over Galilee, and he became known in Mk. vi. 56. both " villages," " cities," and " country."

Jesus met again the more intimate at least of his Ver. 30. followers, as we may gather, at Capernaum. They told Cp. ver. 53. him of great successes in their work; and he exclaimed, " I beheld Satan as lightning fall from heaven." Lk. x. 18.

But even in the midst of such jubilation a fell blow was struck at Jesus. The brightness of success suddenly assumed the aspect of an afternoon glow, and gave warning that the day was passing and darkness coming on. Just as Jesus was in the midst of great prosperity he had to turn and once more meet pain and difficulty, in order that his sublime character might make its grandest achievement, and that God might give him " a name which is above every name : that at the name of Jesus every knee should bow, Phil. ii. 9- of things in heaven, and things in earth, and things 11. under the earth ; and that every tongue should confess that Jesus Christ is Lord, to the glory of God the Father." What happened was this: Herod, Mk. vi. 14- the governor of Galilee and Peræa, heard what was 30. taking place, and gave some good ground for fearing that he might treat Jesus as he had treated John the Baptist. No doubt the enemies of Jesus had gained See Mk. the ear of Herod, had told him of the popular move- iii. 6

ment in his favour, and had made the most of it to his

Lk. ix. 7-9. detriment. As in the words of Luke, " Now Herod the tetrarch heard of all that was done by him : and he was perplexed, because that it was said of some, that John was risen from the dead ; and of some, that Elias had appeared ; and of others, that one of the old prophets was risen again. And Herod said, John have I beheaded : but who is this, of whom I hear such things ? And he desired to see him." At the hearing of the danger which was threatening him,

Mk. vi. 30 ; Jesus withdrew with his intimate friends from public
Mt. xiv. notice, as he had done before on hearing of the capture
13. of the Baptist, first going, as in that former case, to " the desert."

Mk. vi. ; The gospels of Matthew and of Mark tell at this
Mt. xiv. point, for the first time, that John had not only been imprisoned by Herod, but had been put to death. And from the repeated mention of " prison " in the gospels, in relation to John, it is best to take their account literally, and conclude that John had been kept a while in the castle of Machærus before Herod carried his barbarous treatment to the last extremity. While, however, agreeing in this, and indeed presenting the identical story as the account of it, the two

Mk. vi. 14- gospels diverge considerably in the turn they give to
30 ; Mt. xiv. 1-13. the story. Matthew relates that John's disciples came at this point and told Jesus of John's fate, and that having heard of it, Jesus withdrew into the desert ; Mark, on the other hand, makes no allusion to Jesus's hearing of the event, and ascribes his withdrawal to the wish to give his disciples rest. We may decide that it is unlikely Jesus now heard of the Baptist's fate for the first time. The people's calling

him John raised from the dead, points to its having
been popularly known that John was dead ; and also
Matthew's statement about John's disciples bringing Cp. Mt.
Jesus the news, both is itself most improbable and also with Mk.
has the appearance of having been manipulated, in vi. 29, 30.
misapprehension, out of the narrative in Mark. On the
other hand, Matthew, we must say, preserves for us
the true motive of Jesus's withdrawal. All that
followed, as we shall see, fits in exactly to the motive
pointed to by Matthew, and indeed can in no other
way be satisfactorily explained. Jesus learned, we
must conclude, that it had been told Herod how people
were saying he was John raised from the dead, and
that Herod had marked him. He knew the serious
signification of this. Herod himself had shown what
might be expected of him by his treatment of the
Baptist. But also, we may believe, Jesus saw that it
was not only Herod himself he had to reckon with, but
the mistaken zeal of the people, which was likely, in
spite of his own purely moral and religious position, to
give to the rising which had taken place the appearance See Jn. vi.
for such an onlooker as Herod of a political movement. 15.
He therefore withdrew from public notice—wishing
rest for himself and his disciples, no doubt, but also
wishing opportunity to pause and consider the danger
that was seriously standing in his way.

In this second of several withdrawals of Jesus from
danger to his own person, the characteristics of all
these withdrawals strikingly appear. What can be
seen in this case, and indeed in all the cases, is that,
first, Jesus did indeed make escape from danger on its
emergence ; but that, second, having done so, he
concentrated his attention on the special danger that

had appeared, and then, his purpose thus receiving
new special direction, turned and faced the danger.
To suggest, regarding his withdrawals, therefore, their
indicating lack of courage—even had his life not been
crowned by the heroic act which did crown it—would
be to make an outrageous blunder. His withdrawals
showed no lack of courage, but showed an abundance
of thoughtfulness. It is not courage, but foolishness,
to run headlong into real dangers ; and the dangers of
which Jesus had learned were most real. But Jesus
added to the escapes he made this further action, that
when he had had time to fix his thoughts on the
dangers, he in his strength of purpose, though knowing
that they were dangers, faced them again. His
escapes thus became mere times of pause, in which he
formed new special plans to serve his general purpose.

In the case to which we have come, we can discern,
Jesus took the same view of the danger that was
threatening him as he had taken in the first case,
seeing it to be such as arose from the interference of
brute force with the purposes of the thoughtful and
the religious. Either at the very moment of hearing
of the danger or soon after, he likened Herod to a—
fox, as the word is translated, or, as we may say, a
jackal. And so, we may say, the escape which he made
was, in his view of it, as it was in reality, the withdrawal of a Man who had awakened to the consciousness of being a son of God, before the advance of a
man who was no more reliable than that he might
spring on the other like a wild beast.

In this second withdrawal, Jesus took a different
course altogether from that which he had taken in
the first withdrawal, because he had now a different

See Ori-
gen
against
Celsus, I.
65, where
an inter-
esting
illustra-
tion is
given.

See above,
p. 64.

Lk. xiii.
32.

position altogether in relation to his fellow-men, and
he saw in his changed position new responsibilities.
In the former case he had gone right away through
the wilderness of Judæa and entered a new region,
according to the suggestion that had come, as we are
supposing, from the two or three friends who had
accompanied him. In making at that time a complete
escape from the surroundings in which the danger had
appeared, he had left no duty and had forsaken no one
depending on him. This later time, however, his
position was different. He had by this time begun a
work among a particular body of people ; and a large
number of the people, having received him enthusiasti-
cally, were now waiting to learn more of his doctrine.
More than this, these people were, at the point to
which we have come, fairly crowding around him.
The account, indeed, of this period of Jesus's ministry Mk. vi. 31-
has perplexingly mingled the symbolic with the historic, 33.
and so, literal reading of it can but lead one astray.
With care, however, it is possible to detect what took
place. When Jesus sought to withdraw, we can see,
he could hardly get away from the crowd. When he
and his disciples were going towards the desert
"privately," "the people saw them departing, and Vers. 32,
many knew him, and ran afoot thither out of all cities, 33.
and outwent them." Thus, we can read quite plainly,
he put before his mind the fact that now, in a different
way from what had been in the case of the former
withdrawal, he had a number of persons depending on
him. He "saw much people," we read—and saw, as Ver. 34.
we must interpret, that they were people who, should
he go away altogether, would be left morally helpless.
He "was moved with compassion toward them,

because they were as sheep not having a shepherd."
He gave full weight to this fact of the dependence of
the people on him. He gave it full weight, and acted
accordingly. He determined, as we can see quite
well, that his withdrawal should be in the meantime a
very short one.

Mk. vi 45-56.   He went to a mountain near Bethsaida. There he
separated even from his immediate followers, and
communed alone with the Presence that ever sustained
him. Then, having stayed only a very short time, he
came back to his immediate friends. And then he
and they came back among the people in general.

Straight back among both followers and opponents
he came, and then there took place a new altercation,
which has been evidently carefully reported to us. As
Mk. vii.   can be read in the first twenty-three verses of the
seventh chapter of Mark, the scribes and the Pharisees
from Jerusalem renewed their small-minded interference
with his mode of life and its carelessness about certain
ceremonial details which had come to be considered
Ver. 5.   proper. They asked him, "Why walk not thy disciples
according to the tradition of the elders, but eat bread
with unwashen hands?" He replied as he had replied
in former cases. He began by meeting them at their
own point of view, appealing to ancient authority, and
yet at the same time raising the consideration into
freer air. Then he went on to base his position
directly on the grounds of reason. He first retaliated,
Vers. 6-13.   that in the "tradition of the elders" Moses, whom
they professed to follow, was not really followed,
because, for example, that tradition took away from
allegiance to the lovely and rational virtue of honour
to parents, which Moses had enjoined in simple

language; and then he went on to say that what made ^{Ver. 15.} a man pure was not the compulsory washing of hands before meat, but the cleansing of the heart.

He still saw, however, as we may gather, that his person—and with his person his work—was in great danger so long as he waited and disputed with these ^{Mk. vii. 24.} ^{Cp. Mk.} determined opponents. He knew they were in some ^{iii. 6.} way allied now with Herod, who was a still more difficult foe than themselves to meet, with no other weapons than the simple presentation of truth. He saw, therefore, that prudence demanded a more complete withdrawal than he had recently made; and so he set out for a journey to the regions beyond Herod's jurisdiction altogether. We may gather that he determined to make the untoward circumstances that had overtaken him themselves minister to his purpose, by turning this little journey of escape, which had become necessary, into a side-path for the extension of his mission. There is a vague story in Mark—and also ^{Mk. vii.} in Matthew—about a "Syrophenician" woman, which ^{25-30.} we can analyse so as to read in it these facts, That Jesus had spoken to his friends about the plan of going for a little to the more northern parts of Syria and preaching there; that he had said, however, that he was loath to do this, as he felt himself only sent to "the lost sheep of the house of Israel," and as it was ^{Mt. xv. 24.} not "meet to take the children's bread, and to cast it ^{Mk. vii.} unto the dogs;" that, however, some one, probably ^{27.} one of the faithful women who followed him, answered him with the ingenious suggestion, "Yes, Lord: yet the dogs under the table eat of the children's crumbs;" and that the conceit pleased him, as showing that his ^{See App.} follower was beginning to take those broader, those ^{I. (12).}

humanitarian, **not merely** national, views **of** life which
had long been really his **own.** He thus went, we are
to gather, making the best of untoward circumstances.
He went to begin with against his own will, not because
he had any narrow and **purely** Jewish sympathies, **but**
because he believed his own calling was for his own
nation, and still more because **he still** was thinking of
those actual followers whom he **shrank from** leaving

Mk. vi. 34.
See above,
p. 181.
"as sheep not having a shepherd." **But he** accepted
the leaving of his own nation for a little as a necessity
forced on him not from within himself but from the
working of alien **powers** beyond him; and he turned
this necessity to **the use of letting it** enable him to do
a little purely **extra good work, or good** work quite
beyond what he felt **himself specially** called **upon to**
accomplish.

Mk. vii.
24.
He went first westwards to **the** neighbourhood of
Tyre and Sidon. He did not, we can conclude, stay
long there. He came back towards his own country,
striving, **as he** came near it, to keep out of public

Ver. 36,
viii. 26.
notice for a time. But the time did not pass as altogether one **of** public inactivity. There took place at
this time **two acts of** healing which were considered
worthy of record in the Gospel of Mark. These were

Mk. vii.
32-37, viii.
22-26.
the curing **of** a dumb or stammering man at the coast
of the Sea of Galilee, and the curing of a blind man
at Bethsaida. It is plain that both occurrences have

Mk. vii.
37.
See Is.
xxix. 18,
xxxv. 5-6,
xlii. 7, Ps.
cxlvi. 8.
been related as proofs **of** Jesus's healing power and
of his fulfilling, in virtue of it, particular prophetic
promises regarding the blind and other sufferers. And
if, where the early Church saw the fulfilment principally
in the unusualness of the power which he was believed
to have exercised, a modern Church dwells rather on

his spirit of kindness and the opening up of eternal
realities which the sight of that awakens, there is no
falling away in estimation of the importance of the
occurrences, or essential change of view regarding
their significance. These acts of Jesus were, like the
relieving of Simon's wife's mother and the calming of
unstrung minds, instances of the kindness in which
Jesus centered both the nature of God and the ideal
towards which man is called to grow. And this meaning of them may be found not far below the surface
in the record of Mark. In the evidently early accounts
which Mark gives of these actions of Jesus there is in
no way obscured the accessibility to the ordinary
human soul of what they suggest both for faith and
for practice. The recorded use of human means in Mk. vii.
them, brings them as examples within the possible 33. viii. 23-
reach of ordinary human striving, and the gradual 25.
character of the recoveries which they are related to
have brought about, places them as revelations for faith
close to the grasp of the blind and the deaf and the
dumb among ourselves, who are waiting under the
kind overruling of the Eternal Healer.

Having thus come back from the neighbourhood of
Tyre and Sidon to his own surroundings, Jesus seems
to have made the briefest stay. Then he went away
northwards, to the neighbourhood of a town called
Cæsarea Philippi. There he brought his journey of Mk. viii.
escape to an end; for a fresh, clear, unconquerable 27.
resolve had been forming itself in his mind, and had
come to maturity.

CHAPTER XI.

THE BREAD OF LIFE.

Cp. w. this chapter the modern book, "Philochristus," p. 214.

As we saw in the fourth chapter, Jesus's first retreat, in which he escaped from the danger of being captured by Herod as among the associates of the Baptist, had very important issues, both in regard to his teaching and in regard to the course into which he led his action. In the first place, the enforced bodily hardship had occasioned definite thoughts which he imparted to his disciples, regarding the nourishment required not by the body but by the soul. Of these the Temptation story and the aphorisms in the fourth chapter of John preserve for us examples. And in the second place, reflection on what he had met with and on what he had next to face, had occasioned a new directing of his own will. Disappointment, repulse, and sorrow, had not, at that earlier time, crushed his purpose, but had given it new definiteness and new solidity. Similar consequences, as we may now learn from a careful reading of the gospels, arose out of the double retreat which, as we saw in last chapter, took place over some threatened

action of Herod in direct relation to Jesus himself.
By this retreat also there were occasioned, first, special
movements of thought, and, second, a new movement
of will—first, definite teaching, and, second, a definite
purpose. Leaving the latter for next chapter, the
special movements in thought and teaching now
demand our attention.

As in the former case, the teaching rose directly
from experiences of hunger; and also, as in the former
case, it had to do with the higher food, the nourishment for the soul. But it is plain, from the state of
the accounts, that the teaching was delivered in this
case much more solemnly and significantly than in the
former case. All four gospels tell of a *feeding of the* Mk. vi. 34-
multitude, which took place ceremoniously. The ^{44, &c.}
gospels of Mark and Matthew, further, have each two Mk. vi. 34
accounts of such a feeding of the multitude. And the ^{ff., viii. 1-}
Fourth Gospel has given only one account, indeed, but ^{15-21, xv.}
has made it practically fill up his whole presentation of ^{32-39.}
the Galilean ministry, weaving other incidents into a
discourse which elaborates the meaning of this cere- Jn. vi.
monious act, so as to sacrifice their detail to its
importance. Whatever interpretation is to be given
to the particulars in the accounts of this subject, it is
plain that something having to do with imparting food
had sufficiently impressed itself on the first disciples to
have been related as one of the solemn deliverances of
Jesus at this time.

For the actual history of what took place we can
best go to a little notice in Mark and Matthew, in
which there is recorded a saying of Jesus himself,
uttered at a later stage than the exact time of what
came to be called the feeding of the multitude. This

notice claims a special attention inasmuch as it may
be said to be in some measure the Master's own **testi-**
mony in regard to what had taken place. In the
eighth chapter of Mark there occur the following words,

Mk. viii.
14-21.

"Now the disciples had forgotten to **take bread,
neither** had they **in the ship with them** more than one
loaf. And he **charged** them, **saying,** Take **heed,**
beware of the leaven of the Pharisees, and **of the leaven
of** Herod. And they reasoned among themselves,
saying, It **is because we** have no bread. **And when
Jesus knew it, he saith unto** them, Why reason ye,
because **ye have no bread**? perceive ye not yet, neither
understand (*suniete*)? have ye your heart yet hardened?

Cp. Is.
xxxii. 3.

Having eyes, **see ye not**? **and having** ears, hear ye
not? and do ye not remember? **When I** brake the
five loaves among five **thousand, how many** baskets
full of fragments took ye up? **They say unto him,**
Twelve. And when the seven among four thousand,
how many baskets full of fragments took ye **up**? And
they said, Seven. And he said unto them, DO YE NOT
YET UNDERSTAND (*oupo suniete*)?" With this notice

Mk. vi.
51-52.

there may be read a sentence found in the sixth chapter

The por-
tions in
capitals
are from
the Re-
vised
Version.
In the
first case,
the Au-
thorised
differs on
account of
its follow-
ing manu-
scripts not
now
placed

of Mark, namely this, **"And** he went up unto them
into the ship; and the wind ceased: and they were
sore amazed in themselves beyond measure, and won-
dered. FOR THEY UNDERSTOOD NOT CONCERNING THE
LOAVES (*ou* **gar** *sunekan epi tois artois*); for their heart
was hardened." Jesus, then, we find, on speaking to
his disciples about "the leaven of the Pharisees" and
"the leaven of Herod," and on knowing that they
supposed **he was** alluding to material bread, sought to
make them "understand" better by going back on
what had happened in regard to the feeding of the

multitude. Plainly his intention now was to recall highest. Note the same verb in the original, *suniemi*.
what had happened in the case of the great feeding, by
way of giving them an insight into what he meant by
speaking of the "leaven of the Pharisees" and "the
leaven of Herod." Also, we find, they had even before
this been puzzled about the feeding of the multitude
itself; and now Jesus, having reproached them with
possessing eyes that did not see and ears that did not
hear, said, Do ye not *yet* understand? Mark leaves
the case with this question of Jesus; but Matthew
goes on to say that then they did understand "how
that he bade them not beware of the leaven of bread, Mt. xvi. 12.
but of the doctrine of the Pharisees and of the Sadducees." One thing shines out plainly from what is
thus before us, namely that the Master himself regarded
the feeding of the multitude as a spiritual feeding.
And thus when we turn to the gospel accounts of that
feeding, we may legitimately be guided in interpretation by this discovery. There comes before us this
at least, that in the time when Jesus was in the midst
of his second retreat, as he and his disciples were once
more exposed to bodily hunger, he, turning back, fed Mk. vi. 34.
the multitude with spiritual food, and told his disciples
that they must also feed them. With a few loaves only
before him, he showed his disciples how thousands
could be fed, and how baskets full would still remain
over. Whether he did this in a ceremonious illus- With the form in w. the occur-rence is related, cp. the passage in 2 Kings iv. 42-44. which
trative manner, as a literal reading of the accounts
would bid us believe, or whether the original of what
is recorded was just his directing their minds away
from the material and temporal food to the eternal and
abiding, is of small importance in presence of the

Tertullian regards as a proto-type (Ag. Marcion, Bk. IV.). certain fact, that the **spiritual** teaching was that on which Jesus meant attention to be fixed.

The full content of the spiritual teaching which was the food dispensed by Jesus at this time **to the multi-tude, has** not been **made known to us. It was, we** may be sure, like the **rest of his** teaching **which we have** seen, and, for all **we know,** some of the actual utterances which composed it may be in our possession. Of the crumbs that remain, say **in the long unconnected** Lk. ix.-xix. passage in the Gospel of Luke, who can **tell how many** may not have been gathered at this time? But **also** there remain to us in tangible certainty several aphorisms with which the teaching was introduced.

First, **from the critical** survey of the Synoptic account which has just **been before us, we can go on to see that** the Fourth **Gospel** has a strictly historical contribution to present also. In the case **of the first** Above, pp. 62-65, 69. retreat, we found the Synoptic gospels told in narrative form how Jesus had been, in his hunger, " tempted of the devil," and how he had repelled the temptation with the thought of the higher food, whereas the Fourth Gospel preserved something of what he had actually said to his disciples in connection with this experience. A similar state of matters seems to present itself in regard to the second retreat. One aphorism at least comes from the sixth chapter of John, and claims authenticity from several most weighty considerations. First there is the general fact that the chapter is full of notices of events spoken of in the other gospels, too spontaneously occurring to have been taken from the other gospels; so that here as elsewhere we must recognise an independent record to which some attention is to be given. Then we find the aphorism in question is, on the one side, just another expression of what we have seen to be the thought conveyed by Jesus according to the earlier Cp. Mt. vi. 19, &c. gospels, and is, on the other side, in its form like other sayings of Jesus. And finally, there is found in respect to it a state of things which is commonly found in the Fourth Gospel, namely that it is in part *repeated* after See App. various philosophical reflections, suggesting that it was VI. a text on which the evangelist was enlarging. The aphorism is this, "Labour not for the meat which Jn. vi. 27, perisheth, but for that meat which endureth. . . . This 32, 41, 50, 51. is the bread which cometh down from heaven, that a man may eat thereof and not die."

Another aphorism spoken during this period is that which we have already in this chapter had to notice in passing. "Take heed," said Jesus, "beware of the Mk. viii. leaven of the Pharisees, and of the leaven of 15. Herod." He was pondering, one can see, on the persecution that was closing around him, proceeding from an accidental union of bigoted priestcraft with physical force. He was thinking of how there was in both the powers that persecuted him an evil essence directing them, and for expressing this essence he recalled that figure of the "leaven" already See above, used by him for expressing the good essence, which, p. 154. permeating people's hearts, would bring about the "kingdom of God."

Such, then, were the movements in thought and teaching which took place during the second retreat of Jesus. In any way of regarding the detail, there occurred at this time a signal dispensation of the nourishment which man needs because he is no mere

animal creature, but an ever-expanding soul. What
more natural than that the accounts of this occurrence should take the form of the assertion of a vast
miracle, indeed, of two vast miracles? Was the
occurrence anything else than a miracle? Are the
still full baskets and the still increasing multitudes
not witnesses to miracle, in the truest, highest sense?
And what more right than that the philosophising
evangelist who wrote our Fourth Gospel should make
this occurrence the one all-embracing occurrence of the
Galilean ministry, should show forth how the food that
had been dispensed was nothing else than the Eternal
Living Reason that was incarnate and manifest in
Jesus himself, and should bring out that here was the
real beginning of that Christian Communion with the
Divine in Jesus, of which the Last Supper was afterwards to become the symbol? There had, indeed, in
these hurried days of escape from the tyrant's grasp,
been raining from heaven a "manna," a something
beyond naming, the very "bread of life."

Having to do with what thus happened, there also
occurred, as we may reverently discern, an inner
experience of Jesus, which, seeing that he communicated an expression of it, and seeing that it appeals
both to mind and to heart to rouse them to what is
abiding and true, must not be passed over. We have
not, indeed, in the case of this double retreat of Jesus,
as in the case of the earlier retreat, an actual record of
inner experience such as the "Temptation" story supplied. But one thing comes before us plainly through
the narrative of the Gospel of Mark. It is this, that
Jesus experienced real pain and real disappointment at
finding his teaching and his action completely mis-

Jn. vi. in general.

Jn. vi. 46-48.

Vers. 53-56.

Ver. 31, ver. 48, cp. Philo, "Quis rerum div heres," c. 15, the "divine logos," the food (*trophe*) of the soul.

understood. This comes before us, through the manifestly faithful account of Mark, with wonderful vividness. Mark, along with Matthew, relates that at the time to which we have come the Pharisees asked a "sign from heaven" from Jesus, a thing which, according to Matthew, they had also done before. As regards the facts of the case, we must conclude that they really made the demand on both occasions; for both does Mark claim credence here as everywhere in regard to the order of events, and also Matthew's account of the earlier demand is organically related to his account of the other events in the earlier time. But what we are to notice is the way in which, according to Mark's account, Jesus met the demand that was made at the time to which we have now come. Jesus, we read, as he disposed of it, "sighed" over the mental attitude of his "generation" towards religious subjects. We can see that it was not only his opponents that vexed him through want of understanding, but one and all. For there was indeed a misunderstanding among his friends as well as among his enemies. Great as was by this time the influence of his personality, there was little grasp of his ideas. All believed in signs from heaven; all looked for miracles; all were in a state of excited aberration. We do not need the gospels to state this to us directly; the material in the gospels tells us it through the popular forms in which it is conveyed. The Master himself, it is plain, considered no sign of his Divine Mission to be necessary except his teaching and its consequences. The earlier gospels, overlooking, or finding it wisest to disregard, the refusal of "signs" on the part of Jesus, beyond just faithfully recording

Side notes: See above, p. 153. Lk. also confirms earlier occurrence in same way. Mk. viii. 12. With Jesus's severe view of the centering religious faith on "signs," cp. Deut. xiii. 1-3. See Mk. viii. 12; Mt. xii. 39; Jn. iv. 48. Mt. xii. 33, 35; Lk. vi. 44; Jn. v. 36, &c.

it, present his doings as if they themselves were signs of the kind that the populace asked for. The Fourth

Jn. vi. 26.
See App.
I. (13).

Evangelist goes much further in the same direction. And yet it is possible that this latter has been due to an advance in popular opinions in which the Fourth Evangelist has shared just through circumstances. For, strange as the phenomenon is, he seems both to misunderstand Jesus and also to have advanced beyond the popular conception to one which in some

Cp. Mt.
xii. 39 and
41 w. Jn.
vi. 26, then
w. Jn. vi.
27-58.

way returns to Jesus's own thought. The "sign," from being considered by Jesus as sufficiently found in his teaching, came to be looked for in outward powerful action; then later, the outward powerful action was noticed to be symbolical, and so there was some return to the point of view of Jesus himself. But the first movement in reception was deplorable misunderstanding. He whose life and teaching we would here devoutly trace stood alone; ruling, but not yet leading; listened to, but misunderstood. Nothing written by the most conscientious and matter of fact annalist ever bore more assuringly the marks of historical truth than does the whole gospel material, with its mingling of the reception with the giving, of the popular representation with the Master's initiating. And nothing written with the conscious purpose of literary antithesis ever brought out more powerfully two logical contraries than the condition of the gospel narrative brings out these two elements. All in one, yet separate and distinct, the two facts meet our view, both majestic, but the one the creation the other the creator, the one the story from and for the multitude, told in the manner of a multitude, the other the record of the Master's thought, his aggrieved question,

"Do ye not yet understand?" and the simple state- Mk. viii.
21, 12.
ment, "He sighed deeply in his spirit, and saith,
Why doth this generation seek after a sign? Verily
I say unto you, There shall no sign be given unto
this generation."

CHAPTER XII.

JUST as the earlier retreat of Jesus led to his giving his general purpose a more definite form, so it was in the case of the second retreat, which was considered in the tenth chapter. There is, however, to be noticed a development in his purpose as it advanced from the first defining to the second. The purpose which the first retreat led to was a bold and, as events proved, a wise purpose. The purpose led to by this later retreat was the climax of his determination ; it was a resolve which we must call divine.

During the time of Jesus's escape, which was considered in the tenth chapter, there must have been going on within him a most painful mental upturning, in which a resolve was forming itself that was to be for the future the one ruler of his destiny.

Jesus, we can see, with a powerful natural acumen which in his character was combined with more sacred qualities, perceived clearly enough that if he persisted in his mission, reverse upon reverse and most probably death were certainly before him. But to give up the

mission was to him impossible. Also it was impossible
for him to disbelieve that the mission was to be
successful, and that he, as the accomplisher of it,
would be justified and made himself to experience the
fruits of it. There came to be the need, therefore, in
his mind of a new thought which would give new form
to the general purpose that was guiding him; and in
the very facing of the facts before him, looking at their
two sides, this new thought came before him. In his
mind there came to life this conception,—that he must
continue his mission, thereby facing a temporary
discomfiture and temporary suffering for himself, but
that, through the care of God, the end would be certain
—namely, that the work would prosper, and he himself,
even if deprived of life, would be raised up again to
engage still in the work and enjoy still its results.
This became the guiding thought of Jesus through the
working of his mind. It was the thought brought to
him. He could not put it away. It came plainly
before his imagination. Nothing could remove it
unless either a sudden change of action on the part of
the Pharisees and their terrible ally Herod, or an
abandoning of his own aims in life. The former he
saw no possibility of, as he perceived that the whole
characters of his persecutors were permeated with evil
"leaven." The latter was now as impossible as it
would have been for him to become another person
than himself.

In the course of the contemplation which led to this
thought, Jesus was no doubt aided, as it was his habit
to be aided, by the Old Testament scriptures. It is
almost beyond question that he had before him the
picture of the second Isaiah, of the suffering servant of

God, who was "despised and rejected of men." Thus the common identification of Jesus with this ideal person, while it is due to various influences in common with the general identification of him with all ideal descriptions in the Old Testament, can be traced in great measure to Jesus himself, who deliberately took the *rôle* described upon himself. Also, however, we can see, Jesus had before him a passage from another prophet. It was a passage from Hosea, and it reads thus: "Come, and let us return unto the Lord: for he hath torn, and he will heal us; he hath smitten, and he will bind us up. After two days will he revive us: in the third day he will raise us up, and we shall live in his sight." But while these and other passages from the Old Testament guided in some way the thoughts of Jesus, they were not the moving power in his thoughts and intentions. The moving power was his own consciousness. These sayings from the Old Testament held the same place as the Messiah-idea in general, and the conception of the "kingdom of God." They helped him to realise himself and his ideas. He adapted not himself to them, but them to himself.

The resolve to face the suffering and carry on his mission required for its application a special plan; and the special plan which Jesus at this time can be seen to have formed discloses, first, the thoroughness of the resolve, and then also the force of his character. It was nothing less than this: That he would GO TO JERUSALEM, and there assert the very teaching that was bringing death to him even in the freer north. He would go to Jerusalem, though he foresaw it would likely bring death to him. He would go to the centre-point of the nation in which he had been born, and in

the very face of those in authority would declare what
God had given him to declare. Yes, he would bring to
an end this escape from men like wild beasts. He
would openly and seriously proclaim his message and
take what consequences God would allow for him,
knowing that the end would be living again and
conquering. And he would have no stopping short
with the "jackal" that had seized the Baptist. He
would go to Jerusalem.

Jesus took the resolution of facing his persecutors,
defined further by the plan of going to Jerusalem. He
was never to depart from this resolution. So alone,
with no other human mind to direct him and no other
human personality to be comrade to him, he rendered
obedience unto death, only knowing that the Highest
Power was driving him, and was therein caring for
living souls whose very hairs were numbered in
intensity of cherishing, and, with them, for him who
gave the obedience keeping back no thought of safe-
guard for himself.

The thoughts of Jesus which we have thus traced
are made known through the events which, according
to the gospels, next followed in Jesus's life; and we
only perfectly understand the events when we deduce
these thoughts of Jesus from them, and consider them
apart. When Jesus and his immediate friends and
followers, we learn, were in the neighbourhood of
CÆSAREA PHILIPPI, he first put to them the question, Mk.
"Whom do men say that I am?" They replied, 27.
"John the Baptist: but some say, Elias; and others, Ver. 28.
One of the prophets." He then said to them, "But, Ver. 29
whom say ye that I am?" And Peter answered,
"Thou art the Christ." According to Matthew, Jesus

Mt. xvi.
17.

This incident reported in less correct form in Jn. vi. 67-69. See also next page.

Mk. viii. 30.

Also indirectly confirmed in Jn. 1. 42.

replied, "Blessed art thou, Simon Bar-jona : for flesh and blood hath not revealed it unto thee, but my Father which is in heaven. And I say also unto thee, that thou art Peter, and upon this rock [*petra*] I will build my church; and the gates of hell shall not prevail against it." And according to both Mark and Matthew he, as in the words of Mark, "charged them that they should tell no man of him." This, we may say, was the first open appropriation by Jesus of the character of the Messiah. He did now, we must gather, openly adopt the character. The words quoted from Matthew are lifelike and like Jesus's whole manner of thought. He adopted the character, but only—according to his canon of the "fruits" or "works"—because others recognised him as filling it. And also, while adopting it, he did so only in such a general aspect of it as would let it fit itself to his own personality. He still shrank from a public adoption of it, because he knew that such would be taken as meaning not that he filled the general character of deliverer of his people from corruption and from despair, nor the general character of the Anointed, or the Commissioned of God, which the word "Messiah " or " Christ " meant originally, but that he was posing as an opponent of the Roman Government.

After receiving from Peter the recognition which he so dearly prized, Jesus communicated to them the thought of a Path through Suffering to Victory, which he had now embraced as his guiding thought, and the resolve he had formed, to act in accordance with this

Mk. viii.
31.

thought by going to Jerusalem. He told them "that the Son of man must suffer many things, and be rejected of the elders, and of the chief priests and scribes." He even hinted, as we may take it, that he might be killed, and that if so God would, as in the promise in the words of Hosea, "in the third day" "raise him up." _{See note 19 in App I.}

At the very time of announcing his sublime resolution, Jesus showed that he had taken on him an almost unnatural sternness, or abstraction from worldly interests. On Peter affectionately trying to dissuade him from the awful path on which he was determined to walk, or to give a brighter hope for its consequences, he answered, "Get thee behind me, Satan : for thou savourest not the things that be of God, but the things that be of men." It is important to notice that the sternness which thus began and continued till his death did not belong to Jesus's ordinary habit of mind, but was the armour in which he clothed himself, that no affectionate feeling in himself or others might interfere with the purpose he had formed. And so we may notice that through it there were ever breaking gleams of the sunshine of his ordinary nature. A sufficient example to anticipate for illustration is to be found in the fact that it was at the very time in which he was hurrying southwards to his single-handed invasion of Jerusalem, that he took up little children in his arms, and was displeased when they were not brought to him. _{Mk. viii. 32, 33. This also reported, but perverted, in Jn. vi. 70, 71.} _{Mk. x. 14, 16.}

There are reported in the gospels several sayings which we must receive as substantially and almost literally authentic sayings of Jesus uttered at this time.

First, as Jesus was expressing to his disciples his resolve to keep by his mission and abide all consequences, he spoke, we gather, as follows : " For what

Mk. viii.
36, 37.
shall it profit a man, if he shall gain the whole world, and lose his own soul? Or what shall a man give in exchange for his soul?" We have in these words one of many examples to be found of words first spoken by Jesus by way of explaining and justifying his own personal action, and then presented by Christian teachers, from the evangelists themselves downwards, as oracular utterances intended for others. Jesus, we can see, was keenly alive to the awful risk and loss involved in the action on which he was entering; but in the words just quoted he brought out that any other line of action would involve a greater loss, in that it would involve the loss—that is, the degradation—of the soul or self, and that that other loss he would not let come to pass even in exchange for the possession of the whole world.

Taking up decidedly, as he now was, a line of action which led to danger, he had to place anew before his followers the choice of keeping by him or leaving him. And so he plainly indicated to them that to continue following him meant both loss and risk, though at the same time he expressed his certainty that the end of following him in such a cause as he was working for would be not loss but gain. His words, as he spoke
Mk. viii.
34, 35. Cp.
Mt. xvi.
25, and
Lk. ix. 24.
them, were evidently something like these : "Whosoever will come after me, let him deny himself, . . . for whosoever will save his life shall lose it; but whosoever shall lose his life *on account of me* (or, "for my sake," *heneken emou*), the same shall save it." These words certainly, as we may reverently interpret, were a simple expression of his faith in the eternal truth, that those who avoid duty for the sake of self-preservation are only putting a little way off the losses that surely come

in the course of nature; while those who follow duty,
even let it be to death, will live and triumph beyond,
through the care of their Creator, who has given them
both the duty and their lives.

There are added to these words in the gospels further
words, in which Jesus is represented as having spoken
in the manner of thought of the "Apocalyptic" books,
which have been alluded to above, promising that the
"Son of man" would come "in the glory of his Father Ver. 38.
with the holy angels." We shall at once be inclined to ${}^{Cp.~Mt.}_{xvi.~27,~28.}$
say that if the words thus reported are really Jesus's
words at all, they must have been considerably manipulated from what they were as Jesus uttered them.
Their case, however, requires special treatment from
this, that if we recognise that Jesus spoke at all in the
strain of these words as they have reached us, there is
opened up the question, Did Jesus indeed promise his
coming again to the world after his death? or, in other
words, did he indeed originate the belief in what has
come to be called the "Second Advent"?

We may say that while the words as reported are
likely to owe something to the apocalyptic literature of
the evangelists' time as well as to Jesus's own utterances, still Jesus must have said something really like,
in its sound, to what is reported. We may say, accordingly, that he really expressed the idea that the coming
of the "Son of man" was still in the future. And as
we have seen that he certainly called himself by this
name, we are carried to the conclusion that he did
originate the idea that he was to "come" a second
time. But we must think a little what he meant by
Coming. We must by no means impute to Jesus the fan-
tastic, materialistic notions which many have associated

with the phrase " Second Advent." To begin with, any thoughtful reader of the foregoing pages will see that the arrogating to himself, during his earthly life, the position of a supernatural demon-power would have been for him impossible. Further, the supposition that he did so is disproved by positive **facts** about his whole

See espe-
cially Mk.
ix. 11-13.

manner of thought. Apart **from** definite sayings having the mark of authenticity, in **which he** expressly disavowed opinions of the kind we are **dealing** with, his

Mk. iv.;
Mt. xiii.

parables about the " kingdom of God " show that **his real thoughts** were irreconcilable with such opinions. **He could not have** had the view of life expressed by **the parable of the seed and the** parable of the leaven, **and at the same time have** believed that he himself, after death, would **come through** the clouds and make havoc with all nature. **What Jesus really meant in**

Perh.
direct
fr. Dan.
vii. 13.

quoting—as we may say he did **on this** occasion—from some apocalyptic writing, and saying that the Son of man would yet come in glory with his Father, was, **we** must believe, just to enforce further, through the help of familiar phrases, the truth which he had already expressed—namely, that though he had to face suffering and it might be death, still he would certainly live beyond and have his consciousness and **his** mission justified. How his triumph would come he assuredly neither knew nor professed to know. **He** did know, however, that a triumph was sure. **He knew** that fact, because he knew God. And **he used the** pictorial language which all **were** familiar with, to urge **and to** make intelligible that **fact.** Thus we are to **see here,** as all through, **that what Jesus** thought and what he did were due to the development **of** his own life and consciousness—to that and, properly speaking, **that** alone.

All phrases and doctrines which he received and in some way recognised were aids to his expressing himself—that and nothing more.

One other saying, joined to these apocalyptic sayings in the gospels, may be accepted as entirely a saying of Jesus. It is an important one in that it expresses, in general terms, the absolute confidence to which Jesus had by this time attained regarding the success of his mission. This is the saying, " Verily I say unto you, That there be some of them that stand here, which shall not taste of death, till they have seen the kingdom of God come with power." Mk. ix. 1. Cp. Jn. xxi. 22, 23.

After Jesus declared to his disciples his sublime resolution, and explained it through the sayings just quoted, he was, according to the gospels, "transfigured" before the three who were most intimate with him. He was indeed transfigured before them from this time on, as we know from all that followed. The account in the gospels of the "transfiguration" may be looked upon as a materialistic presentation of the change that took place from this time in the attitude towards him of his more intimate followers. Hitherto they had followed him, indeed, in complete allegiance; now, however, they began to look on him as something more than human. We must see in this change of their attitude towards him the last stage reached of that ascendancy over them which his personality obtained. He had so far been asserting himself as one both authoritative and enlightened, acknowledging no leadership from anything but his own consciousness. He had, however, as we have seen, accepted suggestions from various popular ideas, and had expressed himself through various popular phrases; and it is to be Mk. ix. 1-8.

recognised that up to this point the ideas which they
had associated with him had shared with his own
personality the power that bound them to him. They
had at first, while attracted by his personal authority
and the beauty of his personal character, also been
attracted by his proclaiming of the " kingdom of God."
They had even at the last been partly led by him
through having come to associate him with the
Messiah-character. They had thus, to put the matter
in a slightly different way, been so far exacting something from him in return for their allegiance ; they had
been exacting a suiting of himself to an extent to their
preconceptions. But his own new explaining of the
character he meant to realise, his powerful sayings
enforcing what he meant, his confidence in predicting
success, and the unswerving and absolutely independent
pursuit of purpose which he began to show, brought
about that they made at last a complete, unconditional
surrender to him of minds and wills. It was no longer
the preacher of the " kingdom of God " that they
followed. It was no longer even the Messiah or the
Christ. It was Jesus, their friend and master, let him be
or do as he might will. They saw that he was an original
character, a prophet like Moses and Elias. And yet
further, as their thoughts dwelt on him and their hearts
glowed towards him, even Moses and Elias vanished
from their imaginations. They saw that Jesus stood
alone, on a " mountain," to which he had led them up.
They felt and knew that there was something divine
in him. Realising that they were helpless and utterly
ignorant before him, they were yet charmed by him into
perfect subjection. They heard a voice from heaven
saying to them, "This is my beloved Son: hear him."

Mk. ix. 4.

Ver. 8.

Ver. 2. cp.
2 Sam i.
19. 25, Is.
lii. 7, &c.

Mk. ix. 7.

CHAPTER XIII.

THE FAREWELL TO GALILEE.

FOR the events that immediately followed Jesus's resolution to go to Jerusalem, we have abundance of information. And yet the limitations of that information are as striking as its fulness. Reports of what happened have come down to us more detailed than those of what went before; but, on the other hand, these reports give no full indication of time and place. There have come to us strings of narratives independent of one another, but having here and there little circumstances that enable us to guess time and place. Mark and Matthew give us collections of Mk. ix..x ; narratives almost the same as each other. John gives Mt. xviii., xix. only flying notices, hardly to be detected amidst the Jn. vii. 10, idealism of his general account. Luke gives, of all the 14. Lk. ix.-xix. evangelists, the greatest detail. And while it is to be recognised that his account at this stage has become, as scholars have explained, biassed by doctrinal tendency, so far as even to suggest a spreading of Jesus's teaching in his lifetime to an extent to which it Lk. x. 1, really only spread after his death, still a fair estimate xvii. 13.

of the stories he tells will lead to the conclusion that mostly they are trustworthy accounts of real events. The narratives in Luke ix.-xix. are based, we may be certain, on reports preserved without much entrance of error into them from the time of the events to the time in which the evangelist wrote. We can take for our history from Mark and Matthew bit by bit with confidence, adding from Luke with more reserve.

The main general fact that comes to us is this, that Jesus chose the time of the " Passover " as the occasion of his visiting Jerusalem. The Passover was the greatest of the Israelite festivals, and was held in Jerusalem yearly about the beginning of April. It was customary for members of the nation to flock from the northern parts to Jerusalem to attend this as well as the other festivals. Now we have gathered from the Fourth Gospel account that on the occasion of a festival held in the previous autumn, the Feast of Tabernacles, Jesus's brothers had advised him, as we may put it, to use the occasion for going up to Jerusalem and becoming known. Jesus, we have seen, refused to do so; but the gospel adds, " But when his brethren were gone up, then went he also up unto the feast, not openly, but as it were in secret." We can see in this statement — which the earlier gospels do not admit of being taken literally as historical—that though Jesus did not go up to the Feast of Tabernacles as his brothers advised, he so far acted on their suggestion in that he went up to a later festival with very much of the same intentions as they proposed to him. He went up to a later festival, we may gather, not in the open way that probably they intended, but quietly.

Ex. xii., &c. Jos., Ant., xx. 6, 1, &c.

Jn. vii. 3.

Ver. 10.

How long Jesus had to wait for the time of the Passover from the time of his expressing his resolution at Cæsarea Philippi, it is impossible to tell. As, however, the events to which we are coming do not seem such as could have been long drawn out, and as, on the other hand, the events which have been before us as succeeding Jesus's visit to Nazareth must have taken considerable time, it is reasonable to conclude that it was already well on in the spring of the year 35 when Jesus was at Cæsarea Philippi, and that only a few weeks remained before the time of the festival. These few weeks, we learn, Jesus spent in this way: by first paying a final visit to Capernaum, and then going somewhat slowly up to Jerusalem by an indirect route. Mk. ix. 33, x. 1, &c.

Jesus went to Capernaum for a final visit, but not to teach or to show himself in public at all. He went with his intimate followers secretly, having the determination, evidently, to avoid all further collision with the authorities in the north, and leave his further public action for the great city. Conversations, however, took place between him and his intimate friends, which contained some of his most daring, and therein most sublime conclusions regarding sacred truth. These conversations his followers fortunately preserved ; and so there have come down to us many treasures of thought which, as they must now be presented, will give to this chapter a special importance. Mk. ix. 30. Mk. ix. 30. roughly confirmed by Jn. vii. 1.

On the way to Capernaum, we learn, some of the disciples put a question to Jesus regarding the Messiah-subject. They were following him now unreservedly, as we have seen, held bound by his own personality Mk. ix. 11. 13.

14

and no longer expecting that he would shape his
actions to suit their own presuppositions regarding the
Messiah-character. Still, there was a general understanding that he was going to assert himself as the
One who realised what had been meant in the Messiah-
idea. And so, we find, they let their thoughts fall into
the popular plane, even while they looked up to Jesus as
one to be guided by without question. They asked
him—quite ready as they were to have their thoughts
re-shapen in any way that he might indicate—How,
seeing he was the Messiah, had the scribes taught
that Elijah was to come back to earth before the
Messiah appeared? Jesus showed the tact that he
had always displayed in answering unenlightened
questions. He did not assert or remind them—as
he might have done truly—that he was not fitting
himself to any teachings of the scribes, or even of
the prophets themselves, but was exactly what God
had given him to be, so that it was not his concern
to decide what the scribes had meant. He came
down instead, in thought, towards their level, and
Mk. ix. 13. replied, " Elias is indeed come, and they have done
unto him whatsoever they listed, as it is written of
him." The result, we may say, was assuredly as the
Mt. xvii. account in Matthew declares, that they understood
⁕. what he meant, to the extent at least of seeing he
was suggesting that John the Baptist had taken the
part of Elijah.

An interesting little event also occurred as they
travelled towards Capernaum at this time. It was
that the disciples tried to " cast out " a " devil," and
Mk. ix. failed. It is very interesting and important to see
14-29. in this very beginning of the history of Christianity the

same interference of human conditions with religious
endeavour which has continually been repeating itself.
Jesus said, we gather, at this time, that the failure
was to be attributed to want of faith, and also that
a case of the kind before them required "prayer and
fasting"; which meant, as we may interpret, that
faith in the Divine Overruler was necessary for the
conquering of evil, and that for even the partial
victories that could be shown in the present time,
such as he had shown, it was necessary both to
discipline one's own soul and also to seek help from
beyond oneself.   It is also interesting, however, to
see from this event, that those good actions of Jesus
to which the name of casting out devils was given,
required his own strong personality.   He gave the
disciples profitable advice, indeed, as to how they should
set about conquering evil ; but from our point of view
it must be said what was essentially wrong in the
disciples, causing their failure, was that they had not
the Master's strength of character, and were in general
both too weak and too little enlightened, neither knowing rightly how to proceed nor awakening sufficient
faith among those for whose sake they wished to act.

Jesus and his disciples arrived in Capernaum.   And Mk. ix. 33.
the events that took place at Capernaum at this time
are recorded to us in some plainly authentic stories.

First, there meets us the fact that Jesus had to Ver. 33.
redirect the thoughts of his followers, which, under the
suggestions of his new purpose, had strayed out of the
paths of his spiritual teaching, and were concerning
themselves with the expectation of outward triumph.
It would seem that the most intimate of his followers
—the twelve, at least, and the faithful women—had

14 *

decided to accompany him to Jerusalem. But although
he had told them plainly and repeated to them that he
was going in the expectation of meeting persecution
and perhaps death, they evidently took little account
of these sayings, and kept their attention on his confidence of prevailing in the end, with which, further,
there agreed what they had seen in the north of his
power to raise enthusiasm.   They thought, accordingly, as in the words of the Third Evangelist, that
"the kingdom of God should immediately appear."
What that exactly meant for them, we can only guess.
But we may suppose that, religious men as they were,
they were a good deal tinged with the mystical thought
which we see in the "apocalyptic" books of their time,
without the intellectual power to separate the essential
thought in these books from its mystical setting. So
that in all probability they were expecting an actual
interference on the part of God with the world, and
a setting up of Jesus to be ruler over the nations with
more than natural powers at his command. In conversation thus, we learn, it had occurred to them to
speculate as to what kind of places they were to
have in the coming "kingdom." "By the way they
had disputed among themselves, who should be the
greatest."

It is a doubly pathetic incident to contemplate, this
dispute of those poor men. They thought they were
approaching honour and glory, and they were really
approaching insult and dismay. But this contrast
between what they expected immediately and what
came immediately is not so striking as another contrast
that will suggest itself to us—namely, the contrast
between what these men would have seemed to be to

Margin notes:
Mk. viii. 31, ix. 31.
Lk. xix. 11.
Mk. ix. 34.

an ordinary intelligent onlooker of the time, and what they were as we must view them. To an onlooker they would have seemed to be but the deluded enthusiasts of a sect which was about to be crushed by the arm of established power. As we must view them they were, with the exception of their divine leader, who made them what they were, the most notable men among the millions that at that time walked and breathed on the earth, the possessors of the key to peace and power, afterwards to prove themselves heroes and leaders of mankind.

At Capernaum Jesus took these followers to task about their dispute on the way, and gently corrected their conceptions. He told them that in the " kingdom " which he would set up, the greatest would be those who would best serve the others. And to enforce this celestial thought, he " took a child, and set him in the midst of them " : and " when he had taken him in his arms," he said to them, " Except ye be converted, and become as little children, ye shall not enter into the kingdom of heaven." *Mk. ix. 33-37. Ver. 36. Mt. xviii. 3. See App. I. (14).*

About the same time, it would seem, as this took place, the disciple John related to Jesus that he and some of the others had seen some man casting out devils in Jesus's name, and that they had forbidden him, because he did not follow them ; to which Jesus replied, " Forbid him not : for there is no man which shall " exercise power " in my name, that can lightly speak evil of me. For he that is not against us is on our part." *Mk. ix. 38 Vers. 39, 40. Auth. Version," do a miracle," but the idea in the original is that of exercising*

This little incident about the man casting out devils and not following the apostles has got confused, between the two first gospels, with the incident just *power*

related about the child, and the question who should
Mt. xviii.;
Mk. ix.
be the **greatest**. **Matthew** goes on to report more
sayings of Jesus in the line of his remarks about **the**
child, while Mark gives some of the same sayings **as**
arising out of this second incident. And **so it** seems
at first just to be a question **as to** whether this story is
interpolated in Mark and **should not be** there, or
whether Matthew has fused two different collections of
sayings **into** one. But it is best to believe **that both
incidents really** happened about the same time, **and
that the second led Jesus to** develop the thought he
had expressed **in the first.** That is to say, we are met
by this, that at the same time as Jesus rebuked the
disciples on the subject of **who was** to be the greatest,
John told his story about the **man casting out devils.**
Jesus, with the child still beside him, and looking at it,
as we can conceive, further expressed **the** thought
which he had so far expressed in his rebuke. **That**
thought **had** been *the Implicit Greatness, in present
littleness, of a human soul as such.* The thought was
illustrated by **a** living child. And it was further
enforced to Jesus's own mind **by his** hearing of an
earnest man who had **been** trying to do good, and had
only been resisted and injured for doing so. Accordingly **as they sat,** we learn, Jesus proceeded **to** utter
several aphorisms, preserved still for us, to our everlasting benefit, all turning on this one thought that
had arisen in his mind—one of the very thoughts
that he had principally come from Nazareth into the
world to **assert—the** thought of **the** Greatness in littleness of a human soul as such, or the thought of the
Value of Man.

He said that **it** was necessary that offences should

come to the "little ones" whom he loved and in whom Ver. 42.
he believed, but that it was better for one to be thrown
into the sea with a millstone round one's neck, than to
be the person through whom the offence came.   And
on the other hand, he spoke words reported differently
by the two evangelists, of which the meaning evidently
was that one who recognised a prophet to be a prophet
would himself receive the reward of a prophet, that
one who recognised a righteous man to be a righteous
man would himself receive the reward of a righteous
man, and that one who recognised a humble learner to
be a humble learner, and so did for such a one the
smallest kindness, would receive a reward unfailing.
The First Evangelist has presented the words away
from their historical connection, in the list of sayings
to disciples.   Mark, on the other hand, whose report
of the words is less complete, has, by preserving the
historical connection, both made plain that Matthew's
report is the better of the two, and given the key to
the interpretation of Matthew's report.   The words, Mt. x. 41,
as in Matthew, are these, " He that receiveth a prophet 42; Mk.
ix. 41.
in the name of a prophet shall receive a prophet's
reward : and he that receiveth a righteous man in the
name of a righteous man shall receive a righteous
man's reward.   And whosoever shall give to drink
unto one of these little ones a cup of cold water only
in the name of a disciple, verily I say unto you he shall
in no wise lose his reward."

Then he carried further the thought of the offences.
Each one, he said, would not only be offended, but
would have to pass through that "fire" of which they Mk. ix. 43-
had been taught in the popular belief.   But he told 50.
them that that fire would be a cleansing fire.   " For Ver. 49.

Cp. Is. lxvi. 24, also Is. xxx. 33, and see App. I. (22).

every one," he said "shall be salted with fire." He urged them, as we may interpret, to take reverses and evils as fire, or, changing the imagery, as salt. Salt, he said, was good if it really was salt—that is, evils could be made good if they were appropriated in the way of cleansing or disciplining the soul.

Mt. xviii. 12.

He said also, " How think ye ? If a man have an hundred sheep, and one of them be gone astray, doth he not leave the ninety and nine, and goeth into the mountains, and seeketh that which is gone astray ? And if so be that he find it, verily I say unto you, he rejoiceth more of that sheep, than of the ninety and nine which went not astray. Even so it is not the will of your Father which is in heaven, that one of these little ones should perish." And also, we may suppose, he added at this time the similar parable of the lost

Lk. xv.

piece of money. And indeed, for want of testimony to the contrary, we may believe he may at this time also have spoken the parable of the Prodigal Son. If this is so, we can imagine what a thrill must have gone through the frames of those few attached followers, and how the most intimate of them, at least, must have been lifted up suddenly away from the whole plane of the foolish thoughts which they had been expressing, as this benign story fell on their ears from the lips of him who had been "transfigured" to them and become to them the very Son of God.

Telling them such things as these, he went further, and expressed both his own ruling passion and also the promise he felt able to make in the name of God, in

Mt. xviii. 11.

these words, " For the Son of man is come to save that which was lost."

Then, as he always led from faith to duty, and as it

was his way to go from the care of the heavenly Father
to the responsibility of brothers and sisters, he went on
to say to them that they must all reverence their fellow
men and women and consider for them. He told them
how they should spare no pains to win back those that Ver. 15.
might go astray. And he told them they must forgive
their sisters and brethren with a forgiveness — as
we may interpret and analyse Matthew's report—the Ver. 35.
very same as was felt by the heavenly Father Himself.
Peter, it would seem, here interposed with the question,
How often should one forgive one's brother? He Ver. 21.
answered, "I say not unto thee, Until seven times; Ver. 22.
but, Until seventy times seven." And then he put
before them a parable about a servant who had been Vers. 23-35.
freely forgiven by his master, and yet refused to forgive
a fellow-servant.

At one quiet time, we may believe, in which they
were all sitting together, did Jesus deliver all these
teachings. And so in secrecy, to which he was compelled, because if he should speak openly his fellow-
men were ready to fall on him like wild beasts, Jesus
was bringing to a close his Galilean ministry, and was
adding the last master-touches to the sacred exposition
which in Galilee he gave to the world.

On some other occasion, we may also gather, during
the same time, he spoke further in the same strain as
he had spoken in at Cæsarea Philippi, when he had
justified the course he was taking by speaking of the
supreme importance of not "losing the soul." He See above. P. 202.
said, speaking in the same strain, that it was better to
lose a hand, or a foot, or an eye, than to require the
whole self to be cast into the cleansing fire. He illus- Mk. ix. 43-47.
trated his position and the position of all who would

learn from him by saying that one who understood him and did accordingly was like a man whose house was

Mt. vii. 24-27.

built on a rock, and he illustrated his action and the action of all who would follow him, in these words:

Lk. xiv. 28-32. Cp. following verses.

"For which of you, intending to build a tower, sitteth not down first, and counteth the cost, whether he have sufficient to finish it? Lest haply, after he hath laid the foundation, and is not able to finish it, all that behold it begin to mock him, saying, This man began to build, and was not able to finish. Or what king, going to make war against another king, sitteth not down first, and consulteth whether he be able with ten thousand to meet him that cometh against him with twenty thousand? Or else, while the other is yet a great way off, he sendeth an ambassage, and desireth conditions of peace."

It is highly probable that some of the other sayings which make up the collection which we call the "Sermon on the Mount," were uttered also at this time in Capernaum. It was a time in which the disciples were likely to pay a special attention to Jesus's sayings, so as to treasure the remembrance of them; and the fact that so many of the sayings which make up the collection were evidently uttered at this time, confirms the belief that it may have been so also with some of the others. There may thus have been

Mt. vi. 20; Lk. xii. 16-21.

spoken at this time the saying about the "treasures in heaven," and along with it the parable given in Luke about the man who determined to build new store-rooms for his goods, and on the very night that he did so was required to give up his earthly life. But especially we may ascribe to this time the sayings about prayer. This was the early time of the disciples'

actually pupil-like obedience to him. It is very likely
that it was at this time that, in childlike veneration
and in readiness to follow what he would teach to the
last particular, they said to him, " Lord, teach us to
pray, as John also taught his disciples." Jesus, in Lk. xi. 1-13.
replying to their request, told them they ought to pray
to God as children ask of a loving father, or as a friend
in need asks of a friend who can help him. And he
also gave them a few simple sentences of prayer, which
Christians have come to call the " Lord's Prayer," and Vers. 2-4 ;
Mt. vi. 9-15.
to look upon as the model for all prayer.

The Lord's Prayer has been subjected by scholars to
the keenest criticism, and doubts have been thrown
both on the fact of its details having actually proceeded
from Jesus and on the fact of its originality on Jesus's
part, even if proved to have been uttered by him. It
can be said, however, without hesitation, that the result
of the matter is the recognition of the prayer by competent judges in general, as in substance a prayer
actually given by Jesus, and an original prayer. As
for the authenticity of the details, no doubt of any
weight need remain on any of its parts that contain
essential thought, unless on the doxology at the end,
which scholars in general regard as an addition by the
early Church for liturgical purposes. And as for the
originality of the prayer, while we are to believe Jesus
took many of its phrases from what he had heard and
read, its arrangement is certainly Jesus's creation, and
its spirit has been breathed from Jesus's soul. It is a
prayer in which the leading thoughts are the sovereignty
of God the heavenly Father, the coming, in the world,
of a better recognition of the heavenly Father, and the
rightness of each one asking the heavenly Father for

help in ordinary needs, with perfect confidence of being heard and answered.

Before Jesus left Capernaum at this time, we learn, he paid a tax. It seems to have been a tax which from early times had been levied on the Jews for the maintenance of religious services, though some have supposed it to have been a tax levied by the Romans. The detail of the account of this event in Matthew is obviously coloured by popular conveyance. The event itself, however, is guaranteed us by the very existence of an account of the kind, and it is interesting as bringing before us once more Jesus's perfectly submissive attitude towards political arrangements. This it does the more forcibly in that it took place at the very moment that Jesus was on the point of leaving his native province, never to return, as he himself surmised, and was about to perform a bold action which, as he well knew, would be mistaken by many for having a political end.

Mt. xvii. 24-27.

Ex. xxx. 13, xxxviii. 26.

PART III.

THE LAST DAYS.

CHAPTER XIV.

THE JOURNEY TO JERUSALEM.

THE journey of Jesus towards Jerusalem was under- Mk. x. 1.
taken not in any public way. He went quietly, Cp. Lk.
accompanied by his intimate followers, including,
beyond doubt, the faithful women, and very likely Mk. xv.
children belonging to some of them. Once away 40, 41.
Mk. x. 13.
from Galilee, however, he came more and more before
the public, so that, while still on the way, he attracted
attention in many quarters as one who was making
claim to be a great teacher and leader. Mk. x.

The accounts of the course of the journey do not
agree well with each other, and it is not an easy task
to decide what really happened in it. Mark and Ver. 1;
Matthew say that he went by the other side of the Mt. xix. 1.
Lk. xvii.
Jordan. Luke says, on the contrary, that he went 11.

through Samaria and Galilee. Now for the account of Mark and Matthew there is this to be said, that nearly all scholars give one or the other of these evangelists the preference over Luke in regard to historical accuracy in general; and to this general consideration it is to be added that in Luke's account of the journey there is clearly present a doctrinal bias. For the other side, however, there is to be said that one at least of the stories Luke gives of Jesus in Samaria has suggestions too realistic for us to sweep it entirely out of history. The explanations of scholars which treat the Samaritan stories of the Third and Fourth Gospels as idealistic accounts of the universality of Christianity, or as after-events in Church history transferred to the life of Jesus himself, while throwing light on the form in which we have them, are rather far-fetched as complete explanations of their origin. And keeping to the case of the journey through Lk. ix. 51- Samaria told in Luke, the story of the Samaritan
56. village, in which Jesus was not well received, is too lifelike for even unconscious invention. It, further, is suitable to the time in which Jesus had completely left home and country, and was dependent on reception by strangers both for lodging to the body and in great part also for cheering to the mind. And once more, we can see a striking naturalness in the idea See above, that this rejection would be specially noted by Jesus
P. 73. and his more intimate followers, in that it presented a strong contrast to the kind reception he had met with in a Samaritan village a few months before. On the other hand, it is to be noted that the accounts of Mark and Matthew do not really preclude his having gone so far through Samaria, and that their silence

regarding his having done this may be explained by the
fact that they are dealing with the direct ministry of
Jesus. They are more correct, doubtless, in regard to
Jesus's direct ministry, when they confine it to the
Jews; but this does not interfere with the fact of his
having had a merely local relation to Samaria. To
this it may be added that the parable of the Good
Samaritan brings a mass of evidence in itself. This
beautiful parable first recommends itself as an authen- Lk. x. 25-
tic parable of Jesus, as certainly as we can make any ^37.
judgment from internal evidence at all. Granted,
then, that it is an authentic parable of Jesus, its
introduction of a Samaritan, and also of the road
between Jerusalem and Jericho, suggests that Jesus,
before composing it, had been coming in contact both
with Samaritans and with that road, and so suggests
very convincingly that it is likely to have been spoken
. by him just after a journey in which he had gone
through Samaria, and had also gone from Jericho
to Jerusalem. We must, then, harmonise the two
accounts. Jesus and his followers, we must believe,
first went through Samaria so far, then crossed the
Jordan, and then came back and went through Jericho
to Jerusalem.

On starting, then, we are to suppose, Jesus and his
followers entered on the ordinary road to Jerusalem
through Samaria. They left, no doubt, very quietly;
and as they went along the road, they were to all
appearance but a body of people journeying to Jerusalem to the Passover. On seeking lodgings in a Lk. ix. 51-
certain village they were received very inhospitably, ^56.
the inhabitants probably being unaccustomed to put
themselves much out of the way to accommodate

Jewish pilgrims. The disciples James and John, resenting any discourtesy to Him whom they had come to worship, and carried away into a mystical world by ascribing to Jesus divine power such as they believed Elijah and Moses to have possessed, exclaimed, "Lord, wilt thou that we command fire to come down from heaven, and consume them, even as Elias did?" to which Jesus replied, " Ye know not what manner of spirit ye are of. For the Son of man is not come to destroy men's lives, but to save them."

See above. p. 206.

We gather that as they went on they were not able to preserve the quiet progress that Jesus wished. The name of Jesus had become by this time pretty well known ; and no doubt the excited condition of his followers led them to tell many, as they went along, that this was indeed Jesus, the great prophet of Nazareth, with whom they were travelling. Accordingly excitable persons in the country through which they went were beginning to come up and to ask liberty to join them. Amongst such was one who, it would seem, said he wished to follow Jesus, but asked him to delay his journey a little until he had time to bury his father. Jesus is reported to have said, " Let the dead bury their dead, but go thou and preach the kingdom of God." This harsh-sounding reply (made even more harsh in Matthew's form of it) must be accepted in substance as having been really uttered ; but it assuredly does not represent the everyday mind of Jesus. He had surrounded himself at this time with a gloom which was really the gloom of death on his young life. But what is still more important to mention is that the incident, while we must accept it in general, is almost certainly not correctly reported

Cp. Mt. xxi. 11.

Lk ix. 57.

Ver. 60.

to us. The evangelists have turned it into an illustration of the claim of religion on the soul, so that we cannot say how far its original facts have been altered. Probably the saying of Jesus, in its real form, was much less harsh than is reported, and had merely to do with his musing on that better life of man that could triumph over death, as he himself was showing through terrible experience. And further, there surely followed, we may say, some remark in his own real manner, which more than took away the sting that may have been felt by the man.

The First Evangelist adds another saying of Jesus to this one, so as to make two sayings to would-be disciples ; and the Third Evangelist adds two to it, so as to make three sayings to would-be disciples. Of these other sayings, we may almost certainly decide that the extra one in Luke, in its real utterance by Jesus, had a different connection, as the question and answer taken together have an artificial appearance, and are not compatible with Jesus's general teaching. The saying was probably one uttered in reply to some reasoning with him on the risks he was facing. " No man," he said, "having put his hand to the plough, and looking back, is fit for the kingdom of God." The other saying, given both in Matthew and in Luke, was indeed, it is probable, induced by some talk of a person or of persons wishing to follow him. It is, however, principally to be viewed as having been a pathetic expression of musing in which he allowed himself to indulge at intervals in the midst of his heroic determination. He had left everything, he was thinking, because conscious of a dignity in the human soul, and of a care from God for the human soul, and

Margin notes:
Mt. viii 19-22.

Lk. ix. 57-62.

Cp. Lk. x. 29, and other places in Lk. of manifestly supplying introductory words ; and on the other hand, cp. Mk. vii. 9-10, x. 7-10.

Cp. above, pp. 63, 64.

15

because conscious himself of having a special nature giving him a special name and calling—the Son of man, come to seek and to save the lost; and what he had attained to so far was, as he pathetically expressed it, "The foxes have holes, and the birds of the air have nests; but the Son of man hath not where to lay his head."

Mt. viii. 20; Lk. ix. 58.

It is likely to have been the very fact that his journey was beginning to lose all its private character, that induced Jesus to forsake, at a certain point, the common road, and to turn into another way across the Jordan. At all events, we find him, according to the most reliable accounts, having gone to the other side. His journey along the other side was, no doubt, a hurried and uneventful one; and he crossed back again and directed his course towards Jericho. His progress began again to attract attention, and again enthusiasts began to seek to enter into his train. Now, however, probably, he began to make less objection to publicity, as he was nearing the quarter in which it was his intention to make himself known.

Mk. x. 1.

In the tenth chapter of Mark, and in the nineteenth of Matthew, there is related an incident as happening on the journey which is at first sight puzzling. It is introduced by Mark in this way, "And the Pharisees came to him, and asked him, Is it lawful for a man to put away his wife? tempting him." Now it is to be remembered that "the Pharisees" who had been accustomed thus to come up to him had at this time been left behind away in the north; and it is hardly in accordance with the swiftness and unobtrusiveness of his journey, that he could already have roused an opposition among the southern Pharisees. The dif-

Mk. x.

Ver. 2

ficulty may, however, be very reasonably met by supposing that the incident was at the start an incident of the kind just above alluded to, in which excitable persons became eager to follow the little band to Jerusalem. Two or three unsettled men, we may suppose, with whom some of the followers had been conversing, had begun to think of joining in the pilgrimage of which, no doubt, the followers had given a glowing account; but the difficulty had arisen, whether, as they were married, they could leave their wives and children — leave them completely, as it appeared might be the end of the matter, in the way "Christian" in the "Pilgrim's Progress" leaves his friends. The matter was brought before Jesus. The men, or some followers speaking for them—having been, no doubt, of the party of the Pharisees—said, " Is it lawful for a man to put away his wife ? " Jesus said, " What did Moses command you ? " They answered, " Moses suffered to write a bill of divorcement, and to put her away." To which Jesus replied, " For the hardness of your heart he wrote you this precept." And then he went, as usual, from the Law to Reason, and put an end to the whole proposal of the men in these grand words, " From the beginning of the creation God made them male and female. For this cause shall a man leave his father and mother, and cleave to his wife; and they twain shall be one flesh : so then they are no more twain, but one flesh. What therefore God hath joined together, let not man put asunder."

The disciples afterwards asked Jesus further about the general subject which was suggested by the incident just related. As Matthew, indeed, reports

Marginal notes: Mk. x. 3-5. Cp. Mt. v. 31, 32. and see Deut. xxiv. 1.

Mk. 6-9.

Ver. 10.

this after-questioning, there are mixed up with it echoes of some discussions on the subject which must have taken place among Christians much later, indeed long after Jesus's death. And especially the words in verse 12 of the nineteenth of Matthew are to be taken as inquiring words of those later Christians, not as words of Jesus. But the simple account of Mark may be accepted as an account of questionings brought before Jesus himself, by his immediate disciples, just after the incident we have now had under consideration. They "asked him again of the same matter." And he expressed his idealistic view of the relation of husband and wife in these uncompromising words: "Whosoever shall put away his wife, and marry another, committeth adultery against her. And if a woman shall put away her husband, and be married to another, she committeth adultery."

As they journeyed along, several other incidents occurred, of which a record has remained. Of these the first that meets us is one that stands in striking contrast to the incident about the disciple who would bury his father. It is the incident about Jesus calling the little children to him. Assuredly in his old home in Nazareth, simple young life had been his delight, and had stood before his mind in close relation to that kind Father whose name and nature he was afterwards to declare. And now, when it was required of him, for the very sake of declaring the ultimate rule over the universe of a simple childlike kindness, to act himself for the time with more than ordinary sternness, he could still on an occasion turn to delight in the young untroubled souls that he loved, and to tell his followers that their state of mind was like that

See App. I. (15).

Mk. x. 11, 12.

Vers. 13-16.

mind which rules in heaven, which all are called to
enter into and rejoice in.

Another incident which occurred—one small in itself,
but leading to interesting remarks on the part of Jesus
—was that a certain man came and kneeled to him
and asked him, " Good Master, what shall I do that Mk. x. 17.
I may inherit eternal life ? "   Jesus, having first rebuked
him for addressing him as " Good Master," referred
him to the commandments.   But on the man replying
that he had observed all of them " from his youth," Vers. 17.
Jesus first became affectionately interested in him, and 22.
then gave him, as an indication of the direction in
which he might further excel, the suggestion that he
might bestow his wealth on the poor.   When we
notice the spontaneous character of the occurrence,
when we see how the idea of giving his wealth to the
poor was only brought before the man by Jesus in
the second place, on his seeking guidance on sacred
things beyond what " the commandments " could give
him, and, most of all, when we see that Jesus was
specially impressed by this man, and, indeed, seems
to have thought of him as one who might become a
special instrument and enthusiast in his own sacred
cause, we shall perceive that it is quite a blunder to
suppose Jesus was here laying down a universal principle, and that far less was he entering on political
and social questions.   What we have learned of Jesus
all along discloses that he did not urge on people in
general any sweeping abandonment of the worldly
position in which they might be placed.   And what he
said to this man had force only for the case of the
man himself, except that it went on the lines of the
general principle that excellence in a religious life is

attained by caring for the unfortunate. The real point of importance in this incident is to be found in the fact that Jesus took a special liking to this man— indeed, it is probable, saw something striking in his personality, and for a moment entertained the hope that he might have in him a follower of special power, who might play a special part. Thus we find that just after he gave the man the suggestion to sell his goods Mk. x. 21. and give them to the poor, he asked him simply, as we Ver. 22. may interpret the account, to follow him. The man, however, only seemed grieved, and went away. And Ver. 23. Jesus was grieved too, and said to his disciples, " How hardly shall they that have riches enter into the king- dom of God ! " This saying, we must carefully notice, was occasioned by Jesus's disappointment in the man. It was, we may believe, a hasty utterance, and was, as Mark's account records, immediately qualified into Ver. 24 " how hard it is for them that TRUST in riches to enter See, how- ever, App into the kingdom of God ! " And then he added, I. (16). speaking in his own vivid manner, " It is easier for a Ver. 25. camel to go through the eye of a needle, than for a rich man to enter into the kingdom of God." The disciples expressed amazement at this saying, no doubt mistak- ingly giving it a literal and universal application. Jesus Ver. 27. then added, " With men it is impossible, but not with This say- ing echoed God : for with God all things are possible." The in Lk. i. 37. whole incident is to be interpreted as one in which Jesus's strong feelings—first of affection and hope, and then of disappointment—influenced his utterances. So that it is wrong and unjust to give to the utterances an oracular or even intentionally didactic character. At the same time all of them were utterances of un- impeachable goodness and devotion to truth, containing

in them Jesus's own ideas. He taught in them that
the giving to the poor and needy is the virtue through
which man can show his kinship to the divine nature.
He gave a special suggestion, by way of carrying
out this principle, for a special case. On the suggestion being rejected, he made a remark which was to
the effect that for any one's helping that new establishment of religion to which he had lent his own energies,
the possession of great wealth was a stumbling-block.
And then, lastly, in his own manner, he acknowledged that, while this was what a human view of
things disclosed, still God, who was the Father of the
rich as well as of the poor, and the Giver to the rich for
His own ends, would yet save and lead His children in
ways beyond what could be discerned by any human
view taken in connection with a particular time.

This incident, it would seem, put it into the mind of
Peter to say, "Lo, we have left all, and have followed Mk x 28.
thee." From the reply of Jesus, as well as from
our other knowledge of him, we must conclude that as
he heard this remark there arose in him a tumult
of mixed feelings. It sounded, we must believe, almost
like a reproach, as he thought of how some of those
about him had indeed left home, friends, and ordinary
business, for all of which he had himself the warmest See above,
reverence, and on the loss of all of which in his own P. 140.
case he was now looking with keen regret. But still he
was conscious of the faithful care of God, and of the
special calling which he and his followers had received.
His reply was, "Verily I say unto you, There is Mk. x. 29,
no man that hath left house, or brethren, or sisters, or 30.
father, or mother, [or wife?*], or children, or lands, if genuine, must be
for my sake, . . . but he shall receive an hundred- an addi-

tion, not in original remark. See above, p 227. It is not in the best MSS. at all, however.

fold now in this time, houses, and brethren, and sisters, and mothers, and children, and lands, with persecutions ; and in the world to come eternal life."

This whole talk, however, among the disciples about their sacrifices, and what would come to them of high position in consequence, led Jesus, further, to express the general reflection that God gave high places to whom He chose, putting one high up at one time and

Mk. x. 31. another at another time. "But many that are first shall be last," he said, "and the last first." And he

Mt. xx. 1-16. added a parable about workmen engaged to cultivate a vineyard, of which the point unmistakably was that God so gave, out of His own kindness, that He was bound by no laws of only giving to the deserving, but put now one and now another in a position of advantage for His own gracious ends.

After recording the incidents up to this point, the

Mk. x. 32-34. Gospel of Mark makes as it were a pause to tell how, as they went on following their Leader, who was at every step showing his august and imperial character, they "were amazed," and even while they followed, "were afraid." It tells, further, that Jesus repeated

Vers. 33, 34. his predictions of the troubles they were going to face. And then it records another incident, in which we see how the very most intimate disciples, though "amazed" and "afraid," had but little assimilated Jesus's spiritual

Vers. 35-45. thoughts. James and John, no doubt moved not so much by any unworthy motive as by affection to Jesus, of whom they knew themselves to be favourites, came and asked him, in spite of what he had so lately said, if they might sit one on each side of him when he came to his "glory." The other disciples saw in the request more desire of high position than affection to the

Master. And Jesus himself, seeing that the two disciples had indeed let themselves forget for the moment
all consideration for the others, so as justly enough to
offend the others, spoke something as follows : " Ye Mt x. 42-
know that they which are accounted to rule over the ⁴⁵·
Gentiles exercise lordship over them ; and their great
ones exercise authority upon them. But so shall it not
be among you: but whosoever will be great among you,
shall be your minister ; and whosoever of you will be
the chiefest, shall be servant of all. For even the
Son of man came not to be ministered unto, but to
minister, and to give his life a ransom for many."

Jesus and his followers came on the way to JERICHO. Ver. 46.
At Jericho there happened a little event of which all
three gospels give an account. According to the gospel
account, it was an event in which a blind man got his
sight—or, according to Matthew, two blind men. But Mt. xx. 30.
as Luke follows up his account with a much more life- Lk. xviii.
like story, that has, in essentials, a great resemblance 35-43 ; xix.
1-10. As
to the accounts of the blind man, we may conclude justifying
this treat-
that this other story is another version of the same ment, note
the con-
story; that Luke himself, not knowing this, has tradic-
tions in-
inserted both; and that the second is the more volved in
a literal
accurate of the two. As Jesus entered the town, we reading,
are to learn, the appearance of his company caused spec. leaving Jericho
some stir, and especially a wealthy publican, of the name in Mt. and
Mk., and
of Zacchæus, asked what this all was, and was told "that approach-
Jesus of Nazareth passeth by." Very likely, indeed, ing in Lk.
The "two"
this event is the origin also of the story of Nathanael in blind men
of Mt.,
the Fourth Gospel, as there are some striking simi- though
larities between that story also and the story of having
other
Zacchæus. If this is so, then, it would seem it was to parallels
in Mt.,
Philip the disciple that Zacchæus put his question may pos-

sibly be explained by the doubling of the story. SeeLk.xix. 2, 3, 4 ; cp. xviii. 36, 37, and Jn. i. 45, 46.

Lk. xix. 5 ; Mk. x. 49.

Or likely, Behold a son of Abraham indeed. Jn. i. 47. Cp. Lk. xix. 9 ; Mk. x. 47, 48.

Lk. xix. 5.

Ver. 6.

Ver. 9.

Jn. i. 48.

as to what was the cause of the stir, and that he replied to Philip, " Can there any good thing come out of Nazareth ? " At any rate, after being told about Jesus, Zacchæus, being " little of stature," climbed a tree, that he might distinguish Jesus himself amongst his company. And Jesus, arrested by the figure, and seeing, through his power of discerning character, something interesting in Zacchæus, first, no doubt, asked some one who he was, and then called to him. Zacchæus came to Jesus, and as he came, we may believe, Jesus, looking at him, said, " Behold an Israelite indeed, in whom is no guile ! " Then, when he came near him, he, as we may simply receive the account, boldly said to him, "To-day I must abide at thy house." The result showed the delicate perception which he had had of the case. Zacchæus was over-joyed to receive him, and they went into Zacchæus's house together. When they were in the house, Zacchæus, after some conversation, must have shown himself the better of Jesus's visit, and have expressed a new interest in sacred things ; and Jesus said, " This day is salvation come to this house." Also, during the lighter turns of the conversation, Zacchæus evidently asked Jesus how it was that he had marked him out and spoken to him, and Jesus replied that he had seen him in the tree. This episode, trifling as it may seem, was noted and repeated, we may conclude, by the apostle John, who was present, as no doubt the simple-minded little man showed very plainly a delight at the compliment implied in his having been singled out by this com-manding and charming person whom he found himself to be entertaining. When the whole incident was over, the usual murmuring arose, even amongst those people who were following Jesus in perfect allegiance, over the idea "that he was gone to be guest with a man that is a sinner;" and Jesus gently met this murmuring by repeating his saying, "The Son of man is come to seek and to save that which was lost." Thus we may believe that Zacchæus and the blind man who received his sight and Nathanael were all one and the same, and that it was spiritual eyesight which was awakened in the blind man at Jericho. *Lk. xix. 7.* *Lk. xix. 10.*

As they drew near to Jerusalem, they stopped for a little at the village of Bethany, and Jesus went into the house of one Martha. But he did not wait long there, we must believe, at this time. He hurried on into the great city. *Lk. x. 38. Cp. Jn. xi. 1.* *Cp. Mk. xi. 1.*

The enthusiastic followers gave his entry into the city something of a triumphal character. Jesus evidently submitted to this quite willingly. And thus at this point, we must say, we see him for the first time openly and publicly, without any concealment, acting as the "Messiah" or "Christ" of the popular expectation. He rode into the city on a colt; and the followers spread clothes and branches of trees on the way as he rode, crying, "Hosanna! Blessed is he that cometh in the name of the Lord! Blessed be the kingdom of our father David, that cometh in the name of the Lord! Hosanna in the highest!" *Mk. xi. 7-10. Ver. 7, Cp. vers. 2-6, hardly them- selves his- torical. See App. I. (17).* *Mk. xi. 9, 10.*

He made at first just a brief visit to the temple. The followers then, no doubt, dispersed to various lodgings. Jesus himself and the more intimate of them went out to Bethany, where, it may be supposed from what we shall further see, the "Martha" that has just been spoken of had procured lodgings for him, though whether in her own house or in that of some neighbour it is difficult to decide. *Ver. 11.*

CHAPTER XV.

THE BEGINNING OF JESUS'S PUBLIC APPEARANCE IN JERUSALEM.

Mk. xi.-
xiii.; Mt.
xxi.-xxv.;
Lk. xix.-
xxi. WHEN we enter on the consideration of Jesus's short time of teaching in Jerusalem, we are met by a sufficiency of reliable and detailed information. The accounts in the Synoptic gospels indicate, as is to be expected, a still increasing care on the part of the believers in Jesus to preserve particulars, so that we get several passages of considerable length, which can be taken as reports of public teaching, as well as many passages telling with evident truthfulness of incidents containing private teaching. But the advance thus to be noticed in the care of believers in Jesus to preserve reports of what he said has been a little counterbalanced by the uncertainty and hurry of their own movements, causing them difficulty in drawing out a calm and complete statement. This position of matters has brought about that the account of the events in order is broken, even in the early gospels, after the first full day in Jerusalem, only to be clearly resumed at the terrible day of the arrest. To this it is

to be added, as also on the negative side, that the
artificialising forces of Messiah-lore and ecclesiasticism
have, as we might expect, very specially laid hold of
the accounts of this important time, so as to repress
what is spontaneous and personal in Jesus's actions
and utterances, and bring into prominence his superhuman office. In spite of these facts, we meet very
sure ground on which to build up our history of this
time.

Special help for this and the following chapters is
afforded by our secondary informant, the Fourth Gospel.
That book, as all who have studied it know well,
conveys the impression of Jesus having been several
times, instead of only once, teaching at Jerusalem.
In doing so it has left real history behind ; there is no
proper reconciling of its account, in this matter, with
that of the other gospels. But it would be wrong to see
no history at all in its account. Some of its narrative
of Jesus in Jerusalem, no doubt, as has been seen above,
has originated in some account of Jesus's ministry in
Galilee. But most of it has been originally an account
of this one small visit to Jerusalem, which has been
drawn out and mixed up with the writer's own
teaching. In this and the following chapters there
will be an endeavour to show, just through bringing
forward the events, that the Fourth Gospel, from the
seventh chapter of it onwards, is part of a doctrinal
essay, to begin with, but is also a bold handling of a
lost account telling of the same events which the earlier
gospels relate as having taken place in Jesus's short
visit to Jerusalem—the lost account having been
originally an independent account of the one short
visit, probably become mutilated and obscure before it

reached the hands of the evangelist, and the changings of place and the extendings of time having origins in the doctrinal imagination. And recognising in our work here that such is the state of matters with regard to the Fourth Gospel, we shall both be able to confirm points brought forward in the earlier gospels, and also get some extra information through abstracting from the doctrinal composition the lifelike elements.

Mk. xi. 12-15. We learn, then, that Jesus and his intimate followers, having passed a night in Bethany, went back to Jerusalem. On the way a little incident happened which has an interest. They passed a fig-tree, and, feeling hungry, would have gladly had some fruit. There was, however, no fruit on the tree, because, in the simple words of the Gospel of Mark, "the time of figs was not yet." We shall come upon this fig-tree presently again, and we shall then see what further took place in regard to it.

Ver. 13.

Vers. 15-17. On entering the city, Jesus went to the temple, and performed that bold act which, standing out in striking dissimilarity to his general life and teaching, might, only at first sight, seem to disturb the unity of his character. In the outer courts of the temple it had come to be customary for a large trade to be conducted. It is to be remembered that Jesus had come to Jerusalem with a decidedly aggressive purpose. Having found by experience that peaceful enunciation of his ideas only stirred up the established teachers against him, he had now taken the initiative of attack into his own hands, and had come to Jerusalem with the purpose of openly setting himself forward as a higher leader than the established teachers in regard to religious matters. He had come to make a very

special assertion of himself as the Teacher of a simple See above, pp. 197-199.
genuine religion. He had, further, thrown off all the
ordinary considerations by which the inhabitants of
earth guide themselves. He had made himself an angel
of God, and, for the time, not a peaceful but a warring
angel. And so, laying aside his natural sweetness, and
caring not for consequences to his own earthly life, he
went up to the traders who were accustomed to keep
their wares about the temple, threw down some of
their tables, and interrupted their work, saying, "Is it Mk. xi. 17: Jer. vii. 11.
not written, My house shall be called of all nations the
house of prayer? but ye have made it a den of thieves."
At the same time, we are to believe, he began to
address the people in such a way as to command Mk. xi. 18.
attention.

It is unnecessary for us here to give a detailed consideration to the moral bearings of this action of Jesus.
Certainly it was an action unlike his ordinary self; but
so was the whole stern attitude which he had at this
time assumed. And the results have declared that the
seizing of the public attention in the way adopted by
Jesus was such as was rightly calculated to advance
his cause. Whether or not he could have been equally
successful without this action, we need not be specu-
lative enough to inquire. The facts with which we
have mainly to do are, that Jesus laid the foundation
of an establishment of his teaching by forcing attention
on himself through an action which was violent
certainly, but raised above assailableness on moral
grounds in that it was, beyond all question, prompted
and permeated by stainless moral enthusiasm.

The authorities seem to have made no interference Mk. xi. 18.
with Jesus. And this is to be partly explained by the

fact that his followers from Galilee and some of the inhabitants of Jerusalem who had become interested in him had, as no doubt they did, assembled round him, and were supporting him. The Gospel of Matthew, indeed, speaks of "children" calling out "Hosanna to the son of David," and of Jesus, true to his own heart and mind, being keenly touched as he heard their young voices praising him. From comparison of this story of the children with a somewhat similar passage in Luke, it has been argued with much force that the "children" were really the ordinary followers of Jesus, so called from their humble position. This interpretation is, at least, not necessary; and the account in Matthew taken quite literally is very suitable to the whole scene as described by all three evangelists. In any case it is certain that there was some kind of popular movement around him at this time. And this popular movement would itself be enough to explain his being left unmolested after so high-handed an action. But there is also to be taken into account his own dignified bearing, along with the fact that he immediately began to address the people, in that manner of his which, as we have already discerned, must have been irresistibly charming and commanding. Jesus certainly did address the people at the temple on this very day; but of what he said, as is the case with what he said in his first preaching in Capernaum, not one sentence has been directly preserved for us, unless some of the teaching occurring in different parts of the gospels, which we can, by criticism, refer to the Jerusalem time, may have been given on this day. All we can be sure of is—just as in the Capernaum case— that Jesus told the people of Him whose presence had

Marginal notes:

Mt. xxi. 15, 16.

Lk. xix. 37-40. see Wendt, &c.

See above, pp. 101, 135.

Mk. xi. 18; Mt. xxi. 14, 15.

come to hold himself in command, and of the intention
of that ever-present Being that one and all should
grow into His own life; he told them of the Fatherly
care and of the brotherly and sisterly calling.

In the evening Jesus returned to Bethany. And we
must not pass without consideration this and some
following evenings at Bethany that lay between the days
of tumult within the city. Reports of these evenings
we have none, indeed ; but we can with very great
confidence surmise. We learned last chapter about
the "certain woman named Martha" who had received
Jesus into her house, and about the probability that
this woman had procured lodgings for Jesus in Bethany
—either in her own house or near it. We shall
meet, further on, notices of this woman and her sister
and brother, asking our attention with all the claim to
recommend them of speaking likeness to life in general
and to Jesus in particular. And so we can fill up the
picture of the evenings at Bethany. Whether the
family was one with which Jesus had newly become
acquainted, or whether he had known some of the
members before, we cannot tell; but we can say
almost surely that during some evenings extending
over a week or a fortnight, of which we have now
reached the second evening, a friendship of a very
intimate nature was cemented between Jesus and these
three persons. They, no doubt listening during these
evenings in reverent attention to his sublime conversation, gave him what he now sorely yearned for—
some simple trust and affection; he in his turn gave
them, not now but afterwards—what we shall see when
the occurrence comes before us in its proper order.

On the next morning—that is, his second morning

Mk. xi. 19
Mt. xxi.
17.

16

Mk. xi. 20-
26.
in Bethany, but the morning of his third day about Jerusalem—Jesus went into the city again with his special followers, and on the way they came again on the fig-tree. Now in the Gospels of Mark and Matthew there is recorded a little circumstance that naturally must puzzle earnest believers in Jesus of any thoughtfulness—namely, that Jesus had *cursed* this tree the first day, and that now he found it had withered away. The little circumstance cannot be taken as literally historical. Scholars have been able to detect the origin of this story of Jesus destroying a fig-tree in the
Lk. xiii. 6-
9.
lovely parable preserved in Luke, in which we see Jesus telling of a good gardener who *refused* to destroy a fig-tree. We must not, however, go with the scholars the length of supposing that the whole incident in regard to the fig-tree is unhistorical. Rather, there was an incident in regard to the fig-tree, and that led to the parable being spoken. The fig-tree incident led to the parable, and the parable led to a false account of the fig-tree incident, through the carelessness and perverseness of mouth-to-mouth reports. What happened was evidently something like this : The followers, as they approached the tree the second morning, made some remarks, probably half humorous, about that disappointing tree being there again ; and they may have even repeated the kind of suggestion which some of them had made before in relation to the inhospitable
Above, p.
224.
Samaritan village. Jesus, whose mind was now dwelling on the serious future, led the matter into the lines of
Lk. xiii. 6-
9.
serious reflection. He said to them, "A certain man had a fig-tree planted in his vineyard ; and he came and sought fruit thereon, and found none. Then said he unto the dresser of his vineyard, Behold, these three

years I come seeking fruit on this fig-tree, and find
none: cut it down; why cumbereth it the ground?
And he answering said unto him, Lord, let it alone
this year also, till I shall dig about it, and dung it:
and if it bear fruit, well; and if not, then after that
thou shalt cut it down." The thought he evidently
meant to illustrate by the lovely story was the inex-
haustible hope ever attaching to a living soul. And so
we find he added: "Have faith in God. For verily Mk. xi. 23
I say unto you, That whosoever shall say unto this
mountain, Be thou removed, and be thou cast into the
sea; and shall not doubt in his heart, but shall believe
that those things which he saith shall come to pass;
he shall have whatsoever he saith." And then, in his
usual way, he turned from the devotional to the ethical
—from the faith in God to the duty of man—and
gently rebuked the way of thought that would destroy
what for the present gave offence, even were it an
irresponsible fig-tree. He said, "When ye stand Vers. 25,
praying, forgive, if ye have ought against any; that 26.
your Father also which is in heaven may forgive you
your trespasses. But if ye do not forgive, neither will
your Father which is in heaven forgive your trespasses."
The reader will see how disconnected, or indeed how
out of agreement would be the teaching in these words
with Jesus's own action, if we were to read the report
in the Gospel of Mark quite literally. When we read
it, on the other hand, critically, with the help of Luke,
the whole incident comes intelligibly before us, and
brings most precious teaching to ourselves.

By the time Jesus presented himself at the temple Mk. xi.
on this day, the priests and scribes had collected their 27-33.
courage, and had resolved on an interference with him.

They came up and said to him something like this,
Vers. 27,
28.
"By what authority doest thou these things? and who
gave thee this authority to do these things?" Jesus's
answer was in accordance with his usual masterly skill.
He did not choose to involve himself in discussions
with these men about his claims; but still we can see
he was determined to make clear to them the kind of
authority he was claiming, along with the kind of
ascendancy he was aiming at, so that, once for all,
there might be no confusing of his mission with that
of any political revolutionist. What he did was to
choose another concrete example for them to compare
him with. Clear and unmistakable to every class of
intelligence was his answer. *He named the name of*
Ver. 29.
John the Baptist. He said, "I will also ask of you one
question, and answer me, and I will tell you by what
Ver. 30.
authority I do these things. The baptism of John,
was it from heaven, or of men? answer me." They
were silenced, as they were compelled to be. They
Vers. 31-
33.
could not, in the face of the people, object to one
who was only coming with that moral kind of appeal
which had been addressed by a well-known man, and
been recognised by all honest persons as having no
political significance, and as being just a sacred appeal
to the heart. They saw that Jesus was claiming to be
not a revolutionary, but a "prophet"; and so, though
they might not withdraw their secret opposition to
him, they perceived they had no ground for public
interference. We find, accordingly, that they left him
to continue his sacred teaching.

From the Fourth Gospel we get a rather interesting
confirmation of this incident—of the aim of the interference, the course adopted by Jesus, and the failure of

the aim. The Fourth Gospel seems at first sight to
antedate Jesus's action in the court of the temple, and
conveys the impression that it happened at the beginning instead of at the end of the ministry. The fact,
however, is that the evangelist, having evidently had
two different original accounts before him, runs over
the whole ministry in the first two and a half chapters
and then starts anew. In the second chapter of the Jn. ii. 13-
Fourth Gospel, thus, we find an account of the events 22. See
above, p.
now before us, and there we find given as Jesus's 53; and
also see
answer to the objectors a remark which, we shall App. IV.
see, was really uttered by Jesus, but on a later occasion Jn. ii. 19.
than that to which we have come. The Fourth Gospel
also, however, in its second and main narrative, has
preserved a notice of Jesus's real answer to the
objectors, which has just been before us. Yes, far-
fetched as it may seem at the first look, we may surely
see a report of the incident in the following words :
" They sought again to take him : but he escaped out Jn. x. 39,
of their hand, and went away again beyond Jordan, 40.
into the place where John at first baptised." This
statement is, literally read, not historical, for, as
scholars have shown, Jesus did not move about bodily
from place to place as the Fourth Gospel makes him
do. The Synoptic gospels do not give him time for
such journeyings ; and in the matter of time the
Synoptic gospels can be proved to be strictly accurate.
But, as has been said above, we are to see that the
whole of the second and larger half of the Fourth
Gospel is, in its original elements, an account of the
one short visit to Jerusalem. And so there is suggested
that the statement is not a purely fictitious one, but is
a materialised report of what took place in Jesus's

management of his case. We shall see, indeed, in a later chapter, that there is a truth in the fact that Jesus made a slight withdrawal from notice during the Jerusalem visit; so that that event **has** so far entered **into** the statement before us in its development. But what has mainly **given rise** to the statement is evidently the answer **of** Jesus **to the** priests and scribes, which we have **just had before us.** It is quite true in a sense, just as the statement declares, **that the** enemies of Jesus—taking "enemies" of Jesus, Galilean and Judæan, all in a mass—"sought *again* to take him"; and it is true that he "escaped out of their hands," in this way, that he suddenly and unexpectedly went away again (in his talk) "into **the** place where John at first baptised." The disciples, no doubt, who had come to think of late of his own great personality, and of his acknowledging himself **to** be the Messiah, were as surprised as the priests and scribes were at his going "away again" back to John the Baptist. **And so the** story would come to take the fanciful form, in which the fancy was changed to an erroneous assertion regarding the place in which Jesus actually was.

Mk. xii. 1; Jesus began at this point some lengthened teaching
Lk. xix.
47, xx. 1. in and around the temple. But at this point the exact determining of time fails in the gospel accounts, from the natural causes above specified. All we can know about the setting of time is that the whole teaching evidently lasted little over a week. During this week or so, Jesus gave some teaching on which we must enter in next chapter.

CHAPTER XVI.

THE PROCLAIMING OF HIS OWN IDEAS IN JERUSALEM.

THE teaching of Jesus in Jerusalem, in accordance
with the action which we had before us in last chapter, See above,
took a more aggressive form than his Galilean teaching p. 238.
had done. The difference was brought about by the
fact that he was now deliberately laying siege, as it
were, to the religious opinions and feelings of his
countrymen, having it before his mind that he could
only spread his own ideas through making a decisive
stand against the old-fashioned teachers. Thus his
public addresses in Jerusalem seem to have been in
the same spirit as that in which he had acted when he
had overthrown the tables. We shall find, however,
that he made them lead up to the teaching of his own
positive ideas, and we shall also find that he gave in a
more private form much of his own teaching at the
same time. In this chapter we are to attend only to
the public teaching.

Both Mark and Matthew give reports of his attacking
the scribes and Pharisees about their love of high

place. We may take it as certain that Jesus openly
reproached the scribes with loving the dignities
attached to their office, but not acting themselves in a
way worthy of their office.

Mt. xxiii.;
Lk. xi. 39-
52.

Matthew, however, adds to his report a long address
of reproach against the scribes and Pharisees; and
the substance of this address is found in Luke also,
though not given there among the occurrences at
Jerusalem. The address speaks for itself as containing
the words of Jesus, so powerful is it, and so in accordance with his ideas and his way of expressing himself.
Now it is to be recognised that Matthew has the
tendency to make up long speeches out of sayings
really spoken in different connections, so that in the
twenty-third chapter of Matthew there may be
elements that have been woven in to make up the
speech. The speech, however, is such a unity that
we can accept almost all of it as having been really a
speech of Jesus delivered in public. Any additions
must be inconsiderable; the report of Matthew may be
taken as almost literally correct. And we must fix it
to this time at Jerusalem, and not to an earlier time,
as Luke would have us do, both because this was the
time consistent with its fierce spirit, and because
Luke's own report of it suggests the circumstances in
which Jesus now was—that is, engaged in his last
struggle with the authorities. The speech is in the
tone of the old prophecies, but excelling all of them in
power. It is a speech which shows Jesus to have
excelled all others as greatly when speaking as a
moralist as he did when speaking as a prophet of the
higher kind. One after another of the ways of those
who make profession not in accordance with their

practice is laid open in it in plain and cutting language. But along with these are mentioned faults such as Mt. xxiii. are the temptation of the devotees of all systems, 15, 16, 23, 25, 27, 30. and are only likely to be escaped where zeal is elevated through being accompanied by an abundance of charity and wisdom.   The eagerness to make proselytes to one's own system, the disputing over trifles, the centering religion on ceremonies and forms, the outward profession of sanctity disproportionate to the inward attainment, the blaming the men of the past for persecuting their prophets while acting in the same spirit oneself—all these things are trenchantly reproved in this address in Jerusalem.

There is an expression used in the address which we Vers. 17. have just had before us, which is interesting from 19, 24, 26. different considerations.   That is the expression Confirm- "blind" as applied by Jesus to the scribes and ed in Jn. ix. 40. Pharisees.   It is interesting in that it gives an explanation of the form of some of the miracle-narratives. It is also interesting as we shall see it made a strong impression on one at least of the hearers, who, indeed, came to believe in Jesus.   But it is interesting chiefly in this, that it gives a most valuable clue to the nature of Jesus's own religion.   In reproaching the scribes with being blind, he implied, in distinction, that there was a way of dealing with religious subjects, in which one looked and saw what was there to see.   In this, as elsewhere, Jesus assuredly taught that the true subject for the study of the religious is to be found in what is always living around us, and not in any records of the past.   Records of the past, we may say, according to Jesus's teaching, may suggest in a most valuable way how to look for ourselves ; but those who study the records without being able to see any present sacred reality are, in relation to sacred things, like blind men, and if they pose as teachers of others on these subjects,

Mt. xv. 14.
Cp. mar-
gin.p. 100. are " blind leaders of the blind." It is in accordance with this that Jesus's own teaching keeps mostly away from established embodiments of doctrine, as well as from established religious **practices, and** busies itself with **the care of our heavenly Father,** and our duty **to care for** one another—with such **subjects as the** Divine **government of** nature, kindness, mercifulness, honesty, and purity of heart.

Mt. xxiii.
2. In Matthew it is reported that Jesus said, in connection with his attack on the scribes and Pharisees, " The scribes and the Pharisees sit in Moses' **seat :** all therefore whatsoever they bid you observe, that observe and do ; but do not ye after their works : for they say, and do not." For us the fact that he did say, if not this exactly, then at least something like this, is confirmed—strongly, **if** in a rough manner —by our finding **in** the Fourth **Gospel** report the

Jn. vii. 19. following words : " Did not Moses give you the law, and yet none **of** you keepeth the law ?" It is likely that in neither **of** the reports are Jesus's words quite accurately preserved. But two reports so different **from** each other, and yet evidently reports of one saying, compel us to recognise that Jesus really said something like them. The probability is that, in this instance, the Fourth Gospel report is the more accurate, the First Gospel report being led away by the respect **to** Law which runs through the First Gospel. Jesus, it is likely, stated plainly to the inhabitants of Jerusalem that he was not interfering with the Law nor objecting to the scribes teaching the

Law, but wished them, scribes and people, to act in accordance with what they professed to reverence and learn.

In these aggressive addresses, we find, Jesus led up to the presentation of the gracious truths which it was his mission to assert. Our reports of this directly positive teaching are, no doubt, more suggestive than complete : but they are in the highest degree convincing, and are sufficient in extent to give a valuable addition to our knowledge of his ideas.

First and foremost, we have almost perfect evidence for the fact that he proclaimed in public, in simple language, his great ruling idea of the *Fatherhood of God*. According to the report in Matthew, he was led on to do this through attacking the love of high place which prevailed among the "scribes and Pharisees." And we have assuredly in this report of Matthew the original words of Jesus, though a few small additions are just about as surely interwoven from later elucidations given for the sake of the early Christians. The original words of Jesus were at least almost exactly these : " But be not ye called Rabbi : for . . . . . all ye are brethren. And . . . . . one is your Father, which is in heaven "—to which prophetic utterance he added, in his customary way, the ethical counterpart, " Neither be ye called Masters . . . . . But he that is greatest among you shall be your servant. And whosoever shall exalt himself shall be abased ; and he that shall humble himself shall be exalted."

The fact of the prophetic utterance regarding the Fatherhood of God having proceeded from Jesus at this time, is confirmed by the Fourth Gospel, though *Jn. viii. 41.*

Mt. xxiii. 9. Cp. below.

Mt. xxiii. 1-12.

Vers. 41-
44. See
App. I.
(13, 23).
the evangelist has in this case done the most arbitrary
thing we have seen him do in the enunciation of his
dualistic philosophy—namely, no less than put our
Lord's sacred words into the mouth of "the Jews"
themselves, and represent Jesus as having disagreed
with them, preferring to think that "the devil" was
their father, because they did not love him. This, no
doubt, is a case similar to others that have been before
us, in which the evangelist has received words accompanied by no explanation of their definite connection,
and has himself, accordingly, with every intention to
keep to the truth, given the words a setting—in
this case an authorship. Nevertheless what he has
presented to us in this case is Johannine Christianity,
not history. The great words are Jesus's, not "the
Jews'"; and the lesser words are the evangelist's, not
Jesus's. But the finding our words in the Fourth
Gospel report, in spite of the perversion applied to
them, is confirmatory of their having been uttered at
this time.

And, further, the very perversion of the words in the
Fourth Gospel helps us to maintain what we must take
our stand by—namely, that the words were uttered not
merely to the disciples, but to all, not merely to "the
Pp. 38, 98,
164.
Christians," but to mankind. We have seen above
that it was most certainly a universal Fatherhood that
Jesus taught, and that the supposition of his having
communicated his ideas to a favoured few only, is
excluded by the very character of the ideas themselves.
It is interesting, however, to find this confirmed by
a particular instance; and in the particular instance
now before us testimony is borne both by Matthew
and John, independently of each other, to the fact

that Jesus spoke of a Fatherhood for all. The fact that the words had come into the hands of the Fourth Evangelist in so bare a form that he had practically to contradict them to suit them to his own narrow and exclusive view, suggests convincingly that they had not, at first, any qualification limiting them to the disciples, as such a qualification is not of the kind that would likely have altogether disappeared.

Another point seems to have been specially brought forward in Jesus's proclaiming of his ideas at this time, and that was the truth of the RESURRECTION of our spirits after death. This truth had been bound up with his teaching all along, as we have seen above; and in the matter of Jairus's daughter, he had given forcible expression to it. It natur-ally, however, had assumed greater prominence in his own thoughts since the time of his coming to the presentiment that early death was before himself. And thus we should expect a slight distinction between the place it would hold in his earlier teaching and that which it would hold in his later teaching. We should expect that in the later teaching he would oftener and more prominently introduce the subject. This distinction is borne out by the evidence we possess. It is in what is certainly early teaching that we find Jesus urging his hearers to take " no thought for the morrow," and to trust to being clothed and fed by the heavenly Father, like the flowers of the field and the birds of the air. In this last Jerusalem teaching, assuredly the truth of what is to come after death, in the care of that same heavenly Father, was pro-minent. We have not, indeed, much record of his public utterances on the subject, though we shall

Above, p. 165.

Jn. viii. 51
may be a

trace of such. Cp. the following verses, which are certainly founded on incident of the objecting to his teaching the resurrection.
find him expressing the truth forcibly in his private conversations. His parables, however, to which we are to come presently, involve the truth; and both the faith among the people and the opposition among the religious parties which followed his whole appearance, bear witness to the fact that this truth was asserted by him openly and unmistakably. Fixed in his gaze on that Presence which he saw to be all Care for every being that lives and thinks, and burning with an emotion in himself which was so overpowering that he knew it bore witness to the determination of that Presence to accomplish its ends, Jesus, with the "authority" which was attached to his personality, taught that those who suffered and hoped and died in this world would live again.

A few of the grandest parables also were almost certainly spoken and repeated at this time. These, like his other public utterances in Jerusalem, were largely given to begin with by way of attack on the Pharisees and scribes; but most of them were such that they soared far above their first aggressive aim, and became expressions of those eternal truths which Jesus had come to Jerusalem to assert.

There was the PARABLE OF THE WICKED HUSBANDMEN. This is the only one that our chief guide, the Mk. xii. 1-12. Gospel of Mark, has preserved; and it had a special importance from the view of those gospels which had, as one aim, to set up the claims of Jesus to be followed rather than the scribes. It is an almost purely aggressive parable, and it has a peculiar gloominess in that it seems to presuppose the temporary discomfiture of Jesus. There is a self-assertion in it, on Jesus's part, which prompts us at first to suspect it has been

tampered with slightly before it has reached the form
in which we have it. We find Jesus saying in it,
"Having yet therefore one son, his well-beloved, he Ver. 6.
sent him also last unto them, saying, They will reverence
my son. But those husbandmen said among them- Ver. 7.
selves, This is the heir," &c. Probably the report was
very slightly diverted from the original. The remark
about "the heir" especially is not likely to have been
in the parable as Jesus spoke it. But it is best to
believe that the change has been very slight, and that
Jesus did indeed, at this time, speak out his consciousness of being greater than any prophet that had gone
before him. This self-assertion through a parable is
not like the Fourth Gospel self-assertion. And we
have already seen that Jesus's whole conduct at this
time implied an indirect self-assertion, for the sake of
his mission; so that a delicate self-assertion in words,
through a parable, is quite in keeping. This parable
is, however, also remarkable as containing a prediction
made by Jesus about the future of his own name,
which is no doubt authentic. Recalling the words of
a psalm, Jesus said, at the end of the parable, "And Vers. 10,
have ye not read this scripture, The stone which the 11; Ps.
cxviii. 22,
builders rejected is become the head of the corner: 23.
This was the Lord's doing, and it is marvellous in our
eyes?" This prediction, based on his consciousness
of power and of enlightenment, was justified long after
even the gospel's time by a resplendent fulfilment.

Then there was the PARABLE OF THE MARRIAGE Mt. xxii.
SUPPER. This parable, reported and certainly added 1-10, 11-
14 add.:
to in Matthew, and simply reported in Luke, may be Lk. xiv.
16-24.
assigned to this time on Matthew's authority. It
expresses the experience of Jesus all along, of finding

those whose names were "cast out as evil," rather than the professed religious classes, listening to his simple teaching.

Then there was the PARABLE OF THE PHARISEE AND
Lk. xviii. 9-14.
PUBLICAN. We may fix this one to the time we are dealing with from its local setting of the temple. It is a great parable, going far beyond an aggressive purpose in its teaching.

Mt. xxi. 28-32.
Then there was the PARABLE OF THE TWO SONS— the one who said he would go and work, and did not go, and the one who did not say, but went. This, reported in Matthew along with the Parable of the Husbandmen, may be assigned to this time. It is a striking illustration of the point above noticed, which Jesus brought forward in reference to the greater importance of keeping the law than of professing reverence for it. But it also goes beyond its immediate purpose, and is of eternal value.

Lk. xv. 11-32.
Some scholars, furthermore, have fixed the parable of the PRODIGAL SON to the Jerusalem teaching, on the ground of its likeness to the parable of the Two Sons, just mentioned. And it may be that the parable of the Prodigal Son, perhaps the greatest of all the parables, was delivered at the temple at this time,
Above, p. 216.
though, as we have seen, there is temptation to fix it to the last visit to Capernaum.

Then lastly, the parable of the JUDGE AND WIDOW,
Lk. xviii. 1-8.
one with no aggressive element in it, may have been delivered at this time, seeing it is in some way coupled with that of the Pharisee and Publican in Luke's report.

By way of concluding the account of this part of the teaching which comes under the head of pro-

claiming his own ideas in public, there is one small
contribution that may be extracted from the long
disputatious report of the Fourth Gospel. It is in
this sentence, " If any man thirst, let him come unto
me, and drink." In this saying, in which we see Jesus
applying to himself the words of the fifty-fifth chapter
of Isaiah, we have life-likeness and likeness to Jesus.
And we may find here an example of the length to
which Jesus really went in the self-assertion to which he
had a right. There is nothing here of the self-glorifi-
cation which the evangelist's handling has imposed on
Jesus in the general picture. Here Jesus only expresses
his consciousness of religious authority. Here is not
self-elevation, but modest assertion of conscious power.

That such teaching would actually win over the
inhabitants of a city which was the citadel of the
artificial Judaic religion, Jesus himself, as we are
believing, had hardly hoped. But the narrative in
general brings out surely, what we should otherwise
have felt certain of, that it charmed many and set
them a-thinking, as it had done with the people of
Capernaum. A little incident told of in the ninth
chapter of the Fourth Gospel illustrates this and bears
it out. Some man had been so impressed by Jesus's
public addresses, that he had become a believer in Jesus.
His friends were displeased at this, and abused Jesus
to him, saying, " Thou art his disciple ; but we are
Moses' disciples. We know that God spake unto Moses :
as for this fellow, we know not from whence he is."
They further said, in their ignorant indelicacy, that
Jesus was " a sinner." The man said, in reply to this
abuse of Jesus, something like the following: " Whether
he be a sinner or no, I know not : one thing I know,

Marginal notes:
Jn. vii. 37.
Cp. above.
pp. 70, 73, 75.
Reuss compares
Mt. v. 6.

Jn. ix. 28, 29.

Ver. 24.

Ver. 25.

17

that, whereas I was **blind, now I see.**" This was too much for the ruling powers in the synagogue which the man had attended ; and if we can hardly accept entirely the evangelist's statement that they went at once to the extremity of expelling him from the syna-

Ver. 34. gogue, we must believe they warned him that if he persisted in his convictions they would do so. It will be perceived that the suggestions which the man's remark to his friends bears of **Jesus's sayings about**

Cp. above, the Pharisees and scribes in his address that we have
pp. 249. particularly reported to us, is strong evidence for the
250. truth of the incident, in the abridged and purified form in which we have followed it. And indeed we find the

Jn. ix. 40, evangelist's own account gets mixed up with that
41. saying of Jesus about the Pharisees. The giving here the blindness of the man a spiritual, not a physical meaning, need hardly be defended. Not only is it required for the sake of making the whole incident

See vers. intelligible, but it may be said to be proved from the
5. 28. 39, record itself. This incident—which will come before
41. us again in another aspect—helps to show us the *power* of Jesus's teaching at this time.

CHAPTER XVII.

TEACHING SUGGESTED BY INCIDENTS.

IT will by this time be apparent to the reader that the teaching of Jesus in relation to incidents in general is the most valuable part of his definite teaching that remains to us. And the reason for such a state of matters is not far to seek. In such a community as that which surrounded Jesus, his words that were called forth by special incidents naturally made the strongest impression on the memory, and so were best preserved. Now several incidents which took place in the short time at Jerusalem have come down to us, having connected with them teaching which both discloses to us the mind of Jesus and brings sacred suggestions of the highest order for ourselves.

At the outset we must consider one incident, which is different from all the rest in that the report of it, in literalness, though not in its significance when subjected to critical treatment, brings before us teaching of a kind very perplexing as related to the character and mind of Jesus as far as we have discerned them.

Perhaps the only part of the Synoptic gospels which,

17 *

to a thoughtful follower of Jesus, must prove in some
way repellent, is to be found in those passages towards
the end of all three, which are called by scholars
APOCALYPTIC passages, and deal with the subjects of the
destruction of Jerusalem and the end of the world.
They are so evidently compositions of an artificial type
which prevailed in Jesus's time. They have, further,
not that ring of the highest type of prophecy, of
unparalleled religious genius, which is found in the
Sermon on the Mount and the Sermon on the Plain.
Their subjects, again, though in literalness supernatural, are in reality less ethereal than the subjects of
the parables of the Seed, the simple aphorisms, and
the parable of the Prodigal Son. And finally, in dealing
with the end of the world, they so plainly, unless
recourse be had to the utmost ingenuity of interpretation, give an account regarding what was to come
which the facts afterwards proved to have been not
strictly accurate.

We are to be thankful, therefore, to scholars for
being able to hold with certainty that these apocalyptic
passages, so far as they are accounts of the sayings of
Jesus, are largely elaborated and added to by foreign
hands. It is not the work of this book to go closely
into the critical discussion of these passages ; but we
may sum up the truth regarding them in this way :
The fact that the destruction of Jerusalem did not
happen till long after Jesus's death is enough, in a true
understanding of prophetic insight, to put out of the
question the supposition that he really spoke, in any
detail, of that event. The fact that the idea of an
abrupt and judicial end of the world is quite out of
keeping with his whole view of life, as criticism discerns

*Mt. xxiv.,
xxv. ; Mk.
xiii. ; Lk.
xvii. 20-
37, xix.
41-48, xxi.*

*See J. E.
H. Thom-
son's
work on
Apocalyp-
tic books.*

it, disposes, as we have already seen, of the supposition that he really entertained that idea. And as regards the general state of matters, it is to be said that these apocalyptic passages are due to Church expositions of the sayings of Jesus, and that they have been worked up out of original sayings, wrongly interpreted in the light of subsequent events, and filled up through the help of apocalyptic writings belonging to the time.

For us now, however, the important thing is to determine what points of real history are to be discerned through them ; and the answer to this must be that the main historical background is to be found in *one incident.* We can learn what this incident was by reading the one chapter in our most ancient gospel which presents the subject. We can recognise that the longer records of Matthew and Luke, while drawing more from other apocalyptic sources, have also had access to some further true reports of Jesus's sayings in connection with the incident. And we shall learn thus what may make us call it *the Incident of the Disciples admiring the Temple Buildings.* Mk. xiii. 9-11 is from different occasion. Cp. Mt. x. 17-20, Jn. xiv. 16-17. Mt. xxiv., xxv. ; Mk. xiii. ; Lk. xvii., xix., xxi.

The incident has three parts, which we may call *A*, *B*, and *C*.

(*A*.) The disciples, and also, no doubt, Jesus himself, were admiring the beautiful structure and ornamentation of the temple. And as they did so, Jesus made a remark which the Synoptic gospels have reported not very accurately, and in such a way as to suggest, wrongly, that it was an allusion to the coming destruction of Jerusalem. For what he really said we must call in the aid of a notice in the Fourth Gospel, which is supported by a notice in Mark regarding the charge which was afterwards brought against Jesus at Mk. xiii. 1, 2. Jn. ii. 19 ; Mk xiv. 58. Cp. Mk. xiii. 4

with Jn.
ii. 18,
"what
sign."
See also
above, pp.
53, 245.
his trial.   Jesus said, we must learn, that this temple "made with hands" would be destroyed, and that he "within three days" would raise up a temple "made without hands." The meaning of what he said is easily discerned for a thoughtful student of his life. In speaking of the three days, he again quoted his
Hos. vi. 1.,
2. Cp.
above, p.
198.
favourite saying from Hosea, meaning by the "three days" a fixed period which God, who overrules all, would determine.   And the whole remark was as much
With
evange-
list's ma-
terialistic
explana-
tion (ver.
21) cp. Mt.
xii. 40.
as to say, This temple and the work connected with it will perish, and indeed must perish soon ; but let both the temple and the whole worship connected with it go, I, out of my own knowledge and power, will make religion live again.

(*B.*) Afterwards when they had gone out to the
Mk. xiii. 3.
Mount of Olives, on the way to Bethany, " Peter and James and John and Andrew " asked him for some explanation of what he had said about the destroying of the temple, and of himself restoring it.   And it is in reporting his meeting of this request that the Synoptic gospels definitely introduce those considerations taken from later time, in virtue of which they depart from real history.   For the learning what really happened at this point of the incident, we get no help from other sources, but are reduced to making the best of an ordinary critical reading of the Synoptic reports themselves.   Fortunately, however, amongst the reports of the three gospels, there are fragments of information which carry conviction with them ; and the broken pieces fit together so as to make one consistent whole.

First, then, by way of explaining *why* he looked forward at all to a destruction of the temple and of its worship, he spoke, we must believe, those words which the gospels report out of their logical connection, "Wheresoever the carcase is, there will the eagles be gathered together." The meaning of the words is plain. He had seen the whole religious system of his people to be *dead*. He looked at the temple building itself as having degenerated into being the centre of a not very honest trade. And as for the teaching of those in authority, he had given his stern opinion of what it was worth. The words were as much as to say, The whole system is dead. Dead things don't remain as they are. Some power will come forward in the course of nature and remove the carcase.

Then, we are to learn, from speaking of the first part of Jesus's prediction—namely, that the temple made with hands would be destroyed—they went on to ask for explanations regarding the second part of his prediction—namely, that he would raise up a temple made without hands. And in connection with this, there came into the conversation some words of the apocalyptic kind, most likely the words Jesus himself had used by way of expressing the fact of which he was sure, that opposition and even death would not put an end to himself or his mission, but that God would restore himself and carry the mission to success. How this would come about it is not difficult to see. When Jesus was now talking about a restoration, all of them would at once connect what he was saying with the great restoration which they all believed in and called *the kingdom of God*. And when Jesus was now speaking of *himself* bringing about a restoration, they would naturally recall the apocalyptic words which Jesus had already, on a former occasion, used to express his ultimate hopes regarding himself and his mission.

[margin notes: Mt. xxiv. 28. For want of logical connection in gospels, cp. Mt. xxiv. 27 w. Lk. xvii. 36. Mk. xiii. 26 ; Mt. xxiv. 30. See above, p. 203 ff.]

When Jesus now spoke of himself, in the future, building a temple without hands, there would at once recur to them the thought of *the Son of man coming in his glory*. Whether it was the disciples or Jesus himself that introduced the words into the conversation now before us, it is difficult to tell; but it little matters, as we have already seen that Jesus was willing to use such words, though he used them not literally but as mere expressions of his own thoughts. What happened, then, was that they went on to seek explanation of what Jesus had meant by speaking of restoring the temple, connecting that with the great restoration and with the resurrection and ultimate triumph of Jesus. Jesus's sayings, by way of supplying the explanation which they thus desired, stand out from the report quite plainly to a thoughtful reader. He said that the time and ways of the coming restoration were not to be accurately foreseen by human minds. He said that all things come in unexpected ways and at unexpected times. And he gave two illustrations of this general fact. First, he reminded them of the old story of the flood, as a vivid illustration of how things happen in the eternal rule of God. And then, second, he appealed to ordinary experience. He said, " Two *are* in the field ; the one *is* taken, and the other left." Two *are* grinding at the mill ; the one *is* taken, and the other left." That the gospels have misunderstood these words, and so slightly manipulated them, is sufficiently clear from the fact that they present them in such a way as to have no logical connection with the words which they make to follow them. They were assuredly, as Jesus uttered them, words expressing the ordinary facts in the continual government of God,

Mk. xiii. 32.

Mt. xxiv. 36-41.

Cp. ver. 42 w. Lk. xvii. 37.

brought forward to be examples of what was to be
expected in the future, and were not oracular
apocalyptic sayings. Jesus further, we may believe,
at this time, impressed upon his disciples the fact that
the restoration of what is good was not to be looked
for as to be accomplished altogether by external means,
but required the growth of what is good in the souls
of men themselves. For the report of this point,
indeed, we are indebted to a notice in Luke, in which
it is said that it was to the *Pharisees* Jesus said this. Lk. xvii.
But the notice seems to belong to the report of this 20, 21.
incident that is before us. The words attributed to
Jesus in it bear all the marks of genuineness, and are
these, " The kingdom of God cometh not with observa-
tion : neither shall they say, Lo here ! or, lo there ! for,
behold, the kingdom of God is within you." And then,
lastly, he added that indeed he looked for a great
immediate establishment of what was good in the
world, as he had always taught. He grounded the
belief in such a thing coming on the fact of so much
earnestness having appeared all over the nation. He
said, " Learn a parable of the fig-tree ; When her branch Mk. xiii.
is yet tender, and putteth forth leaves, ye know that 28, 29.
summer is near : so ye, in like manner, when ye shall
see these things come to pass, know that it is nigh, even
at the doors." In the gospel report of these words
they read as if the "these things" alluded to were the Vers. 24-
realisations of awe-striking apocalyptic notions, such as 27.
the sun and moon ceasing to give light, the falling of
stars, and the coming of the Son of man in the clouds.
The utter unsuitability of the parable to such things,
viewed as facts, and indeed its utter pointlessness
when supposed to start from such things as facts,
will be patent to the reader. The connection of the

words has been lost in the apocalyptic composition
Cp. above, pp. 7¹, 7². which meets us in the gospel. The "these things"
which Jesus meant were assuredly the quickenings of
earnestness and devotion which had taken place in
connection with the preaching of himself and of John
the Baptist.

Thus here as elsewhere the "apocalyptic" element
in what is reported as Jesus's teaching is to be
detected as having been partly later filling up of the
report, and as having been, even in the part in which
it really belonged to what he said, mere material or
imagery there to his hand. On the other side, what
really proceeded from Jesus's mind on the subject is
to be looked for first, no doubt, in the declaring that
the imagery in question expressed a real fact, but,
second, in those thoughts which we have just had
before us, which gave to the imagery and the fact
presented by it a spiritual and rational explanation.

(*C.*) And finally, as regards this incident, it is as
plain as it need be for any fair reader, that Jesus went
on to turn the conversation which had arisen out of
the incident into the lines of taking lessons for ordinary
life. What he went on to say, we can see, was to this
general effect: While it is right to remember the fact
that God will bring in the end the triumph of what is
Mk. xiii. 33. good, the main thing for men and women to attend to
is their *duty in the present*. And this thought he
developed in several parables which are more or less
pointed to in a brief notice by Mark, and are preserved
by Matthew, in forms through which, though they are
more or less influenced by the apocalyptic beliefs of
the time of the gospel, we can read the original.

Vers. 34-37. There was the PARABLE OF THE WATCHMEN. This
seems to have been a short parable. Its meaning

clearly is that God has given each one a *trust* for this world, so that each one should be alive and attentive. This parable is reported in Mark.

From the Parable of the Watchmen he likely hurriedly went on to the PARABLE OF THE VIRGINS. This parable is hinted at, but not properly preserved, in Mark. In Matthew there is a long presentation of it; but in that presentation it must have been changed since its utterance by Jesus. The Parable of the Virgins in the severely dualistic form in. which the Gospel of Matthew gives it is not in accordance with the teaching of Jesus, but is in accordance with the tendency of the Gospel of Matthew. We can suppose the parable was originally a short parable similar to that of the Watchmen, to the general effect that each one has something to do before God sends the times of rest and joy, and that *when* God brings the good times it is right to be found not in an idle state, but attending to one's duty, even if that duty only consist in such a thing as keeping a lamp burning.

Ver. 35; Mt. xxv. 1-13.

Mt. xxv. 1-13. Cp. Lk. xii. 35-40.

Then there was the PARABLE OF THE TALENTS. This splendid parable, containing in itself the whole system of a moral philosophy in accordance with religious faith, is preserved both by Matthew and by Luke—probably more faithfully by Matthew, but very correctly by both. It was to the effect that all of us have trusts to attend to in our common surroundings, so that our commonest surroundings should be sacred to us.

Mt. xxv. 14-30; Lk. xix. 12-27.

And lastly there was the parable—as parable it may rightly be called in its original utterance—of the SHEEP AND THE GOATS. The passage containing the reminiscence, as it must be expressed, of this parable, is

Cp. Bruce's "Kingdom of God," p. 326, "fire,"

&c.,
" figures."
Mt. xxv.
31-46. Cp.
Ezek.
xxxiv. 17,
Zech. x. 3.

one of the most remarkable in all the Bible. It presents, perhaps, an unparalleled collocation of the contraries of thought. On the one side is fancy, presenting a state of things for the future such as, in the record of knowledge, no daylight experience, but only perhaps some terrible dream, has ever brought before the mind of man ; on the other side is promise, which at once is justified by and transcends the best that experience, imagination, and aspiration have touched. And the collocation is no blending. The weirdness of the one factor throws into relief the winning gentleness of the other. But just from this state of matters it comes about that the passage is one of the dearest trophies of a victorious Biblical Criticism. The separation of the factors is historically justifiable, and Biblical Criticism is to be thanked for

Cp. Mk.
ix. 49 w.
Mt. xxv.
41; Mk.
xiii. 36-37
w. Mt.
xxv. 10-
13; Lk.
xiv. 24 w.
Mt. xxv.
28-30, and
specially
Lk. vi. 46
w. Mt. vii.
21-23.

it. Comparison of the teaching of Jesus in Mark and Luke and of other treatment of teaching in Matthew, can place it beyond question that the awful dualism which is found in this passage is to be referred either to the evangelist or to the didactic school of which his gospel was the outcome. The original parable has been treated something as the parable of the Virgins has been treated ; and a closer correspondence can be found in the case of the parable of the Tares. The

Mt. xxv.
41-46. Cp.
Mt. xiii.
36-43.
See also
App. I.
(18).

second part of the passage is, at least in its present, extreme form, a didactic offset to the first part, intended by the early Christians as a warning to evil-doers. On the other hand, our canons of investigation unhesitatingly ascribe the rest of the passage, in substance at least, to Jesus ; and the form also may be allowed to be his own, from a broad view of its distinctiveness and its likeness to his other teaching,

along with an appreciation of the character for faithfulness belonging to the First as to all the three earlier
gospels, keeping them from departing, more than in
"tendency," from the historical original.   Returning
to the scene of the delivery of the parable, what comes
before us is that Jesus continued and, in all probability,
concluded his lessons for ordinary life at this time by
telling his disciples that, above all things, the main
interest for them was to be found in being kind to one
another.   When the King would come in glory, he ^{Mt. xxv.}
said, He would say to his own "sheep," "Come, ye ^{34-40.}
blessed of my Father, inherit the kingdom prepared
for you from the foundation of the world : For I was
an hungered, and ye gave me meat : I was thirsty, and
ye gave me drink : I was a stranger, and ye took me
in : Naked, and ye clothed me : I was sick, and ye
visited me : I was in prison, and ye came unto me."
" Then shall the righteous," he continued, "answer
him, saying, Lord, when saw we thee an hungered,
and fed thee ? or thirsty and gave thee drink ?   When
saw we thee a stranger and took thee in ? or naked, and
clothed thee ?   Or when saw we thee sick, or in prison,
and came unto thee ?   And the King shall answer and
say unto them, Verily I say unto you, Inasmuch as ye
have done it unto one of the least of these my brethren,
ye have done it unto me."   See App.
                                                      1. (22).
    The other incidents having teaching connected with
them are easily made sure of.   They are, most of them,
related in simple language, and may be accepted as
having happened much as they are related.

    A certain scribe came and asked him what he taught
to be the first commandment of all.   He answered, ^{Mk. xii.}
" The first of all the commandments is, Hear, O Israel ; ^{28-34.}

The Lord our God is one Lord: and thou shalt love the Lord thy God with all thy heart, and with all thy soul, and with all thy mind, and with all thy strength. This is the first commandment. And the second is like, namely this, Thou shalt love thy neighbour as thyself. There is none other commandment greater than these." The scribe was evidently impressed with the teaching, as well he might be, and said, agreeing with Jesus, that indeed to love God first and then to love one's neighbour, as Jesus had said, was "more than all whole burnt offerings and sacrifices." Jesus, in his turn, was pleased with the scribe, and said to him, "Thou art not far from the kingdom of God."

Luke gives—in the long disconnected chapters in the middle of his gospel—a story very like the account of this incident in Mark and Matthew. It is evidently another account of this incident, seeing that the essential points are much the same. And though Luke has related it out of its true historical connection, he has told that it led to Jesus speaking a parable which most naturally fits to the time here recognised as the true time in which it occurred. It is very likely, as Luke relates, that this incident led to the Parable of the *Good Samaritan*. How exactly it did so we cannot be quite sure, as it is not likely that, as Luke suggests, this earnest scribe made an endeavour "to justify himself." Probably Jesus led on to it by way of making plain what he meant to teach, himself stating the question, "And who is my neighbour?" At any rate, the parable is beyond question a parable of Jesus; and in accordance with what we have already seen, its names of Samaritan and Jericho seem

Lk. x. 25-37.

Lk. x. 29. For similar mistake cp. ver. 25. "tempted him." Luke's explanatory phrases

to fix it to this time of Jesus's ministry. The road have been
on which Jesus had lately travelled had, no doubt, subjected to much
suggested it, and now he stated it in its complete investiga-tion.
beauty, to the instruction and admiration of ages to See above,
come. p. 223.

Again, they were near the treasury of the temple on
one of the days, and Jesus noticed a poor woman
giving her offering. He said to his disciples words
that need no comment. "Verily I say unto you," he Mk. xii.
said, "that this poor widow hath cast more in than 41·44.
all they which have cast into the treasury : for all they
did cast in of their abundance; but she of her want did
cast in all that she had, even all her living."

The incidents that come to us through the Fourth
Gospel account are, of course, less easily made sure of
than the two just noticed. Even they, however, can
be traced and accepted through criticism.

The story of *Nicodemus*, who came to Jesus by night, Jn. iii.
must for our present purpose be bereft of all the
teaching given by the evangelist in connection with
it, as it is certain all that teaching is, in the main,
the evangelist's own, not Jesus's, and any little echo
in it of Jesus's teaching is too faint for us to make
anything of it for our history. The stripped hulk
which is left us is such as to suggest that it has been
originally one and the same with the story of the
earnest scribe related above, though on that we
need not make certain. The mention of Nicodemus,
however, by the Fourth Evangelist has its special value.
The evangelist himself evidently introduces Nicodemus
by way of showing how a learned man was in essentials
quite unlearned in comparison with Jesus; and that
point even is not without its importance. The chief

value, however, of the story of Nicodemus, stripped of its unhistorical accompaniments, will appear further on, when we see how Nicodemus comes forward again in two notices most worthy of acceptance.

Jn. viii. 1-11. The well-known story of *Jesus and the woman taken in adultery* may be accepted as the account of a real incident, and one that happened at this time. There are great difficulties, indeed, in regard to accepting it. It is recognised by Pfleiderer, however, and a good many others. Most commentators do not recognise it as an original part of the Fourth Gospel itself, because it is not found in the best manuscripts. And it has been very ably explained as being a later particularising of the general fact of Jesus associating with " publicans and sinners." Keim. We may recognise it, however, as a genuine account— whether it belonged to the Gospel of John originally or Eusebius's Hist., iii. 39. Interesting on this subject is the attempted reconstruction of the " Gospel of the Hebrews " by Nicholson. Some scholars take the passage as having been original in the Mark text, comparing Lk. xxi. 37-38. See Wittichen and Holtzmann. Jn. ix. not—from its naturalness, and from a suggestiveness in it too great to have its origin in anything fictitious, and in consideration of the fact that, though it is not allowed by most scholars to be a part of the original Fourth Gospel, it is sufficiently attested as being an ancient story.

Another incident comes to us from the Fourth Gospel as having happened at this time. It is one that has got mingled with an incident already noticed here ; and it seems to have been the occasion of some very important teaching of Jesus. We had before us, at the end of last chapter, a certain man confessing that he had been "blind" before Jesus came, and that Jesus had opened his eyes. The narrative in the Fourth Gospel which presents this has obviously been freely applied by the evangelist. But there seems to have been in some way connected with it—perhaps as one of the sayings of Jesus which

influenced the man—an utterance claiming Jesus's
authorship by its fitting to much else that he said,
as a link in a chain. It is an utterance that plainly
must have been given in relation to some sufferer,
quite probably a literally blind man, and it is this,
" Neither hath this man sinned, nor his parents: but Jn. ix. 3.
(he suffers, understood) that the works of God should
be made manifest in him." It will be seen by the
reader how the miracle related by the evangelist spoils
the general meaning of these most suggestive words.
Except for the miracle, the words might suggest sweet
comfort to the many afflicted who know they have no
miracles to depend on, but can only depend on the
ever-unfailing care of the heavenly Father. Criticism,
however, restores those words of Jesus to the class of
people to whom Jesus dedicated his life and teaching
—the blind, the lame, the captives, the broken-hearted.
The miracle taken literally is unhistorical, as has See above,
partly appeared above. The words, on the other hand, p. 258.
are evidently genuine, and besides being themselves of
deep meaning, they show how Jesus had now quite
thrown off all adherence to the popular belief that
sufferings were the punishment of special sins. Sufferings, Jesus now taught explicitly, were not necessarily
to be looked at as punishments; they were, on the other
hand, however, to be looked at as opportunities for
the kindness of God. Probably it was at this time
that he spoke further in the same strain, as Luke
relates. The disciples were, no doubt, interested in
what he had said as suggested by the case of the
afflicted man; and so Jesus went on to give further
examples. Talking of some Galileans whom Pilate,
the governor, had caused to be put to death, he said,

18

Lk. xiii. 2-
5. We
find, in-
deed, a
small
trace of
these very
sayings in
the Fourth
Gospel ac-
count in
the word
" Siloam "
(v. 7).
The word,
left alone
like one
wall of a
ruined
house, has
been over-
grown
with
legend.

" Suppose ye that these Galileans were sinners above all the Galileans, because they suffered such things? I tell you, Nay." And then he added, " Or those eighteen, upon whom the tower in Siloam fell, and slew them, think ye that they were sinners above all men that dwelt in Jerusalem? I tell you, Nay." Luke, we may be sure, has not caught the point of these sayings, when in his account he has added the words, " But, except ye repent, ye shall all likewise perish." These words, we may be sure, are a filling up either by Luke himself or, more likely, by a church exposition in which the whole passage reached Luke. The real point of the sayings, assuredly, has not to do with repentance, but with the Divine Care, which is above the range of small retributive considerations, and will in the end be seen to have been kind to all.

CHAPTER XVIII

SELF-DEFENCE AND TEACHING IN CONNECTION.

It is pleasant to dwell on the cases that have come before us in the last three chapters, of successful receptions with which our Lord met in his visit to Jerusalem. The crowd strewing his path with leaves to honour him, the children shouting in praise of him, the man who through his teaching received new sight, and, last not least, the earnest scribe who recognised the value of his teaching, are all pleasant to contemplate. We have now, however, to turn to the other side of the picture. We have to fix our minds on the fact that from the first there had been growing a determined and vindictive opposition on the part of the legally appointed priests and scribes in general. It could not well have been otherwise. Jesus, having had former experience of the class they belonged to, had not this time waited for interference from them, but had himself begun with a direct attack on them. Besides this, it is almost certain, as we have seen, that the priests and the scribes of Jerusalem had been in communication for some time with those in the north, so that they had been for some time prejudiced against

Mk. iii. 22, vii. 1

18 *

him. It was inevitable that now they would act as
his sworn enemies. Enemies indeed they were, we
find, and as enemies indeed they acted. They, partly
openly, but more quietly, set themselves from the first
to destroy, if not his life, at least his position in the
minds of the people. And at the same time they
began to look to getting him into trouble with the
political authorities, the representatives of Rome. As
in the case of the oppositions in the north, we are
now to see, this opposition called forth some of the
finest teaching of Jesus, and led to the assertion of
his character.

The chief weapon which the priests and their allies
used against him was one that was well chosen; and
how they used it comes before us in the gospels very
plainly. Those enemies of Jesus knew well that what
gave him his immediate influence with the many—let
alone what would give him a lasting influence with
the many—was the connection of him in the people's
minds with the *Messiah-character*. This connection,
therefore, they set themselves to destroy, and they
managed their attempt ably. The Messiah! Who
was the Messiah? A certain expected deliverer, told
of in the Scriptures! They, who were practised in
interpreting the Scriptures, then, had surely a mastery
of the subject in comparison with the ignorant populace! Thus they set themselves to show, from their
study of the letter of Scripture, how it was impossible
for Jesus to be that " Messiah " who was described in
the Scripture. The Messiah, they pointed out, was to
be a son of David, and to be born in Bethlehem.
How then, they asked, could he be recognised in this
man of notorious Galilean parentage and birth? The

venomous power that this sort of reasoning exercised
on the minds of the people is made plain to us by
the very fact that the earlier gospels seem to avoid
emphasising it, as well as by the two later of these
gospels having prefixed to them stories which, if we
take them literally, gainsay the Galilean parentage
and birth of Jesus. But the earlier gospels, with that Mk. xii.
honesty which really never deserts them, have given 35-37.
us a short notice in which it is possible for us to
read the facts. And the Fourth Gospel, which was Jn. vii. 26-
written in a quarter where the question, as we may 28, 40-43.
believe, no longer appeared to be one of much 52.
importance, discloses much more fully what took place.

On hearing of the opposition being placed on the
basis thus indicated, Jesus, we learn, said something
like this: " How say the scribes that Christ is the Mk. xii.
son of David? For David himself said by the Holy 35-37.
Ghost, The Lord said to my Lord, Sit thou on my
right hand, till I make thine enemies thy footstool.
David therefore himself calleth him Lord ; and whence
is he then his son ? " This saying may at first seem little
raised above the scribes' own plane of thinking. But
there is in it a thought in accordance with the mind
that produced it. Indeed, as we have seen repeatedly,
it was Jesus's way to answer his objectors first on
their own ground, and then to lead them to a higher
plane of thinking. And here, we can see, there was
a thought of real worth expressed even in his words
which seemed to be limiting themselves to the scribes'
dark wanderings in interpretation of Scripture. The
thought was that this Messiah, or deliverer, being one
that was to be greater than David, should surely have
a freedom attached to his appearance. If a deliverer

was coming to them from God—the words meant—
that deliverer must not be tied down, in the way of
his coming, by the likeness of men who had gone
before, but must have a way of coming of his own.

We must learn also, however, from our careful
sifting of the Fourth Gospel account, that Jesus said
something more than this in regard to the opposition
placed on this ground. He had all along, we know,
been demanding that his claim to be heard be judged
by his "works" or "fruits"; that is, by the natural
outcomes of his personality, showing forth the soul
and mind there were within. He had also ever been
angry and grieved at this canon not being applied to
him. And so we shall be inclined to recognise as
really his own these words of indignation, spoken
evidently in answer to the repeated murmurings about

Jn. vii. 28.
Cp. ver. 27
w. ver. 28;
regarding
ver. 27 see
App. I.
(13). For
language
cp. Mk.
xii. 14.
his origin not being the right one for a Messiah, "Ye
both know me, and ye know whence I am : and I am
not come of myself, but he that sent me is true."

While the priests and the scribes thus sought to
undermine his influence with the people, they also
began to try and involve him with the political
authorities. That they were dishonest when they
did so is clear. He had taken pains, as we have
seen, to impress upon them that his aim was not a

Above, p.
244.
political one. But honesty seems to have had little
to do with their motives. What they did in the
direction of bringing him into trouble with the
political authorities is thus related by Mark : "And
they send unto him certain of the Pharisees and of

Vers. 13-
17.
the Herodians, to catch him in his words. And when
they were come, they say unto him, Master, we know
that thou art true, and carest for no man; for thou

regardest not the person of men, but teachest the
way of God in truth : Is it lawful to give tribute to
Cæsar, or not ?   Shall we give, or shall we not give ? "
Who the " Herodians " were is not known.   From
the name it is plain they would be a party attached
to the house of Herod.   But it is uncertain whether
they were a party so far loyal to the existing government, submitting, for the time, like the Pharisees and
Sadducees, or were a party specially suspected of
readiness to rise in rebellion ; and the determining
of this point makes a difference as to what was
meant by the priests and their allies in employing
them.   On the whole, the account leads to the opinion
that they were a rather suspected party, and that the
priests actually stooped to the meanness of employing
them to try and lead Jesus on to utter something
which might be reported in such a way as to give it
a rebellious import, through his supposing that the
less respectfully he spoke of the government the more
he would please these men.   Jesus, however, simply
answered them by calling for a coin, pointing to the
image of the Roman emperor on it, and saying these
words, now famous, " Render to Cæsar the things that Mk. xii.
are Cæsar's, and to God the things that are God's." [17]
They " marvelled at him," the account adds ; and
this is doubtless quite true regarding these men who
directly spoke to him.   As regards the priests, however, the failure of their treacherous aim did not,
as we find, prevent them from proceeding farther
more determinedly in the same direction.

We may accept the little notice which the Fourth Jn. vii. 50.
Gospel contains, in which *Nicodemus*—that learned [52]
man who was impressed by Jesus—tried to intercede

for him with his own fellows. It is in every way probable that Nicodemus did say a good word for Jesus to some of those who were against him, and that he informed some of the followers of this, thus bringing about the recording of the fact. It is also most probable, as our record declares, that when Nicodemus did this he was answered with the taunt, "Art thou also of Galilee?"

We shall not meet Nicodemus again in our little history of Jesus's ministry; but we may pause here to remember that there is one more notice of him in the Fourth Gospel, which convincingly recommends itself to acceptance. It is to the effect that after Jesus's death this man assisted another man of position, named Joseph of Arimathea, to bury the body of Jesus, and brought spices, according to "the manner of the Jews" "to bury."

The whole story of Nicodemus, as it remains to us after criticism, is a natural one and a valuable one. A learned writer of our own time has expressed the belief that Jesus must himself have belonged to the higher classes, so cultured was his teaching, apart from being sublime in character. Evidence is against this belief regarding our Lord's class position. But surely here, in this story of Nicodemus, we have the nearest approach in fact to that supposition. If Jesus really did not belong to the classes that have the most leisure for education and study, he at least could attract to himself one who did belong to these classes. Nicodemus was not the only man of the higher classes who, even in the lifetime of Jesus, was impressed by him. But he seems to have very specially appreciated him, more, probably, than Jesus himself learned before his death.

(marginal notes:)
Jn. xix. 38-40.

Conway, Essay on Christian- ity. (He appeals also to 2 Cor. viii. 9.)

It was no easy thing for a man of position to get into touch with Jesus, so short was his public life, and so separated from conventional lines was the path on which he chose to travel.   But we are to believe that this Rabbi Nicodemus visited privately the Teacher who had charmed him, tried to save him from the tiger-like attack that was made on him, and finally paid to him in his death a last tribute of reverence and affection.

A piece of opposition, of little account in itself, but leading to an important reply from Jesus, was made by some of the party of the Sadducees.   This party, as we learn, was a worldly and somewhat aristocratic party. Its members accepted offices in the priesthood, but were not very religious, not believing, indeed, even in the resurrection.   Some flippant members of this party, having listened to Jesus's prophetic sayings telling of God and of a world to come, asked him, as they met him, Suppose, as Moses taught, seven men should, one after another, marry the same woman, whose wife would she be in the resurrection?   Jesus answered, "Do ye not therefore err, because ye know not the Scriptures, neither the power of God?   For when they shall rise from the dead, they neither marry, nor are given in marriage; but are as the angels which are in heaven."   And then he added: "And as touching the dead, that they rise; have ye not read in the book of Moses, how in the bush God spake unto him, saying, I am the God of Abraham, and the God of Isaac, and the God of Jacob?   He is not the God of the dead, but the God of the living: ye therefore do greatly err." This latter saying of Jesus, in his own concrete manner as it is, contains, we may say, both of the two

Mk. xii. 18-27.

Acts v. 17. xxiii. 8.

Deut. xxv. 5.

Mk. xii. 24, 25.

Vers. 26, 27.

This incident reported in doctrinised form in Jn. viii. 52-59.

eternal bases on which a belief in the immortality of
the soul rests—namely, the truth of *the value of each
living soul*, and the truth of *the Care of God for each living
soul*. These two truths, we know, were both ruling
truths in Jesus's mind. And now we must discern
that the Old Testament words which at this time he
quoted, had on some occasion come before his mind,
influenced as it was by these two truths, and that,
reading them as an expression of both the truths, he
had noticed that they presented a quaint and forcible
illustration of the truth of immortality. The care of
God was Jesus's supremely ruling truth. And we may
say he had seen this truth, to begin with, expressed in
those old words about Abraham and Isaac and Jacob,
so far at least as Abraham and Isaac and Jacob
were concerned. He had then argued, we are to
believe—and he now meant the Sadducees to argue
similarly—How could such a Care as he discerned to
exist in the Divine Presence forsake those it watched
over and enriched, after a few short years? This was
involved in the remark he now made after quoting the
old words. When he said God could not be the God
of the dead, he certainly did not mean to refer the
matter to written testimony, and that through the
means of a logical quibble; his words, in their real
meaning, were as much as to say that the Care of God,
which had been so far expressed in the old words
quoted by him, was such that it was ridiculous to
think of it as extended to its objects only for a mere
span of time. The truth of the value of man, however,
was Jesus's second truth; and we must say he had
seen this also expressed in the Old Testament words.
Abraham, Isaac, and Jacob were, to the Israelite mind,

names of the Great. And we may suppose he now felt that their names might appeal even to these flippant Sadducees, seeing they were still Israelites, and inspire in them something of that belief in Man which was moving himself. It had been implied then, also, in the argument which he had on some former occasion had before himself, what he also now meant the Sadducees to be influenced by, that the names of those Great Ones—names that raised indescribable emotions in their hearts—surely could not be the names of some-thing dead only. And this was also involved in the remark he now made after quoting the old words. When he said God could not be the God of the dead, there was also contained in this the idea that it was ridiculous to think of beings that had been singled out to be the recipients of care on the part of God, so majestically expressed in the ancient words, as having been themselves nothing more than passing phenomena, breathing for a few years and then vanishing away.

This truth of the value of man, or value of the soul, used thus by Jesus as a ground for the belief in immor-tality, was similarly used by Plato, the Greek philoso-pher, and perhaps by Socrates before him, though of course it was stated by Plato in a very different way from the way in which Jesus stated it. In the book called the ' Phædo,' in which the subject of immor-tality is keenly and thoroughly discussed, there is a point emphasised in passing, in a poetical rather than a ratiocinative way, so that the matter is referred, something in the manner of Jesus, to what is generally implied in the facts of life, rather than to the deduc-tions made in the particular arguments of the book. This point is that the souls within us are existences that *govern* or *initiate*, and thus are not like perishable things.   In the ' Phædo ' Plato represents Socrates as

Jowett's transla- tion, i. 473.

speaking of the soul, and saying that the soul is to be found " leading the elements of which she is believed to be composed ; almost always opposing them and coercing them in all sorts of ways throughout life." The ground of belief in immortality here made use of, is the fact that the nature of the soul is such that the soul is too great to perish.   It is so far the same ground of belief as was pointed to by Jesus when he solemnly named the names of Abraham, Isaac, and Jacob, whom all reverenced and God Himself cared for.   And one and all of us will be able to see specially the strength of this ground of belief, when we may become impressed by certain personalities that have gained general reverence and have shown themselves beings of a value which is more than can be measured.

And now we must conclude this part of our subject by mustering forth a number of more general sayings of Jesus, which were occasioned by the opposition to him in general.   These are mostly *private sayings.* They are found principally in the Fourth Gospel alone, and there only by a careful process of separation from other material ; but one or two of them can be traced also in the earlier gospels, and they are all in striking agreement with the whole contents of the earlier gospels.   They bring their own guarantee of authen- ticity.   They are words of genius, and at the same time words of strong personal emotion.   That they are indeed words of Jesus, the presentation of them now must be left to show.

First, then, we learn, as he was oppressed by the unreasonableness and unkindness of the opposition, and as, in accordance with all we have seen of his character, he hated the self-assertive position in which for the time he was placed, he spoke some words of which, we must believe, the following sentences give at least a nearly correct report: " My doctrine is not mine, Jn. vii. 16. but his that sent me. . . . He that speaketh of himself 18, viii. 28 seeketh his own glory ; but he that seeketh his glory that sent him, the same is true. . . . When ye have lifted up the Son of man, then shall ye know that I . . . do nothing of myself; but as my Father hath taught me, I speak these things."

As, again, he felt the greatness of his soul and the grandeur of his teaching assuring him, were it against a whole nation opposing him, of his worth as a teacher, and of the certainty of his ultimate recognition as such, he said words that in John are reported this way : " Yet a little while am I with you, and then I go unto Jn. vii. 33. him that sent me. Ye shall seek me, and shall not 34. find me ;" and in Matthew this way : " I say unto you, Mt. xxiii. Ye shall not see me henceforth, till ye shall say, 39. Blessed is he that cometh in the name of the Lord." Quoting Ps. cxviii. The words are in both reports practically the same ; 26. it hardly matters which, if either, is the literally correct report. The saying, as it was originally, must be looked at as representing Jesus's *consolation* in his distress at not being received by the people he loves.

Again, as he felt the loneliness and the horror of his situation, supported as he was only by men mostly uninfluential and ignorant, and ominously opposed by the whole strength of those in authority in a great city, he gave utterance, we must believe, to these words, " He that sent me is with me : *my* Father hath Jn. viii. not left me alone." It was very natural that such a 29.

simple and affecting utterance as this should go home to the hearts of the hearers, and that, as we find Ver. 30. recorded in the gospel, "as he spake these words, many believed on him."

Again, probably after his Parable of the Good Samaritan had been uttered, some miserable man came up to him with the coarse and stupid exclamation, Vers. 48-50. "Say we not well that thou art a Samaritan, and hast a devil?" He answered, "I have not a devil; but I honour my Father. . . . And I seek not mine own glory."

Then, lastly, as he felt keenly disappointed at the unimpressionableness he had met with in the city, he spoke some words which have been lengthened out and formed into an imaginative doctrinal discourse in the tenth chapter of John. He sought to explain a little to himself the facts that had led to his disappointment. For this he had recourse to the familiar Hebrew imagery of *Sheep and Shepherd*, and through that imagery expressed a thought which he had once before Jn. x. 1-6, used to explain oppositions. He said that he was a 26-29. Shepherd; that he was a good Shepherd, who would even give his life for the sheep; that his own sheep would follow himself alone, because they knew his voice, and knew not the voice of strangers; that those that did not listen to him were not his own sheep; and finally, that his own sheep had been given to him, and that because they had been given by his Father, who was greater than all, they would never perish, and no one could ever pluck them out of his hand.

That these sayings, which we can separate from the rest of the tenth chapter of John, are genuine sayings of Jesus, uttered at this time, will strongly recommend itself from the fact that, according to the early Gospel Mk. vi. 34, of Mark, not only was the imagery in them used by xiv. 27. Jesus in a similar connection, but we find him dwelling on this imagery a very short time after the point to which our history has now brought us. Their authenticity will, however, further recommend itself when we notice how, in the simple meaning which they bear when separated from the rest of the chapter, they accord so well with Jesus's character, and fit so exactly to the circumstances in which he was now placed. In the evangelist's discourse, indeed, the idea is just the Old See Ezek. Testament idea of God watching over His people as a xxxiv. 11-15. shepherd watches over his sheep, Jesus being identified with God. In the separated words, on the other hand, the idea is a very different one. As we have seen, it is an idea that was evidently resorted to by Jesus by way of explaining the opposition which had pained him. Having appealed to the people, having reproached them, having in some way consoled himself for their not receiving him, he in the end *explained* their opposition to him ; and his explanation was this, that, as we may put it, only certain souls were, for the time at least, *given him*, and that these received him joyfully.

We have before seen Jesus explaining to himself the irrational opposition which he had met with in Galilee. In Galilee he first rested on the partial Mt. xii. explanation that, at least, it was not so bad in the 31. 32. See above, p. people as if they had been resisting the Divine Spirit 152. itself, independently of any connection with a particular man. But when he went to Nazareth, and found an Lk. iv. 23. opposition which surprised him less than in other 27. See above, p. places, he brought forward the very same idea for 169.

explanation which now again meets us—namely, that,
like other prophets, he had limitations imposed on his
immediate mission.   This time he expressed the idea
through the imagery of sheep and Shepherd ; once
more before his death, as we shall see, he expressed it
dissociated from the imagery again.   This time he
said that some were given him to be his own sheep.
And it may be he really also introduced the idea
contained in some words about entering the fold by
the door, which have got confusedly mixed up with
the words under consideration in the evangelist's
account—the idea, namely, that he had got his influence over these sheep by nature touching nature, or by
power and consideration entering through the natural
responsiveness of the heart.   The thought of these
sheep, who were his own, afforded him joy amidst all
the painful opposition.   If others than these would not
receive him, then these, on the contrary, listened to no
other than himself.   He alone was their own, and they
his own.   With an intensity that drove it beyond this
world's limitations, his affection for these special ones
asserted itself.   "They shall never perish," he said,
" neither shall any man pluck them out of my hand. My
Father, which gave them me, is greater than all; and
no man is able to pluck them out of my Father's hand."

Of such a nature, then, was the teaching of Jesus,
which was occasioned by his defending himself against
the authorities of Jerusalem during the few days that
he spent in the city as a prophet.   The dire events
which quickly followed must be left to be entered on in
another chapter.   Let this one close with our last
look at Jesus in that position of command to which
his personality entitled him.

Jn. x. 2.

Vers. 28,
29.

CHAPTER XIX.

WELL may earnest worshippers of Jesus have a wish for a moment to stop the contemplation of his life at this point. Why, they may ask, must they look at him in his humiliation? and what good can arise from dwelling in thought on the sufferings of his sensitive spirit, and on the brutality of his unworthy contemporaries? Better, they may be inclined to say, to stop with the impression of his majestic humanity, which demands from those who look at it a belief in its duration beyond the span of time in this world, and, taking for granted the break, the wrench, the interruption of power and beauty which came to his person as to the person of every one, go forward in imagination to dwell on the glories beyond. But the wish thus to escape the sight of what now asks our attention, excusable as it is arising and lasting for a moment, is to be overcome, on the promise of this, that Jesus, as he walks through the valley of the shadow of death, shows at their very best both the greatness and the sweetness of his character. Jesus must be seen in his last extremity to be known and valued. The repellent nature of the surroundings is not more marked than the grandeur of soul that appears within the surroundings. And though sympathy for the awful sufferings of Jesus will rigidly prevent us from drawing out the portrayal of them further than may be necessary, the chapters which tell of them must be faced, because they are at the same time chapters which tell of his glory.

Mk. xiv. 1.   The priests, or appointed ministers of religion, and along with them, the scribes, or recognised teachers of religion, decided, soon after Jesus's public appearance in the city, to have him destroyed. Destroyed—yes, made away with in any manner. They had formed a plan well fitted to accomplish this. They were going
Mk. xii. 15. xv. 1.   to make out to the Roman governor that he was a rebel against the Roman Power, at the same time as
Mk. xii. 35: Jn vii. 52. &c.   they made out to their own people that he was a false Messiah. They saw, probably in a few days, that they had him in their hands. The first excitement of the people over him was subsiding, and the venom of their
Above. pp. 276, ff.   own pedantic arguments against him was taking effect. They set themselves against him, therefore, boldly, with an appetite to tear him asunder.

Why did they do it? and how could they do it? are questions which arise in every honest mind. That men could act so wickedly, and that One so great and good could excite such merciless hostility, are considerations which arouse the wonder of succeeding ages. The explanation is to be found, no doubt, simply in the idea brought forward as explanation in
Mk. xv. 10.   the gospels, namely, that *envy* was at the root of their conduct. And if we cannot understand an envy so

demoniacal, we are to remember what was the state of development which these men had reached. They were half barbarians, these men. Jesus himself gave the most kindly estimate of his persecutors when he suggested the likeness between the one he first feared, Herod, and a *jackal*. These men were little different from Herod in moral restraint and spiritual enlightenment. _{Above, p. 180.} They had some knowledge, indeed, and had a religion; but their knowledge was of things little worth knowing, and their religion was itself both formal and super-stitious, and also had not sufficient power over them to elevate them above the passions aroused by injured conceit and the sense of being supplanted. They were half-barbarians, these men. They were not fiends, plotting dramatically against all that is pure and good; but they were only half-civilised men, who, finding themselves disturbed by a Being of a superior character, and knowing that they could kill their dis-turber and get rid of him, without much troubling of conscience, because they were stupid and vainly satisfied with their own rightness of conduct, embraced the opportunity, as a wild animal might turn on a Man that had disturbed its rest.

See Renan, c. 1 p. 159 in Eng. Transl.

So had those priests and religious teachers deter-mined to destroy Jesus; and Jesus knew full well of their determination. What it meant for him to know this is repressed in the gospels; but it may be brought out of silence for a moment and thought of quite consistently with the deepest reverence, as without this being done we should miss a link in the chain of events. What it meant for him we can know, though the gospels do not express it. It meant disappoint-ment to the death, the vanishing of the last flashes

Mk. xiv. 27, &c.

19 *

that had made returning light a possibility, the
remaining of nothing to be seen ahead in this world
but a vista of black darkness. He had weeks before
formed his heroic resolve, with a full appreciation of
its almost certain consequences; but power is never
exercised without a lingering hope of achievement, and
no thoughtful mind can entertain the notion that Jesus
proclaimed his message in Jerusalem with all hope of
worldly success gone. He had come to Jerusalem,
seeing possible two alternatives, of which one, alas!
was very shadowy, but still there. The few days had
brought before him which of the alternatives it was to
be. It was to be the one he had been all but certain
of from the first. His heroic action was to mean his
death. And Jesus flinched not in his resolution. He
had come to take what God would allow to befall him;
and now he turned not back.

And if there must present itself to our minds the
question, Could not all this have been avoided; could not
Jesus have lived many years unmolested, a teacher of his
great ideas in Galilee, had he but taken up a less aggressive position? the answer is on the surface. He could not
have done this and yet have remained true to his ideas,
in that the ideas themselves involved his taking the
best means in his power to have them made known to
mankind. All, indeed, that we have seen of him, from
this point backwards, takes its rise in the principle
Mk. iv. 21, expressed in the " candle " saying, with which, as we
22. Above, have deduced, he first left Nazareth. His whole
p. 41.
conduct and his whole thought form together an
organic realisation of that principle; and there is not
one weak spot from beginning to end. Even the
foresight, discerning that death would not prevent the

spreading of his ideas which his bold appeal to his
countrymen was meant to accomplish, was itself an
outcome of this principle, and organically related to
his action. It was as much as to say that, seeing
God had given him a message to declare, he knew that
when he did declare it nothing would be permitted to
triumph against him.

But did he accept the personal discomfiture without
a moment of pause to consider? That would show a
departure from the custom which we have hitherto
seen observed by him. All, therefore, that we have
seen urges us at this point to scrutinise the accounts, in
search of evidence for Jesus having made some small
retreat from his enemies, of the kind we have before
had knowledge of—some small retreat in which, now
that the outlook had become more definite, he might
pause and consider what he was facing. Artistic unity
asks for this. And it is now to be added that the
records, when critically observed, will be found to
supply what we are thus urged to seek.

It is, indeed, the Fourth Gospel alone that gives us
the detail of this last withdrawal of Jesus. But keeping
to the way of reading the Fourth Gospel which we
have all along been following, we must have, to begin
with, an expectation of finding some real history in the
long passage made up by the eleventh and twelfth
chapters; and on reading the passage carefully and
critically, we shall find ourselves not disappointed.
We shall find a sacred historical reality, which is not
less revealing, not less commanding, and more winning,
than would be the state of facts were the representation
capable of being taken with absolute literalness.

Nor are we even here altogether deserted by the

earlier gospels.   They have themselves, indeed, nothing to tell us of the little **event now to** engage us; but their account is in absolute agreement with its having taken place, and indeed may, in some measure, be said to confirm its having taken place.   For—taking Mark, the earliest and most trustworthy—

Mk. xiv.
1, 2.

(1.) Mark leads up to his description of **the** events connected with the Passover-day in these words: "After two days was the feast of the passover, **and of** unleavened bread: and the chief priests and the scribes sought how they might take him by craft, and put him **to death.   But they said, Not on** the feast day, lest there **be an uproar of the people.''** Now these words may quite **well be interpreted, and** indeed, when **one** thinks a little, are **most simply** interpreted, **as being** an indication of a two **days' gap in** the evangelist's narrative, the doings of Jesus **on the two days** meant having not been suitable to be recorded for the evangelist's purpose.   Even if they were taken to mean **that** at the point to which the narrative has come it was **two days** to the *night* of the Passover, there would still remain **large parts of** Jesus's time not recorded and evidently **not** having **been** taken up with teaching in Jerusalem, **and** there would also still remain a gap **in the** narrative, inasmuch as **it** is in no way indicated why Jesus stopped teaching in Jerusalem.   When, then, **we** remember that hitherto Mark has not been specifying the time taken up by the events he has been recording **(the events** involved **in the** twelfth and thirteenth **chapters** being far too **many** to have happened in one day), we may conclude, and reasonably conclude, that **he** is not here, any more than before, specifying the time of **the** events he is relating but is

Cp. Mk.
ix. 2. See
App. I.
(19).

Cp. also
Mk.xiv.49,
"daily."

indeed indicating a complete gap in his narrative, leaving unrecorded the events of two days. This conclusion is greatly supported by the fact that we find it in striking accordance with what meets us in the Fourth Gospel. In the Fourth Gospel account there comes the following sentence, in a connection so utterly different from that of the sentence just quoted in Mark that it is impossible to regard it as having been adopted by the evangelist from Mark, " When he had heard therefore that he was sick, he abode TWO DAYS still in the same place where he was." This sentence, as we shall see presently, has all the appearance of having been originally a separate account of what Mark relates, a little more full, and made intelligible by its relation to the other material which we are to extract from the Fourth Gospel. *Same holds, taking Mt. instead of Mk. Jn. xi. 6.*

(2.) Mark proceeds to give, in something of a want of connection, the account of Jesus sitting in a house in Bethany, and of a woman coming in and honouring him. This story, as presented in Mark, reminding one of the Galilean period, very much requires explanation, as the idea of Jesus having calmly sat in a house, with people coming from the outside to do him honour, seems out of keeping with the time in which the storm was raging that was to take away his life. The explanation is given, as we shall see, in a critical reading of the Fourth Gospel account. *Mk. xiv. 3-9.*

And (3) there is a decided confirmation of a withdrawal of Jesus at this time in the idea introduced by all the gospels, that Jesus was *betrayed* to his enemies. Betrayed, we ask, from what? If he was still going daily to and from Bethany and Jerusalem, where was the difficulty for his enemies to take him? Now the *Ver. 10.*

Lk. xxii.
2-6 ; Mk.
xiv. 1, 2.
question is so far answered in the earlier gospels, in that they say the priests wished to get him in private, in order to avoid the chance of the crowd making a resistance in his favour. But Jesus was not, at this time, always surrounded by a crowd ; and it would have been easy, according to the accounts, for them to have him followed to his night's lodging at Bethany, where he would be nearly alone. The betrayal becomes intelligible when it is believed that they had indeed thus had him followed, and that Jesus, knowing of that as well as of their resolve to destroy him, had avoided Bethany for some two days.

To all this it is to be added that here, as everywhere, the Synoptic gospels are dramatic, and that so their silence is explained. The presentation of the last act in the appearance of the Messiah made little account of this withdrawal of Jesus, before he would yield to those men that were like beasts of prey. The event, however, has a keen historical importance and interest. And we are to be thankful that he whose aim was to portray not the *appearance of the Messiah* but the *incarnation of the Logos* has retained a record of the event in a form sufficiently clear and convincing for the establishment of credence in regard to it.

Gathering, then, what happened as regards the withdrawal, we are to say something as follows :—

Above, p.
241.
As we saw in a previous chapter, Jesus had evidently during the evenings at Bethany been forming a close friendship with one Martha, along with her sister and Jn. xi. brother. It is by reasoning back from the events and the account of them which are now to engage our attention, that that conclusion is reached. The names of the sister and brother, we are now to learn, were

Mary and Lazarus. All mention of Lazarus has been left out in the earlier gospels—except an indirect reference in Luke, to which we shall come presently; and the reason for the silence we can take to be this, that Lazarus, from the time of the arrival of Jesus, had been nothing but a poor invalid, whom even the followers of Jesus probably, with one or two exceptions, had never seen. We can imagine, however, that Jesus was specially drawn in sympathy towards the poor man, from the very fact that he saw how both he himself and the poor man were approaching very nearly, though by vastly different ways, the mysterious "sleep" which ends all this world's experience. In Jn. xi. 11. the course of a week or so, then, Jesus and his immediate followers found themselves tracked to Bethany. And we may learn that some of those who thus tracked them threw some stones at them. On this happening, Jesus turned and said, "Many good works have I showed Jn. x. 31-38. Cp. you from my Father; for which of those works do ye xi. 8. stone me?" To this some bold fellow replied: "For a good work we stone thee not; but for blasphemy; and because that thou, being a man, makest thyself Ver. 33. God." And Jesus, in reply, appealed, according to his custom, to the Scripture, for the conception of the Vers. 34-36. relation in general of man to God, and to his own works for his own special relationship. It was then, however, we gather, that Jesus saw he could not safely remain about his lodging in Bethany, and so Ver. 39. resolved upon a last retreat, to consider his position.

Where he went this time, we do not learn exactly. The Fourth Gospel gives two statements about it; but the evangelist has evidently become confused in applying his material. He rightly relates the retreat

Vers. 39, 40.
first as having taken place before the incident about
Lazarus. But it would seem he has found, in the
material in his possession, another assertion of Jesus
having retreated. This is likely to have been originally
a repetition by the narrator, after adding that Jesus
had indeed good cause for retreating, inasmuch as the
authorities were determined to put him to death. The

Jn. xi. 54. Cp. previous verses.
evangelist, however, mistakenly makes out that there
was a second retreat in the midst of the events about
Lazarus. Then, again, it would seem, he has also
had either a record in his possession or a floating idea

Jn. x. 40, xi. 54.
in his mind, to the effect that Jesus escaped from his
persecutors at this time, first by going to where John
the Baptist taught, and then by going to "Ephraim."
He accordingly assigns these two localities separately
to the two statements about Jesus's retreat, and makes
his account read as if Jesus had first gone away to the
Jordan, then come back to Bethany, and then gone
away to a "city" called Ephraim. The records, however, or traditional reminiscences about John the
Baptist have been misunderstood by the evangelist,

See above, pp. 244-246.
as we have seen. The reference to going back to
where John the Baptist taught is a confused account
of Jesus's answer to the scribes when they asked him
by what authority he acted so boldly. And in view
of this—added to the difficulty of harmonising with
the Synoptic accounts—the "Ephraim" also becomes
hardly a guide. The going to Ephraim may also have
been a going in thought—perhaps the going to the

Some identify with little town about sixteen miles
country of ancient Ephraim in the very important parable
of the Good Samaritan. Thus taken altogether these
names of places in the Fourth Gospel give us no sure
information regarding the place of Jesus's retreat. In

the evangelist's second statement, however, he says north of
that Jesus went to "a country near the wilderness," Jerusalem.
and this may be accepted as a so far true reminiscence.
Once more, we are to learn, he sought for a place
where he might be, comparatively speaking, away from
men and alone with God.   It is likely he went to
some quiet spot pretty close to the city.

He went, we may further gather, accompanied only Ver. 11.
by one or two of the disciples, but left two or three
others with a knowledge of the direction in which they
had gone, and with the instructions that they should
follow in a day or two, bringing provision for their
bodily wants, and also conveying any news that might
transpire.   Now it is to be noticed Jesus had gone
away knowing that Lazarus was very ill, and probably
had not long to live.   The Fourth Gospel, we may
believe, tells so far truly, when it asserts that, knowing
how Lazarus was ill, "he abode two days still in the Ver. 6.
same place where he was."   Then, we are to learn,
the two or three friends who were to follow arrived
at the place were Jesus was, and brought, among other
things, the news that Lazarus was dead.   *Jesus at once* Ver. 11.
decided to return to Bethany.   Not, of course, without Vers. 7-16.
the opposition of the disciples.   He said, by way of
giving his reason for going, "Our friend Lazarus
sleepeth."   And they were not, surely, so obtuse as
quite to make the remark which the evangelist, accord- Jn. xi. 12.
ing to his manner, attributes to them, but rather
tried intelligently to dissuade him.   They reminded
him, in all probability, of the stones that had been
thrown at him ; and Thomas, seeing he was not likely Ver. 8.
to be easily moved, made the bitter remark, "Let us Ver. 16.
also go, that we may die with him."   This remark of

Thomas, no doubt, vexed Jesus; but it did not succeed in turning him from his purpose. He went back to Bethany.

We must not miss the beauties which are to be seen in this last retreat of Jesus, with the return that followed retreat. As in the case of the earlier retreats, Jesus only waited in concealment till he made sure of what his duty was in the circumstances, which had assumed distinctness. And in this case, that took a very short time, as he had been previously well prepared for what had come about, and had from the first made up his mind what he was to do if it did come about. But in this case a new force arose, and combined with his duty in bringing about his return. That force was personal affection, or call it friendship, or call it kindness to friends. So his character opens up to us and the more arouses our reverence and devotion. And so also we see how God gave himself a gleam of sunshine to light him in the darkness that was closing around him. With a brighter outlook, we can see, he would take that deliberate walk back into the power of his persecutors, in that he was going to comfort two poor women in great trouble, and at the same time to feel the fellowship occasioned by the nearness of one whom he had known and loved, who had already made the plunge which he had resolved he would allow himself soon to be forced to make, and had reached what awaits all on the other side.

CHAPTER XX

LAST MEDITATIONS.

JESUS and his disciples came to Bethany, and Jesus saw the sisters. They were in great distress, and one or both of them said to him, "Lord, if thou hadst Jn. xi. 21, been here, my brother had not died." Jesus told them [32.] that Lazarus would RISE AGAIN. And he told them Ver. 23. this with his own tone of "authority" which enforced conviction. He told them it with that tone of authority which had in Capernaum made him the spiritual king over a whole town in a few weeks, had in Galilee generally made multitudes throng around him like sheep around their shepherd, and had in the circle of his intimates made him become "transfigured" so that they were ready to worship him. He told those sisters that Lazarus would rise again in a way that aroused a faith which was as satisfying as certainty. He made them believe simply and unquestioningly in a new life beyond, which awaited their dear brother. He made them, we may say, see in imagination their brother risen again. How exactly he spoke so as to do this we cannot say. Certainly he

Vers. 23-
26, 40.
cannot have disputed with Martha in the way the
gospel makes him do. Most likely he spoke in a
convincingly vivid manner of the present Father, and
Jn. xi. 34-
36.
of the certain restoration of His children. With the
sisters he then went to the grave in which, according
Ver. 17:
the "four
days"
should
not be
where it is.
See note
App. 1.
(20).
to the Eastern fashion of early burial, Lazarus had
already been placed. He went to the grave, and at
the presence of the hidden form of him whom he had
but a few days before affectionately talked with, shed
tears. Those who saw him were impressed by the
sight, and said, "Behold how he loved him!"

Lk. xvi.
19-31.
On the way back from the grave he talked musingly
over the loss of Lazarus, as we may gather, and let
his musings lead on to his telling a most thoughtful
imaginative story. It was, we may believe, something
like what we read in the sixteenth chapter of Luke;
but we must believe that the exact form which it
bears in Luke is partly due to an influence from
the thoughts of the evangelist himself or of those
from whom the parable directly came to him.

Scholars have very generally explained the Fourth
Gospel story of the resurrection of Lazarus as being
a transference to fact of one of the mere suppositions
See note
11 in App.
1.
contained in the Parable of the Rich Man and Lazarus.
We must accept this explanation, only adding to it
that Jesus's authoritative teaching at this time regarding a resurrection for Lazarus and for all, must have also
contributed to the rise of the story—that authoritative
teaching which is part of what is represented when the
Jn. xi. 25.
evangelist pictures Jesus as saying, " I am the resurrection and the life: he that believeth in me, though
he were dead, yet shall he live." We must not,
however, go with the scholars the length of holding

that the whole incident about Lazarus originated in
the parable, or in the teaching. Rather, as in the
case of the Unfruitful Fig-tree, there was a real See above,
p. 242.
incident about Lazarus, the incident led to the parable,
and the parable, in its turn, led to the unhistorical
additions. The Parable of the Rich Man and Lazarus,
as it is found in the Third Gospel, is one of the least
pleasant to read of all the parables. We may apply to
it a treatment such as we are now applying to the
whole account as found in a gospel less correct than
that in which the parable is found, and see in it, first,
an original element, and next, later additions. While
valuing most highly and receiving most thankfully the
attempt of the Third Gospel to bring into special
prominence Jesus's enthusiasm for the welfare of the
poor and of needy persons in general, we may suppose
that in the case of this parable he has himself in great
part created its hard antithesis between rich and poor,
and that its real point, as it was spoken by Jesus
himself, was one quite different—namely, one having
to do with the subjects of death and resurrection.
We must suppose that the story was told by Jesus
at the time to which we have come, and that it was
occasioned by the death of Lazarus. We need not
suppose him to have characterised Lazarus as a
" beggar." It is enough, in that direction, to believe
that he indeed called him a poor man. He was
thinking, we may suppose, of his lost friend having
been cut off, and he was recalling how Lazarus, in
his conversations with him, had shown a character
that might have been of real value in the world. His
mind dwelt on the thought of the beyond to which
Lazarus had gone; and he pictured him meeting there

an evil-living **rich man**, who **had on earth** been
"clothed in purple **and fine linen."** He brought out,
in the story to the disciples, how in that **meeting**
Lazarus **was** the greater of the two, and was able
to give to the other what could quench the thirst
of the soul. He had further asked himself, **Might**
not Lazarus, were he allowed to come **back** to earth,
be a great power of good among all **careless men ;** and
he brought this **out** also in his story, **representing**
the rich man on the other side of death as saying **to**
Abraham that he had "brethren" still on earth who
might be saved from **great troubles if** Lazarus could
only be sent **to them and let** them drink the life-giving
water. **But he had answered** himself, **and he made**
Abraham answer the **rich man,** "If they hear not
Moses and the Prophets, neither will they be persuaded
though one rose from the dead." **Thus** he left the fate
of Lazarus and the value of his life in the hands of the
all-ruling heavenly Father. It is easy, **however, to** see
how among a people in a state of **excitement there**
might grow out of all this expression of reflection what
would help to **create,** if not the *whole* account of
Lazarus which **we find** in the Fourth Gospel, as some
critics would **make out,** then certainly that part of it
which **relates to a** calling of Lazarus back to the
vanishing life **of this world.**

Thus out **of a** narrative in most respects perplexing,
we redeem one of the most beautiful pictures of Jesus's
life. Instead of the literally received story of the
"Raising of Lazarus," of which it is not too much to
say that it neither contributes anything to the universal
hope of mankind, nor presents what Jesus must have
really promised **to** the sisters and to Lazarus, we have

Lk. xvi. 19-31.

Cp. above, p. 257.

Lk. xvi. 31.

a natural human story, in which we see Jesus almost
literally facing death to comfort his friends, see him
comforting them with the only comfort which the
circumstances admit of—namely, the trust that the
vanished brother will, like all, live again—and see
him, finally, weeping at the grave of him whom in this
life he will meet no more, whom he will soon follow by
a dreadful path which his own self-forgetful love has
helped to bring near him.

We are able now to take up the early gospels again,
though still we are the better of the Fourth Gospel
account to aid us. We come now to the impression Jn. xii. 9.
made in Bethany by Jesus's return, and by his conduct
and teaching. There was, no doubt, a most strong
impression made in his favour. He had revealed his
true self in his kindness to the sisters, in his vivid,
his authoritative, and, we may say, his passionate
assertion of the truth of a resurrection, and in his
affectionate bearing at the grave. He was, in Bethany
at least, regaining his position as a popular hero. But
also a consequence of another kind followed. The
Fourth Gospel relates it in this way: "But some of Jn. xi. 46.
them went their ways to the Pharisees, and told them
what things Jesus had done." And Mark relates it in
this way: "And Judas Iscariot, one of the twelve, Mk. xiv.
went unto the chief priests, to betray him unto them." 10.
The thoughtful reader will see how those words from
John are intelligible when the account is critically
sifted as above, whereas they would have been unin-
telligible had there literally happened the miracle
which follows in the account. Did sane men go to the
authorities to try and get into trouble a person who
could play with the great fact of death, as the Fourth

Evangelist makes **Jesus** do? What really happened, on the other hand, is quite easily understood. **The** traitorous Judas, now **that Jesus was** back in Bethany, seeing that he would sooner or later fall into the hands of his enemies, sought **to** get on the prevailing side by going and offering to the priests to bring them to where they would find him. And at the same time **probably** some others, not disciples, **went** and told **that** Jesus had appeared again at Bethany, **and** that **there was a new** stir **in** his favour. The priests accepted **the offer** of Judas. And in doing so they evidently **believed** that Jesus, having appeared, would withdraw **again, or else** imagined, from what they heard about **the rising in his favour in** Bethany, that even there by this **time it** might be difficult to find him sufficiently alone and unprotected.

If, however, the priests believed that Jesus would withdraw again, when they thought it worth while to **buy** over his unworthy associate, they were wrong. **Jesus** remained over this night in Bethany. And one incident happened in the evening which all the gospels **have in some** way recorded. This incident was a supper of which Jesus partook along with those devoted friends **to** whom he had returned. There is an account **given of this** supper in Mark **and in** Matthew. In Luke an account of it has got mixed up with his narrative of a quite distinct—a Galilean —incident, which, as we have seen above, is also in all likelihood historical; but also **we must discover a** separate account of this supper in **Luke in his general** remarks about Martha and Mary **given** in the tenth chapter, **as** these remarks contain essentially the same points as are contained in the other accounts of this

Mk. xiv.
3; Jn.
xii. 2.

Mk. xiv.
3-9.

Lk. vii.
36-50.

Lk. x. 38-
42.

supper. In John also there is an account so like those Jn.xii. 2-8.
of Mark and Matthew that advanced scholars have
made much of the state of matters in support of the
theory that most of what is historical in John is See espec.
directly taken from the other gospels or from the O. Holtzmann.
accounts which they contain ; but even if it be true
that this account has been influenced by the Synoptic
accounts, it is to be said there are certainly independent historical touches in it, showing an independent
source of information on the subject. What took
place, we may gather, was something as follows :—

The sisters Martha and Mary accompanied Jesus
and his most intimate followers to the house of a man
known as *Simon the Leper*. There all sat together at
supper. Whether this was the house in which Jesus
had been staying all the time, or whether he had been
staying in Martha's house, we need not determine.
At all events, Simon no doubt was, like Martha and
Mary, if not an earnest believer in Jesus, at least an
admirer of him. There was some excitement about
this supper. Extravagant stories about Jesus and Jn. xii. 9.
Lazarus had gone among the neighbours, and the
house was full of people. Attention came to centre
itself very specially on the two grateful sisters, who
were in different ways devoting themselves to the
honouring of Jesus. Martha was showing the more
practical ministration, interesting herself in supplying
his material wants. In the words of the Third Gospel, Lk. x. 40.
she "was cumbered about much serving." Mary, on Cp. Jn.
xii. 2.
the other hand, had chosen a different way for showing
her devotion. She had, in accordance with a very
widespread ancient usage for showing honour, brought
a most expensive kind of ointment, and had anointed

20 *

Jesus with it—as an expression, evidently, of her regarding him as the Messiah, or Anointed of God. Her action was not altogether approved of by some of those present. Luke, indeed, is likely mistaken when he suggests that it was Martha that was displeased, as also when he makes Jesus out to have rebuked Martha. His account stands alone among all the accounts in regard to these two points ; and it is highly unlikely in itself that Martha would object to her sister at such a time, or that Jesus would at such a time give the semblance of a rebuke to Martha in her kindness to him. Luke has rightly brought out the difference of character between the two women, but has overdrawn the details. It was some of the disciples, not Martha, that expressed disapproval ; and all that they did, in all probability, was, while professing admiration of the costly ointment, to remark, with a mere innuendo of disapproval, that many poor people might have been relieved by the money which had been spent on that ointment. Jesus felt the indelicacy of the remark. He was himself keenly grateful, in this time of his terrible trial, for such an act of personal kindness, and the more so as he felt that he would have few more acts of kindness shown him in this world. At the same time a strange fancy flitted across his ever-imaginative mind, to the effect that this anointing might be thought of as the anointing of a body about to be buried. He said to those around him, " Let her alone ; why trouble ye her ? she hath wrought a good work on me. For ye have the poor with you always, and whensoever ye will ye may do them good : but me ye have not always. She hath done what she could :

Mk. xiv. 4.

Vers. 6-8.

she is come aforehand to anoint my body to the burying."

The remainder of the night, no doubt, passed quietly. Jesus went to rest; and next day he awoke to the principal day of the Passover, "in the first month, . . . the fourteenth day of the month," which has been identified as a day in our month of April. Two Aprils before, Jesus had been a Galilean carpenter, outwardly little distinguished, inwardly most gentle, most generous, most appreciative, and most wise. One April before, Jesus had been a teacher regarding sacred things to the people of Galilee, who, as he stood and walked on the shores of a beautiful lake, received him with enthusiasm, and said that no man had ever spoken so commandingly and so sweetly as he. This April, the April probably of the year 35 of our reckoning, Jesus was showing the divineness of his nature by an unflinching upholding of his message to the world, in the knowledge that through such action he was walking into the jaws of death. He and his disciples prepared to partake of the passover-feast this day in the city where he knew his death-warrant was signed. How he passed the day we have no information to tell us accurately. In the Fourth Gospel account, however, there is related and attributed to this time a little incident which, in spite of certain suggestions, seen in it by some, of later history, claims credence for its essentials. Some men, we learn—and they may, indeed, as the evangelist says, have been Greeks who happened to be in Jerusalem—came to Philip the disciple, and said they would like to see Jesus. Jesus, always sensitive to appreciation, and always pleased when it came to

Ver. 12.

Exod. xii 18.

Mk. ii. 12.

Jn. xii. 20-22.

him, said, on hearing of the incident, something like this, "The hour is come, that the Son of man should

Ver. 23.
Jn. xii. 25, 26.
be glorified." And there are also in the Fourth Gospel account one or two sayings attributed to Jesus and to this time which we must accept. He repeated, we are to learn, his great words with which he had left Galilee, to the effect that they who will save their lives at the expense of duty do not gain in the end. And we must also believe that he spoke the following

Jn. xii. 24.
great words: "Except a corn of wheat fall into the ground and die, it abideth alone: but if it die, it bringeth forth much fruit." Suspicion, indeed, has been attached to the authenticity of these words,

The question of how far Paul may have influenced the Johannine writer is interesting, and requires much study.
This suspicion, however, would imply more than mere influence.
See Paul at his best in Rom. viii.
1 Cor. xv. 36.
Cp. ver. 36 w. vers. 51, 52.
Cp. also 1 Thess. iv. 17.
owing to their close resemblance to certain words of Paul. This suspicion, however, is unjust. The words are certainly Jesus's, not Paul's. For one thing, it is highly unlikely that the evangelist would put into the mouth of Jesus here a saying from so well known a source as the epistles of Paul, especially as the saying contains a doctrine quite out of the lines of the evangelist's own philosophy. But besides this, on the one hand, the saying employs favourite imagery of Jesus, is in accordance with Jesus's whole manner of thought and expression, and is in strict accordance with the view of life which we have otherwise perceived him to have entertained; on the other hand, the saying is not in accordance with Paul's lines of thought, which are much more abstract than those of Jesus, and, indeed, the words in Corinthians which form the counterpart to the saying are palpably out of natural connection with the rest of the passage in which they are found, and so have all the appearance of a quotation. The saying is a saying of Jesus; and

Paul, having heard it, throws it into the midst of an argument of his own on the subject of the resurrection, as a general contribution, without very intelligently applying it. What, then, did the saying mean in Jesus's lips? Not, assuredly, what modern philosophy has made much of, that the individual lives in its influence on the general. Jesus's interest was far too much centered on personal lives for him to have cared much about that modern doctrine. The saying is to be looked at as Jesus's own teaching on the subject of personal immortality. He believed, we learn from these words, in a resurrection, but in one quite consistent with the study of nature. He believed, evidently, that the spirit which dwells in a human body, as it returns at last into the arms of its mother-earth, receives new life there. Like a grain of wheat, if it does not thus return into the ground, it abides alone, and its own single strength is soon spent; but when it does return, it receives from the parent-substance new life and new strength. *Cp. Jn. xvi. 21, and the elaborating of Jesus's teaching there, which is found in 2 Esdr. iv. 40 ff.*

This kind of reflection, of everlasting value to the human race, was to Jesus himself, assuredly, of importance beyond estimating. Along with the thoughts that centered on the death of Lazarus, it was the armour with which he faced his unjust death. That he made much of such thought, and that he had need to do so, come both clearly before us. His obedience was to the Divine Voice. His stay was the Divine Care. But a spirit so sensitive as his and so acute in thinking sought something intelligible to the human mind to light its path. And this was granted in reflection of the kind which has just been before us,

bringing into clearness that human life not bounded
by the grave, in which "neither moth nor rust doth
corrupt," and "thieves do not break through nor
steal."

CHAPTER XXI.

THE LAST SUPPER.

In the evening of the day before that midnight-time in which the Passover lamb had to be eaten, Jesus and his special disciples came into the city. And it is most likely that it was as he went into the city on this day, with an outlook so different from that with which he had first entered it, that he spoke these still faithful and affectionate words, " O Jerusalem, Jerusalem, thou that killest the prophets, and stonest them which are sent unto thee, how often would I have gathered thy children together, even as a hen gathereth her chickens under her wings, and ye would not! " Arriving at a house in the city, they all partook of the passover meal; and that meal of which they partook had its importance as a passover-meal lost in the fact that it was also the *Last Supper of Jesus.*

At no place in the history of Jesus is the state of matters which prevails generally in relation to the information we possess more marked than in that having to do with the Last Supper. Here most distinctly we have two sources to be made use of in

Mk. xiv. 17.

Mt. xxiii. 37. Cp. Lk. xix. 41. Also cp. Jn. x. 31: and see above, pp. 297, 299. Mk. xiv. 18.

distinctly different ways. The account in the earlier
gospels is simple, and, as usual, evidently reliable ; at
the same time, all spontaneity and all natural development of events are sacrificed in it to dramatic presentation. The account in the Fourth Gospel again, though
the hand of the evangelist has plainly been brought to
bear on it, still retains touches of nature such as the
earlier account lacks, which criticism is able to separate
from the doctrinal whole and make use of for history.
The account in the fourteenth chapter of Mark is clear
and evidently trustworthy, but requires filling up.
The account in John, chapters xiii. to xvii., is in its
complete form a doctrinal presentation by the evangelist ; but yet it contains most palpable touches of
history, which must be carefully severed from the rest.
The whole scene comes before us through such uses of
our two sources of information, in a perfectness which
will leave little inclination in us to doubt the trustworthiness of our perception. And to begin with, the
two leading incidents of the supper can be made
sure of with the greatest certainty.

The first incident was that Jesus expressed his grief
at the desertion of Judas. That Judas was present at
the meal and retired in the middle of it is, we may
believe, a mistake. In the earliest account the
suggestion is otherwise ; such a course of events would
itself have been most inexplicable ; and it is easy to
see that the mistake arose from the later accounts
giving a literal signification to certain imaginative
words of Jesus. Judas, we may believe, had already
gone quietly away from the company, and Jesus either
suspected or in some way knew what was his purpose.

Mk. xiv.
18-21.

Ver. 10.   He had been in the city the day before on his own account; he had likely enough been back with them this day, pretending allegiance and gaining knowledge of the plans of Jesus; and Jesus had not failed to detect the falseness in him. Now, when all but he were seated together, and when the ceremonial observances in which they may have engaged were mostly past, the bitterness of the desertion arose within Jesus and caused him an overpowering melancholy. "One of Mk. xiv. you which eateth with me," he said—that is, one of [18.] you who are accustomed to eat with me—" shall betray me." And it is most likely a true reminiscence that Jn. xiii. 23. the favourite disciple John was at the moment sitting next him and leaning on him affectionately as he spoke the pathetic words. For a moment, doubtless, as the accounts declare, the question, "Is it I?" started, as such things happen, into every mind; but it is not likely that they quite expressed such a question to him for whom they all felt ready to give their lives. The question would only flit across their minds for a moment, and then they would know quite well who it was to whom he was referring. "It is one of the twelve, Mk. xiv. that dippeth with me in the dish," Jesus added; [20.] and the words must have roused in the whole company conflicting emotions which would bring silence over them all.

And now a careful and at the same time reverent criticism may see in its real spontaneous occurrence a historical incident which has played a wonderful part in the succeeding history of the world. We have already seen, through our critical reading of the Fourth Gospel, that Jesus explained the seemingly unreasonable opposition to him by comparing himself to a Above, shepherd to whom was given only a certain number of p. 286.

sheep. Similarly now we may see, through critical reading of the Fourth Gospel, that he sought for explanation of the conduct of Judas, and found it through the help of another figure, as familiar to the Israelite mind as that of the sheep and Shepherd— namely, that of a Vine. The Fourth Gospel tells us that at this last supper Jesus compared himself to a Vine. The other gospels tell us that at this last supper he compared his own blood to the fruit of the vine. Modern criticism has cleverly brought out the connection between the two reports, generally con- cluding that the Fourth Gospel passage about the Vine is largely worked up out of the report in the other gospels about the wine. We must recognise the connection thus brought out by modern criticism, but, according to our whole way of understanding the Fourth Gospel, we must not attribute the connection to later working up out of the earlier reports, but must see it in the original events as they spontaneously occurred.

Jesus, then, we may say, after the pathetic words we have found him uttering about the desertion of one whom he had believed to be his friend, sat for a few moments in silent suffering of the inward pangs which that desertion occasioned him. Then he partly threw off, as it were, the burdening thoughts, and spoke to the disciples. But still what had occurred was filling his mind and oppressing him; and the words that he now uttered were as melancholy as those which he had spoken before. Lifting up the wine-cup which stood before him, he said he would not drink again of the fruit of the vine till he drank it anew in that region beyond in which he was going to live anew. It was

Mk. xiv.;
Jn. xv.

For order,
Lk. xxii.
18.

then, we must believe, as he still gazed on the wine, and as all were silent, knowing not what to say, and as the thought of the desertion of Judas was still gnawing at his soul, that his mind—his mind ever inclining naturally to express its thoughts through imagery— came on the fancy which he expressed thus : *I am a Vine, planted by God, and God has removed a branch that was bearing no fruit.* The further remark attributed to him in the gospel account about burning the branch is altogether improbable. But we must believe that the fancy roused him to turn to the friends who were still faithful, and to address to them something in the spirit of his own care for them. They were the branches that still remained ; we are to learn that, as the Fourth Evangelist relates, he urged these "branches" to " abide " in him. He may have done this literally and directly as the Fourth Evangelist records ; but at any rate he did so through a request which was more powerful than a direct injunction could alone have been. He told them to regard this wine as his blood which was about to be shed, and *when they drank it, to do so in remembrance of him.* Then he carried fancy a little further, said of the bread also, that it was his body, and asked that also in the breaking of it he might be remembered. Not one, we may say, of the melancholy company assembled round Jesus ever forgot the affectionate request that he made of them. 'Those poor simple men, unable as they were to say anything of comfort or hope in reply 'to his mournful utterances, understood at least the language of friendship, and determined with one mind never to forget to do as he wished them to do. No wonder that the eating and drinking in

Margin notes:

Jn. xv. 1, 2. Probably Mt. xv. 13 is also from a report of this saying.

Jn. xv. 6.

Jn. xv. 4.

Mk. xiv. 24 ; Lk. xxii. 19 ; 1 Cor. xi. 25.

remembrance of Jesus became the most sacred act in the worship of the first Christians. It was bound to become so with such an origin.

How far, if at all, the doctrinal turn which was after-wards given to this incident, may have been present in the mind of Jesus, it is difficult to be sure. Certainly much of the Church doctrine on the subject was later development, if not indeed later accretion; and espe-cially the representations both in mediæval art and in modern declamation, of Jesus's flowing blood and of the cruel sufferings to which he was subjected in his death—which reverent followers, one might think, would rather see buried out of sight—are far from the simple thoughts which have just been before us. But this at least of the doctrine was in germ in the original occurrence, that Jesus desired his disciples to recognise in the bread and wine the showing forth of a sacrifice, which arose out of faithfulness towards heaven and love towards man. And we modern believers in Jesus and followers of Jesus may engage in the instituted cere-mony of eating and drinking in Jesus's name, calling to

See App. I. (21).

mind not only the historical sacrifice but also an eternal sacrifice of which the historical was a revela-tion, even while, at the same time, our first thoughts may be those of simple discipleship and devotion to Jesus, such as he sought and will never despise.

The Gospels of Mark and Matthew tell us no more of much importance as having happened at the Last Supper. But a broad comparison of all four gospels brings us to some further occurrences which, with practical certainty, may be fixed to this point in the history.

What of the Fourth Gospel? The Fourth Gospel,

in its chapters xiii. to xvii., gives a lengthened conversation, with the names of the different speakers introduced—different disciples making remarks, and Jesus answering them, just in the way that things must really have proceeded. But upon examination the whole passage promises very little. As has been said above, it is a doctrinal presentation by the evangelist, just like the rest of the gospel. Even the notices of the remarks of individual disciples give very little on which to lay hold. One remark, indeed, that of Philip asking Jesus to show them this "Father" whose presence always upheld him, may have historical truth in it, as also the reply of Jesus, to the extent of his having expressed disappointment that Philip, after being with him so long, should make a request so materialistic. This is likely, indeed, to be a historical reminiscence. And, accepting it as such, we may gather that Jesus further answered Philip's question in words like these : If a man do "the will of my Father which is in heaven," my Father will make his abode with him. But the other remarks and answers, however they may have taken their rise, are, as we now have them, but the didactic expression of the evangelist's own ecclesiastical philosophising. In the sayings attributed to Jesus, however, we shall still be tempted to think there must be some remains of Jesus's real utterances at this time ; and in seeking to find these out, we may make one more appeal to the Synoptic gospels in the hope of finding some touches which we may connect with the Johannine report, in the same way as has been done above in the case of the wine and the Vine.

We find two passages in the Synoptic gospels which

Jn. xiv. 8-10.

Combination of testimony from Jn. xiv. 9, 23, and Mt. vii. 21 ; connecting-link between Jn. xiv. 9 and Mt. vii. 21, in Lk. vi. 46.

we may use in this way. Though there is almost nothing more in the accounts of the Supper in Matthew and Mark, there is a little piece of material in Luke confirmed by the account in John. And though there is almost nothing more in the accounts of the Supper in Matthew and Mark, we are not to forget the collected *Speech to the Disciples* which is to be found in the tenth chapter of Matthew. That, as we have seen, is collected out of sayings to the disciples uttered at various times; and now we shall find that some of it fits, and only fits, to this Last Supper, is confirmed in its connection with the Last Supper by the Fourth Gospel account, and is confirmed as belonging to the real sayings of Jesus by its having slipped into the " apocalyptic " passage in Mark, with which it has no natural connection.

The piece of material in Luke begins with the statement, " And there was also a strife among them, which of them should be accounted the greatest." Now this statement cannot be taken just as it stands. The idea of a strife about which of them was to be considered the greatest having arisen among them at a time in which, as we have just seen, they must have been silent in amazement and helplessness and yet burning with devotion to the Master, is out of the question. And indeed we find that what Luke here relates is just an event which we have already had before us as having happened in Galilee, reported by Mark and Matthew in its proper place. The suggestion, however, arises, May not Luke have had in his possession some fragmentary report of sayings of Jesus at the Supper, to the same general effect as those that are led up to by the strife about who was to be the greatest, and so

Lk. xxii. 24-30.

Ver. 24.

have introduced the passage about the strife in this place, wrongly indeed, but for the purpose of filling up a similar passage which really belonged to this place? This suggestion is borne out by the facts. The passage about the strife, including Jesus's words which it led to, is given by Luke, and then come the words, " For whether is greater, he that sitteth at meat, or he that serveth? is not he that sitteth at meat? but I am among you as he that serveth. Ye are they which have continued with me in my temptations." These words are not found in the other accounts of the strife, and they have no connection with it further than that they enforce the same general idea. Now we find in the Fourth Gospel account of the Supper a passage enforcing the same idea, having no connection with that " strife," but having a great resemblance to those last words of Luke's account just quoted. The passage in the Fourth Gospel account tells of Jesus having at the Supper *washed the disciples' feet*, and of his having taught them to do the same to each other. Now literally this passage can hardly be historical. While it does not overstate the length to which one should go in carrying out Jesus's teaching regarding kindness one to another, still, viewed as an actual event happening at this time, its presents us with a picture not of spontaneous kindness, but of forced and uncalled-for doing for others, such as does not seem in keeping with what we otherwise learn of Jesus. The feet-washing, then, depending as it does entirely on this late Fourth Gospel, cannot be easily regarded as literally historical. Still the fact of both Luke and John having in their accounts of Jesus's sayings at this time passages so dissimilar and yet urging, both of them,

Lk. xxii. 27.

Ver. 28.

Jn. xiii. 4 ff.

the same mental qualities—namely, those of humble-
ness, kindness, **and** friendliness — suggests most
convincingly, in the circumstances, that there was a
historical background for them both. We may find
a clue to what really happened in two further notices
in the Fourth Gospel account occurring further on.
The first of these (which also is repeated) **is** that in
which it is said that Jesus gave to the disciples as a
Jn. xiii. 34, **"** new commandment " the injunction that they **should**
xv. 12. **"** love one another."   **This** notice is, indeed, too **like**
the First Epistle of John in its language to be accepted
just **as it** stands. The expression " new commandment," **we must believe,** originated not in any actual
utterance **of Jesus, but in the** application of Jesus's
Cp. Gal. teaching by the writer of the Fourth Gospel and of the
vi. 2 ; 1
Tim. i. 5. epistles of John, and also **by others of the** early
Above, Christians.   And we might **be** inclined to treat the
p. 269. whole notice as just an expression, in the evangelist's
own free fashion, of Jesus's teaching **to** the earnest
scribe. This latter, however, would **be** going too far.
It is best to believe that this repeated notice, explaining as it does **so** well the feet-washing story and the
fragmentary **words** in Luke, is historical in so far as it
tells us **that** Jesus at this time went back in some way
on what he had said to the earnest scribe. We shall
presently, then, find help from this notice for our
search after what really happened at this time. The
other notice is that in which Jesus is reported to have
Jn. xv. 15. said, " I have called you friends." In the gospel that
sentence is mixed up with material which is certainly
more or less the evangelist's own composition ; but,
in accordance with what we have several times seen in
the Fourth Gospel, we may take it that the evangelist

has separated these words from their right connection
to allow of doctrinal interpolations, and we may find
their original connection to be with a saying to which
the feet-washing story is made to lead up—namely,
this, "Ye call me Master and Lord." This also brings Jn. xiii.
help to us for learning what happened at this time. 13.
And now we are able to reproduce what took place. It
was, we may say, as follows :—

The melancholy silence which, as we have seen, had
fallen on the company was broken, we may gather, by
some small kindly action on the part of Jesus to one
of the disciples—indeed, it would seem likely, to Peter. Jn. xiii.
The action was performed, shall we not fancy? by
way of gracefully turning the attention away from the
gloomy themes with which they had been engaged.
Peter, it would seem, deprecated the action of kindness
on the part of Jesus towards himself, addressing Jesus
in a distant and reverential tone as *Master*. Jesus
then, we may gather, answered something like this :
Ye call me Master and Lord ; I have ever called you
friends. Ye are they who have continued with me Lk. xxii.
through all my trials. The reverential tone of Peter's 28.
remark, and the very word " Master " had somewhat
jarred on Jesus in the state of mind into which he had
come. He was feeling so keenly the parting from
those faithful men ; he would have preferred that they
should feel as he felt, that what was threatening them
was the parting of friend from friend, rather than the
removal of one to be looked upon with awe. There
was hardly, however, a rebuke in his reply; there was
just an indication of his own fervent feelings in relation
to them. Then, we further learn, he went on to
remind them that in his whole teaching he had dis-

couraged emphasis of the relation of master, and had
taught that the stronger should rather be kind to the

Jn. xiii.;
Lk. xxii.
weaker.   And as he wished them to continue his
teaching and his work after he would be gone, he urged
on them to remember this point themselves.   He said
he would leave with them this precept, that they should

Jn. xiii.
34.
" love one another."   And we may believe he really
added words very like these words which the evangelist

Ver. 35.
gives us : " By this shall all men know that ye are my
disciples, if ye have love one to another."   It is interesting to notice how, even in this most trying time, he,
in his eagerness to impress his teaching on those whom
he was leaving to spread it, showed his usual acumen
in fixing on a word or phrase which they could not
mistake, and could carry away with them to hold in
their memories.   It is also to be noticed, in relation to
all these sayings which we have just had before us, that
the near approach of death took away any constraint
that might have prevented him talking so plainly of
his own personal feelings towards them.

Keeping still by the little piece of information in
Luke, we find another sentence attributed to Jesus—
namely, "I appoint unto you a kingdom, as my Father

Lk. xxii.
29, 30.
hath appointed unto me : that ye may eat and drink at
my table in my kingdom, and sit on thrones judging
the twelve tribes of Israel."   This, we must decide,
has been altered from the original by Luke, not with
the intention of doing so, but on account of the

Jn. xvii.
18, xx. 21;
Lk. xxii.
30. Cp.
also Rev.
iii. 21.
saying reaching him in an incomplete form.   We can
reconstruct the original, with the help of the Fourth
Gospel account, so as to have it this : As my Father
hath sent me, so I send you; "that ye may eat and
drink at my table *in the kingdom of heaven,* and sit on

thrones judging the twelve tribes of Israel." He was
continuing the expression of his wish that they would
teach his ideas to the people; and he recurred to the
old conception, half practical and half fanciful, which See above,
he had put before them in Galilee, according to which p. 138.
they were his twelve *Apostles*, or *Sent-men*—twelve
according to the twelve tribes of Israel. Thus through
Luke and John another episode comes before us; but
this one is not only confirmed, but given us in extra
detail, in that other passage spoken of above, as
available for us from the earlier gospels—namely, a
part of the dramatic Speech to the Disciples, which
forms the tenth chapter of Matthew.

Within the tenth chapter of Matthew there is one Mt. x.
small passage made up of warnings on the part of 16-31.
Jesus regarding troubles which were before his disciples.
Now this passage is quite unsuitable to the first
sending of the apostles in Galilee. At the early time
in which that event happened, Jesus had no such
gloomy outlook as this passage expresses, nor is it
conceivable that he would make such prognostications
as this passage contains in relation to the very first
attempt to spread his ideas over his own province.
When, then, we consider that Mark, the earliest
gospel, has no trace of the words of the passage as
having been addressed to the disciples at that time,
and when we remember that the speech, like other
speeches in Matthew, is plainly made up for dramatic
effect and didactic purpose, from various sayings, we
may conclude that it was not at the Galilean sending
of apostles that the words of this passage were spoken.
We might then be tempted to look upon the passage,
in the way of advanced scholars, as being a description

of after-events put, with literary liberty, into the mouth
of the Master himself ; and this, indeed, we must do
in the case of some of the detail of the passage. But
seeing the passage taken generally agrees so well with
the Johannine report as critically sifted, and seeing it
is so very suitable to the circumstances we have now
come to,—seeing further that, as we have just had
before us, it fits in to the report of Luke, critically
read, **we** may take it as giving a report—genuine in
general, though slightly influenced in particulars by
after-events—of what further took place at the last
supper of Jesus.

We have **just seen,** then, that Jesus had come back
on his old idea of his most intimate disciples being
"apostles," or "sent-men," the number being twelve
according to the twelve tribes of Israel. **I** have sent
you, he said, as my Father hath sent **me.** And then
the darkness of the outlook which had come to exist
influenced what he had to say on the subject. He
recurred—as he would do yet once again—to that
fancy which, as we saw in last chapter, had first
presented itself to him **by** way of explaining how only
a few listened to **his** teaching—namely, that these few
were his special "sheep." He thought of the sheep as
they would **be** without their shepherd, and he said,
Mt. x. 16. "Behold, I send you forth as sheep in the midst of
wolves." Sheep in the midst of wolves! he seems to
have thought for a moment ; and then with a gleam of
humour even in the midst of the great sadness, he
added that they must then not be like sheep altogether,
but must **be** like "serpents" in wisdom, and like
"doves" in harmlessness. To justify the fear which
was expressed in this saying about the wolves, he gave

the reason for it in these words, or something like
them, " The disciple is not above his master, nor the ^Mt. x. 24 :^
^Jn. xiii. 16,^
servant above his lord. It is enough for the disciple ^xv. 20.^
that he be as his master, and the servant as his lord."
They would hardly altogether escape, he said, when he
had been so treated. The disciple would be as his
master. The next two verses in Matthew's account,
after that about the wolves and sheep and doves and
serpents, giving the *detail* of what would come to them,
cannot be taken as literally historical. One morsel,
however, may be abstracted from them. It is this
clause : " They will scourge you in their synagogues." ^Mt. x. 17.^
This likely tells of real words of Jesus, but not quite
accurately, the after-experience of Christians having
given a turn to the words. As the words stand, they
give a piece of detail which would have been quite
unlikely to be mentioned by Jesus. The original, however, is, we may say without doubt, preserved for us in
the Fourth Gospel account, and was this, " They shall ^Jn. xvi. 2.^
put you out of the synagogues." We can see how the
thought in these words was suggested to Jesus. He
was thinking, evidently, of that man of Jerusalem who
had been threatened with being put out of the synagogue for saying publicly that he had been blind before ^See above,^
he had heard Jesus, and that Jesus had opened his ^p. 258.^
eyes. Then he faced one more certainty which was
before them—namely, that, like himself, they would
have to answer the objections, and possibly objections
backed up by threats and injuries, of those in power.
And this led to his uttering the grand words, " But ^Mt. x. 19,^
^20.^
when they deliver you up, take no thought how or
what ye shall speak : for it shall be given you in that
same hour what ye shall speak. For it is not ye that

speak, but the Spirit of your Father which speaketh
in you." In this simple form these words, supported
as they are by Mark, are certainly genuine words of
Jesus. The Fourth Gospel has had, evidently, a
report of them which has been almost word for word
with this of Matthew, as we find all the ideas of this
one in the Fourth Evangelist's account ; but he has
given us much more than Matthew. Most of what he
has given us is put into form by the reflection of a new
generation—as is, to begin with, his calling what Jesus
named " the Spirit of your Father " the *Representative*
or the **Advocate** (*Parakletos*, translated in the English
version, as " the Comforter "). (He has preserved the
original idea that it was their *Father's* Spirit they were
to trust to, in these forms, " whom the Father will
send in my name," " whom I will send unto you from
the Father," and "which proceedeth from the Father.")
But we may take it as a historical fact—as this
evangelist tells us—that he also bid them *pray* to their
heavenly Father—as he had, doubtless, often bid them
do before, that he said he also would pray for them,
and that he assured them that after they had prayed,
and he had prayed, God would give them that great
boon, the help of His own Spirit. And we may also
take it as a historical fact that he added it would be
good for them to lose him for a time, because in that
case the Spirit of their heavenly Father would come
and teach them. This is borne witness to by the
very growing up of the materialistic belief which is
centered on the day of *Pentecost*. It could not well,
indeed, have been the intimate disciples themselves,
but rather later tradition, that gave to those sage
words of Jesus the aspect in which they seemed the

Marginal notes:

Mk. xiii. 11. Cp. also Lk. xii. 12. Jn. xiv. 16, &c.

Ver. 26. Jn. xv. 26.

Jn. xiv. 14, 16.

Jn. xvi. 7

Acts. ii. 1-4.

prediction of a magical gift, and supposed that the gift came on the day of Pentecost. Those intimate disciples of Jesus, most surely, were able to see in some way, in the words, the meaning which is so clear to any one now—namely, that when he was gone they would have to think for themselves, and so would be brought into more direct communion with the ever-present God.

Thus far we have gained our knowledge of the Last Supper from the early gospels as confirmed and illumined by the Fourth Gospel read critically. Dare we now attempt to get one or two touches of information from the Fourth Gospel alone? We have been walking with one foot on the firm ground and the other on the ice. Dare we, just for a moment, venture a little way out, and let the ice alone bear us? Assuredly, if our method of reading all along is the right one, there is still, in these chapters of the Fourth Gospel, much, beyond what the earlier gospels directly confirm, to be attributed to Jesus himself. It is difficult to abstract; and any full or detailed abstracting cannot be satisfactory. But there are at least a few of the sayings presented of which we can be particularly sure according to the canons which have been generally guiding us. We can be virtually sure, for one point, that Jesus did say, "Let not your heart be troubled"; that he said, "In my Father's house are many mansions"; and that he said, "My peace I give unto you." We may be sure that he said—in answer, probably, to some deprecating objection to which the disciples may have roused themselves, "Whither I go ye know, and the way ye know"—meaning that they all knew pretty well the kind of movement that was going on against him, and knew that the Roman death by crucifixion was before him. We may be sure that

Jn. xiv. 1-2, cp. ver. 27, where the words " Let not your heart be troubled " are repeated. See App. VI. Jn. xiv. 4.

Jn. xvi. 17. he spoke of their meeting again, and that—in his own
22.
way—he gave the illustration which compared death
Jn. xvii.   itself to the pains of travail.   And lastly, we may be
sure that, even in the presence of them all, he sought
relief in prayer to Him who was sustaining him.

Yes, let us still refer the lovely elements of the
prayer in the seventeenth chapter of John to Jesus our
Lord.   We have really, according to the view of the
Fourth Gospel which we have been taking, everything on our side when we do this.   First, it is most
probable—indeed, from our knowledge of Jesus, we
may say it is certain—that Jesus would pray with his
friends at this last supper, as he knew he was going
from them.   And further, the earlier gospels may be
Mk. xiv.   said to give some confirmation.   Mark and Matthew
26.
both relate that before leaving the supper-room they
"sang a hymn."   And even if that refers to a ritualistic
observance having to do with the Passover, we must
feel sure, from what we have learned of Jesus, that he
would connect with it some individual contribution of
Lk. xxii.   devotional expression.   Luke, again, in relating what
32.
certainly happened after they had left the supper-room
(although Luke himself is not clear on that point),
reports Jesus as having said to Peter, " I have prayed
for thee, that thy faith fail not."   In the circumstances,
all things considered, it is most likely that the conversation which we have had before us would lead up to a
prayer on the part of Jesus.   It is, further, more than
probable that the disciples would remember the chief
points of Jesus's farewell prayer, and that some preser-
vation of it would be made, corrected by the remembrance of one and another.   And it is intelligible why
we do not find it in the earlier gospels.   It is enough
to notice that, as they were presenting the " Christ "

as a general object of faith, this prayer, with which really his friends alone had concern, would not seem to them of the importance which it possesses to us who are inquiring anew regarding the personality of Him whom we have worshipped. The Fourth Evangelist has evidently had in his hands a report of it which he has worked up into a longer form in his own way. How can we separate the elements? Only, perhaps, at all to an extent which leaves a vague idea of the original; but so much of a separation can surely be accomplished by the methods that have hitherto guided us. The dualism of the "world" and the chosen is not of Jesus: if Jesus said, "I pray not for the world," it must have been because he left the world to the Eternal Father and His care. The allusion to the "son of perdition" is not of Jesus; if Jesus alluded to Judas in his prayer, it cannot have been with the calmness of the evangelist's presentation. But Jesus, we may learn, did pray for those whom God had given him in the time of his earthly life, did entrust them to his Father's keeping, did pray for their sanctification, did say, "the hour is come," did speak of love which he had himself known from God, and did fervently implore such a realisation of that love as would bring to all a meeting again.

With this prayer, in all probability, the occurrences at the Last Supper ended. After this prayer, we must believe, rather than in the middle of the conversation, as the Fourth Evangelist perplexingly relates—after this prayer, which must have caused to reign among those devoted and affectionate men who surrounded Jesus, a silence even more profound than had been before—after this prayer, amid utter stillness, Jesus said, "Arise, let us go hence."

Marginal notes:
Ver. 9; the soi eisi (they are thine) may originally have referred to the "world."
Ver. 12.
Vers. 2, 6, 9.
Ver. 11.
Vers. 17, 19.
Ver. 1, cp. Mk. i. 15.
Vers. 26, 24.
Jn. xiv. 31.

CHAPTER XXII.

THE TRANSLATION.

Mk. xiv. 26. JESUS and his disciples, or rather, as he made known his wish to have it expressed, Jesus and his friends, went out from the house in which they had supped, and walked as it were back towards Bethany, but not to lodge there any more, as Jesus had only too good grounds for believing. They reached the Mount of Olives. And the stern supernatural humour settled down upon Jesus, only to be relieved by expressions of solicitude for his disciples' welfare, and of craving, in return, for assurances of their community in his aims and their devotion towards himself. He said, " All ye Vers. 27, 28. shall be offended because of me this night : for it is written, I will smite the Shepherd, and the sheep shall be scattered. But after that I am risen, I will go before you into Galilee." Peter said in answer, Vers. 29-31. Cp. Caspari on Mk. xiii. 35, in his "Einleitung," p. 4. " Although all shall be offended, yet will not I." And Jesus rejoined—as we may simplify the report, which has been slightly moulded by after-events,—Before the cock-crow, thou shalt be offended. Peter "spake the more vehemently," protesting that he was ready to die with Jesus. And here we must find a trace of real ^{Ver. 31.} history in a narrative which not only is to be found in ^{Cp. Lk. xxii. 33.} the Fourth Gospel alone, but also has been seriously questioned as belonging to the Fourth Gospel. In the twenty-first chapter of John, held by many scholars to have not been an original part of the Fourth Gospel, there is an isolated story which so perfectly fills up and gives life to the scene now under consideration, that our canons of inquiry are hardly strained if we find part of its origin in its having been an account of this scene. True, it is in its present form a narrative of experiences after the death of Jesus, and there is a likeliness in its details which recommends them to consideration as having had a historical reality. But the form of the story may be explained by the idea that, in the resurrection experiences which it recounts, the apostle Peter may have remembered the other scene just before the translation of Jesus, so as to dwell once more on its particulars, and that accordingly the narrative of the resurrection experience which was preserved blended the two scenes into one. And so we may gather, what took place was this : Jesus, after his remark about even Peter being sure to be offended before the cock-crow, went on to say to Peter, in allusion to his strong asseverations, "Simon, son of ^{Jn. xxi. 15-17.} Jonas, lovest thou me?" Peter, aggrieved, replied, "Yea, Lord; thou knowest that I love thee." Then Jesus said, "Feed my sheep." Then, more affectionately and more trustingly, we may gather, he went on to say what Luke has preserved for us: "Simon, ^{Lk. xxii. 31, 32.} Simon, behold, Satan hath desired to have you, that he may sift you as wheat : But I have prayed for thee, that thy faith fail not : . . . strengthen thy brethren."

There is a clause in **Luke's** report **of** this saying **which, as** he reports it, is not intelligible—namely, "when thou art converted" (strengthen thy brethren). **The** appearance of this clause suggests that its origin may have been in another remark of Jesus **at** the same time, which Luke became confused over. This we may **take to** be the case, from the fact that **we** find an exceedingly lifelike remark which might easily have thus originated the clause in Luke, in the twenty-first chapter of John. Another remark, then, of Jesus, **we** may say, which Luke became confused over, is preserved **in John, also in a** confused form. The remark originally, we **may gather,** was something like this:

Jn. xxi. 18. When thou wast **young, thou** stretchedst forth thy hands, and another girded **thee;** but now thou must gird thyself and gird others. The scene comes before us clearly, and very touching **it is.** Jesus, knowing **that** his days on earth were about at an end, had only this **poor** fisherman to look to to continue his work and his teaching. Only this one; for **he** saw, no doubt, that his was the only very striking religious personality among them, and that, while the others were earnest, faithful, and in some ways well instructed, they had not sufficient enthusiasm to make them leaders. And this Peter himself, he knew, had up to this point been never the least like a leader, but had been of an impressionable and indeed somewhat wavering character. It was not a confident outlook, had he had no power other than his disciples to trust to. But Jesus had more to trust to. He left his cause in the hands of Him who had given it to him. And God **both led** Peter and these other faithful friends in the paths of success, and also raised up, in the great Paul, a man such as Jesus now wished for, who carried his name and his message triumphantly over the world.

The rest that happened is easy to tell. The account in the Synoptic gospels is a plain, evidently trustworthy statement. The Johannine account becomes much freer than before from doctrinal and traditional influences, and contains some most valuable reminiscences of its own, which at this stage of our work may be presented to the reader as they come, without apology or much explanation.

Jesus and his disciples entered a piece of open ground, called GETHSEMANE. This may have been Mk. xiv. either a garden or a piece of waste ground or a 3²; garden, Jn. plantation of trees. In this place Jesus parted a xviii. 1. little from the disciples, and gave way to a terrible outpouring of anguish. The Presence that had inspired him now sustained him. He knelt in prayer as we may behold him, revere him, and love him—the Elder Brother of the human race, who was the true Son of God. His disciples overheard him say: "Abba, Mk. xiv. Father, all things are possible unto thee : take away 36. Less correctly this cup from me: nevertheless not what I will, but reported what thou wilt." in Jn. xii. 27-29.

In Gethsemane his persecutors, led by Judas, found Mk. xiv. him out. They came up to him, and as they came, he 43-52. said bitterly, "Are ye come out, as against a thief, with swords and with staves to take me ? I was daily with you in the temple teaching, and ye took me not." And he added, " But this is your hour, and the power Lk. xxii. of darkness." The devoted Simon Peter drew some 53. Cp. Jn. xi. 9, weapon, and made an attempt at defence ; but Jesus 10; Mk. xv. 33. rebuked him, repeating in calmness the words that Mk. xiv. had lately burst from his soul in his agony. He said, 47; Jn. xviii. 10.

Ver. 11. " **Put up thy sword into the sheath**: **the cup** which
my Father hath given me, shall I not drink it?"   The
slight resistance, however, was enough to make some
of the officers begin to lay hands on **the** disciples also.

Vers. 7. 8. But Jesus said, "Whom seek ye?" and on receiving
the answer, "Jesus of Nazareth," continued, "**I am
he. If** therefore ye seek me, let these go their way."
We must not miss the heroic majesty of these words.
We have indeed presented in these words a com-
manding picture.   **He** who has lately been praying
that his friends may not be taken away from him,
now **gives the request** from **his own** lips that they
may be allowed **to leave him.**   Because he sees that
their welfare leads **them for the time away from him,**
he demands that they **may be** separated from him,
even till the coming of all to **the hidden world** beyond.

Mk. xiv.
50, 51.
The disciples at this moment **let** fear overcome all
other considerations, and fled—in **such** panic, indeed,
that one, who had been seized by an officer, left his
cloak, or covering of some sort, in the officer's hand,
and ran off **without it.**

They took him before the high priest *Caiaphas.*

Vers. 53;
Mt. xxvi.
57.
Witnesses against him were called, even in the middle
of the night, **as the** time was.   They got two men to
testify to his having said he would destroy the temple,

Mk. xiv.
55-64.
and rebuild it **in** three days.   **What did it** matter,
before such judges, that the testimony was both in-
accurate in detail and misunderstanding in general?
The high priest gave him opportunity to defend himself.   But he answered that he had nothing to bring
forward, saying that he had spoken openly of the
matters which he had come to Jerusalem to teach,
and that those who had heard him could tell what

he had taught. At this, one of those infatuated men Mk., Jn. xviii. 22.
struck him. The high priest then, by way of bring-
ing the matter to a point, asked him : "Art thou the Mk. xiv. 61.
Christ, the Son of the Blessed?" Jesus met his
challenge boldly, and said, " I am : and ye shall see
the Son of man sitting on the right hand of power. Ver. 62.
. . ." The high priest then said : "What need we Cp. Lk. xxii. 69.
any further witnesses? Ye have heard the blasphemy:
what think ye?" And, in the words of Mark, " they
all condemned him to be guilty of death."

The disciples had, some of them, gathered round Mk. xiv. 54 ; Jn.
about ; but they were too terrified to acknowledge con- xviii. 15.
nection with him. Even Peter was heard to deny any
acquaintance with him. But soon that really devoted
friend was found bitterly weeping. His fault would Mk. xiv. 66-72.
surely have been tenderly dealt with by the Master.
And for us it may be said in regard to him, that,
remembering his after-conduct in suffering and dying
for the cause of Jesus, no disciple of Jesus has the
right to speak of him with anything but respect and
admiration.

As the passover-meal, in which both Jesus and his
enemies had been engaged, had extended, according
to custom, till past midnight, they had not long to
wait till the new day was upon them. When the Mk. xv. 1.
new day's business was begun, the whole circle of
priests, along with the whole company of scribes,
held a meeting with regard to him, and decided, as
they had before intended, to bring him before the
Roman governor, Pilate, on a political charge. They Vers. 1, 2.
hurried him away, accordingly, before Pilate, alleging Lk. xxiii. 2, 3.
that he professed to be the King of the Jews. Pilate
said to him, "Art thou the King of the Jews?" He Mk. xv. 2.

Mk. along
with Jn.
xviii. 36-
38.
Cp. Mk.
xii. 14.
replied, "My kingdom is not of this world." "Art thou a king then?" Pilate rejoined; and he said, "Thou sayest that I am a king. To this end was I born, and for this cause came I into the world, that I should bear witness unto the truth." Pilate replied, "What is truth?" Whether he meant to ask for a further explanation of Jesus's own words, or meant to express a sceptical opinion about matters of conviction in general, we cannot tell. One thing, however, we can gather plainly; and that is, that Pilate understood Jesus—understood Jesus, and understood the case which had been brought before himself. He did not, however, boldly and honestly acquit Jesus. And in this can we judge him harshly, knowing so little of the extent of power which in his peculiar Mk. xv.
3-5. position he possessed? He first got the priests to state openly their charges against him, and asked Jesus to answer them. This request, however, Jesus refused to comply with. He would answer nothing to the charges of the priests. Why? Partly, no doubt, because he knew that it would do no good, but partly also because he could not throw off his view of them, in which he saw them to be practically at the time just "jackals," or creatures that it would be unworthy of him to argue with. Then Pilate tried to free him through subterfuge. He suggested, as we may gather Lk. xxiii.
5-12. from a somewhat perplexing report in Luke, that as Jesus was a Galilean he should be sent to Galilee to be judged by Herod. This suggestion, however, the priests managed to overcome. And then he tried that compromising plan which it is difficult to believe could have been successful. It had been the custom, Mk. xv. 6. it would seem, to release a prisoner at the time of

the passover. Pilate accordingly attempted to get
rid of the case by avoiding the question of right and
wrong in regard to Jesus, and proposing that he
should be the prisoner to be released. He addressed
the people who, it would seem, had begun to assemble
round the judgment-hall, saying to them, "Will ye Vers. 6-15
that I release unto you the King of the Jews?" The
fickle people, however, were now against Jesus, and at
the bidding of their long-respected priests. Perhaps,
indeed, they were now on their own account also
somewhat indignant with him. It may be, as is suggested in Dr. Keim's account, that his failing to fulfil VI., 95-
the hopes they had associated with him of his being 99 (Eng.
a political " Messiah," or deliverer, now inflamed them Tr.).
against him. At all events, they rejected Pilate's offer,
and said they preferred to have released a certain
leader of insurrection who happened at the time to
be imprisoned. In the words of Mark, "the chief Mk. xv.
priests moved the people, that he should rather release 11.
Barabbas unto them." Then as regards Jesus, there
got up among these savage beings the awful cry
" Crucify him!" And at the same time the priests
surrounded the governor, saying that by their laws,
which Pilate was expected to respect, Jesus had incurred the penalty of death. " Why, what evil hath Ver. 14.
he done?" said Pilate. They answered him, doubtless, with pendantry such as they were accustomed to
use, and at the same time from the streets there rang
again the horrid cry that called for the death of Jesus.
Pilate here, it would seem, in his weakness tried, as
another expedient, to get Jesus to speak out and defend himself. Jesus was silent, however, and Pilate
said, " Speakest thou not unto me? knowest thou not Jn. xix.
9-11.

22 *

that I have power to crucify thee, and have power
to release thee?" Then we must learn, with all our
admiration even especially aroused, Jesus *excused* this
perplexed judge in something like the following words:
"Thou couldest have no power at all against me,
except it were given thee from above: therefore he
that delivered me unto thee hath the greater sin." But
again the cry arose from the streets; and the priests
kept harassing Pilate, and said, "If thou let this
man go, thou art not Cæsar's friend." Then Pilate,
saying he "washed his hands" of the matter, yielded,
and delivered Jesus to his soldiers to be crucified.

They took him to the place called *Golgotha*, and
women followed him, weeping and wailing. He was
subjected to the death to which the people on the
streets had sentenced him, one of the most fiendish that
barbarian cruelty has ever devised. With his dying
lips he was heard to speak words of forgiveness for his
murderers, and to send some loving message regarding
his mother. His bearing impressed even two men who
were dying by a similar death beside him, and one of
them at least roused himself to turn to him and say
something like this, "Lord, remember me when thou
comest into thy kingdom." The people who had
followed in enmity at first mocked and abused him;
but soon this was changed, and their deepest feelings
were aroused as they saw further the grandeur of his
death. Nature began to break down, and his spirit
turned to God, praying for help. He who had been
gentle and childlike in his life faced his death like a
soldier. On some one offering him a draught that
would have lessened his sufferings he refused to receive
it. He died. The chief officer in charge bore witness

Cp. Lk.
xxiii. 34.

Jn. xix. 11.

Mk. xv.
13, 14;
Jn. xix. 12.

Mk. xv.
15; Mt.
xxvii. 24.

Mk. xv.
16-25.
Lk. xxiii.
27.

Ver. 34;
Jn. xix.
25-27.

Lk. xxiii.
42, much
more
probable
than Mat-
thew's
form of
the tradi-
tion. xxvii.
44.

Mk. xv.
29; Lk.
xxiii. 48.

Mk. xv.
34.

Ver. 23.

to his greatness and goodness; and the people around Ver. 39;
Lk. xxiii.
47, 48. —friends heart-broken and foes awakening a little to their better nature—"smote their breasts and returned."

He went into the Beyond, into which we have all to go; and if we could not have hopes there for ourselves alone, we should still have to feel it must be well there for Him, and well there for all whom he loved.

He went into the Beyond, and went, as he had prophetically known and said, to live again. That his spirit was not held bound by the tomb into which he was soon to be reverently placed, but only disappeared to rise again, has been the faith with which his disciples in all ages have connected their dearest hopes. And it is a faith by which any one in full sympathy with this little book will take the very firmest stand. It is a faith to be rightly grounded on the perception of many spiritual realities. Details, however, regarding the resurrection of Jesus are beyond the purpose of this book. He went, like all other human spirits that have for this present world died, into regions yet hidden from us which he, in his prophetic insight, had looked forward to as other "mansions" of his Father. That in these mansions his spirit rose again into active personal life is the fact on which we must lay hold. How that happened is a consideration going past the limits of this work. All that need be said here is that, while the resurrection of Jesus, like the general renewal of life of which it has come to be looked on as a type, must have happened in ways far beyond our present understanding, and while accordingly all representations of it are but pictorial and are inadequate, yet the fact of a resurrection for Jesus and for all whom he loved stands fast, and is the better grounded when it is dissociated from superstitions, which obscure and confuse everything they touch.

He went into the Beyond; and he left behind him a number of " apostles," who for a short time became scattered in dismay, but soon rallied themselves, and with the Divine aid became worthy of the hopes he had rested on them. God made known to them that their Friend and Master, in real personality and activity, was alive again. And his words came back upon them : " Peace be unto you : " " as my Father hath sent me, even so send I you." So with new faith, centered on Him in everything, they pursued bravely the Mission which had been his and had been left to them.

Jesus went into the Beyond. And what fancy can even suggest the peace and the happiness which had been won there for a life such as his had been ? He sat down at the right hand of God, and his sorrows were turned into joy.

PART IV.

CONCLUSION.

CHAPTER XXIII.

THE CHARACTER OF JESUS.

WE have gone through the materials in our possession affording a knowledge of our Lord Jesus, making every effort to be honest and thorough in the treatment of them ; and what conclusion can we have come to but the one, that we have been brought face to face with a Character so sublime as to be worthy of the recognition given to it during so many hundred years, as being the human ideal and the manifestation to us of what is above the human? We have brought criticism to bear on the records that have come down to us ; and criticism ends its work by giving way to silent admiration. It has no faults to find. It places before our view a completely beautiful and noble Soul. There have indeed come before us, in the course of the work, human weaknesses and earthly

limitations; but we have seen these caught up by the
master-spirit within the man, and absorbed in all that
received a heavenly glow from his heavenly enthusiasm.
The whole is perfect.   The end of our study is worship
and transportation among things sacred.

That Jesus's character was sublime—so sublime as
to lead those who contemplate it into regions higher
than the human—has been made known to us through
the impression which, made on the age just after his
death by his spiritual grandeur, has never faded away.
Our critical study, as must come to be the case with all
critical study, while giving a certain consideration to
the impression for its own guidance, in its turn also
renews the impression.

What, in character, was He who has been the
subject of our consideration ?

He was one, plainly, whose own character was
turned straight in the direction which he indicated
when he spoke of the two chief commandments for
men, that they should, first, love God, and, second,
love their neighbours.   He was a Soul whose whole
interest was the Divine Presence.   Perception of the
Divine Presence in its self-existence and transcend-
ence made him what he was so far.   Perception of the
Divine Presence as having imparted its nature to the
living and thinking beings of earth, completed what he
was.   Perceiving God with him, he loved God.   Perceiving the good, or the divine, in the men with him,
he loved man.   So was Jesus, as we have seen him.

In detail, what we have seen mainly is this : After a
quiet and unobtrusive, but most contemplative boyhood and early manhood, he comes into the world to
teach men about One who cares for them.   He appears

Mk. xii.
28-31.

first at the Jordan, listening, with many people, to another teacher, a man only like himself in earnestness and in being of commanding personality. While at the Jordan he excites the interest of persons assembled to learn of that very different teacher, and also gains the respectful notice of that other teacher himself. He shows honour to that teacher most unstintingly. He is appalled at the triumph of brute force over that devotee to what is good and true ; but he never wavers in his faith that things are ruled by One the Best and Kindest. He has attracted to him a few earnest and high-toned men ; he says to them that that other teacher has been a sower, and that there is still the reaping to do. In so speaking he is most humble and most respectful ; for what he is able to do is no mere reaping, but is very enchanting. With a small body of admirers around him, he in a few weeks arrests the attention of a whole town. He shows himself a great Power ; sickness yields to him, nervous excitement yields to him, foolishness yields to him, human beings open their hearts to him. He remains still humble in this success ; he retires to think and pray. Having done this, he comes back among men, to continue his work which he has taken on himself. And similarly the rest of his course is run. In unflinching devotion to God and unshared enthusiasm for the elevation of man, he deliberately continues his work till at the last he crowns it by submission to an agonising and horrible death, at the instigation of men debased and heartless, whose relentless purpose he has clearly foreseen. But in the path which he thus pursues he does many little things that declare his character to us in ever-increasing completeness. He is disappointed often at reverses ; but he always explains the reverse, and still is faithful to Him who has sent him forth. He is touched and made sorry when he sees any human suffering or any human fault. He is touched and made glad when he sees a pure soul, when he hears an honest word, when he looks at young children, and, perhaps most of all, when he is himself the receiver of a piece of genuine kindness, let the giver of the kindness be saint or sinner. He is roused to disapproval and rebuke at every littleness of view, every animosity, and every needless interference with the earnest. He is roused to open triumph both at the awakening of earnestness and at the awakening of considerateness. He prays as no one else has been known to pray. He says at one time that he is able to give his fellow-men an easy yoke to bear. He says at another time that he can give them meat to eat and water to drink which will satisfy them for ever. He comforts those who have lost friends by death in a way that even those who have learned from him his solace can but feebly imitate. He is time after time very affectionate, and very solicitous of a welfare for each that will not pass away, but be an everlasting possession. He forgives those who murder him. He excuses the poor judge who condemns him. He comforts his friends, whom it almost breaks his heart to part from. All this and much more we have seen. And so we see Jesus first devoting his whole powerful mind and his whole rich heart to God, and next desiring, in such a way that we may call it demanding, all attainment for every personal life. We see him valuing every personal life, finding an original sacredness in every personal life, and promising an everlasting care for every personal life. We see him, inasmuch as to begin with he measures the worth of any possession by the idea of accordance with the Divine Purity, demanding accordance with the Divine Purity for every personal life. The full activity of his soul, as it comes before us, takes the form of an unlimited Sympathy, or Compassion, which seeks out the unfortunate first, be they suffering or erring, bodily fallen or spiritually fallen, but cares for every one, rich or poor, old or young, elevated or depressed. Such was the soul of Jesus.

We find, indeed, in the material telling of his life, so far as we have been able to discern it in its genuineness, a certain passivity, or humanness, in which the great spirit feels the weakness of an individual, and prays to and waits on the Eternal Disposer. And it is important to notice this human weakness, for our religion's sake as well as for truth's sake ; for it helps us to see the more completely the divine power which was also in his character. What meets us in Jesus is this, that having a nature inquiring, sensitive, and craving for affection and recognition, he, even when his path was dark and when he was completely abandoned by all outward stays and encouragements, followed the path of his Mission unswervingly through pain and weariness, and trusted the Divine Care unhesitatingly from first to last.

This humanness, or passivity, is to be discerned both in his position as a prophet of the Unseen, and also in his general relation to his fellows as a man among men.

There is a perfect humanness presented by our material in regard to his position as a prophet of the Unseen.

To begin with, his very sayings themselves, spontaneous as they are, royal as they are, proceeding as they do direct from his own commanding soul, are

occasioned and helped to come into expression by
circumstances. We can in several cases detect the
stages in their genesis into expression; and what is
acutely interesting is that he seems, when once he had
come on a fine thought, to have gone back on it afterwards, in a perfectly human manner, in a beautifully
simple and winning manner, in new applications or on
new occasions. Thus, after the imprisonment of the
Baptist he had compared the Baptist to one who had

C. iii. *sown,* leaving others to reap; soon after, in Capernaum,
he gave to the same thought a general application in

C. viii. his great Parable of the Sower. So when turning from
C. iv. Nazareth to begin his work in Capernaum instead, he
had said that a prophet had not honour in his own

C. ix. country; afterwards, when actually in Nazareth and
actually rejected there, be recalled the same thought.

C. xxii. And so in the garden of Gethsemane, to which he had
gone straight from drinking of the cup of friendship at
the Last Supper, he had given utterance to a passionate
but perfectly devoted prayer regarding the different
"cup" that was before him; soon after, when some
would have defended him from his persecutors, he
prevented them, going back on that same imagery
which made his sufferings a "cup," given him and not

Mt. xxv. to be shunned. But while all this shows humanness,
40, and
Jn. xiii. 20 shows passivity, shows receptivity, it at the same time
may be helps to show us his divineness. To begin with, his
another
example divineness is in no way interfered with by the fact that
of this. his thoughts developed themselves in a process which
we can partly follow. As the world of nature reflects
the Divine even though processes are discovered in it,
so the thoughts of Jesus are divine even though we
can in some way trace their growth. And besides this,
the very manner of their growth which has just been

noticed, attracts us to his sacred person, and so
ministers to our belief in his divineness. It speaks to
our sympathies, making us interested and charmed ;
and then when we have become so, we discover that in
what is interesting us and charming us there is to be
found a Soul worthy of our worship.

Most strikingly, however, does his humanness come
before us in relation to his position as a prophet of the
Unseen, in the plain evidences that reach us of his
having fervently wished for recognition as a prophet of
the Unseen.   As he comes before us, we find him
feeling keenly that his people will not " know a tree by
its fruit," and will not receive him simply as the
prophet Jonah was received by the men of Nineveh. Above, c.
We find him also feeling keenly that his own town ^{viii.}
does not honour him, and that his own family will
not understand him.   Quite plainly to critical reading
of the gospels, he experiences pain at not being
recognised for what he is conscious of being.   But at
the same time how divine is he in this humanness !
How beautiful are the reflections with which he
silences his own disappointments !   He says, wrong as
his countrymen are, they can be forgiven if it is something about his human personality that they object
to, and not the Divine Voice which speaks in him.   He
recalls how it has always been the rule that a prophet
has only a limited sphere.   Then he remembers, with
a very gratefulness, how some success has indeed been
granted to him.   Some, indeed, are not his sheep, he
says ; but then, he says, he has some sheep that listen
to him, and to him alone.   He receives with a simple
joy the inquiries of a few about him, and with a simple
faith the confession of his disciple Peter that he is the
Christ, the Messiah, the Anointed of God.   Besides all

this, he knows the recognition is only a question of time. His countrymen will yet say of him, he asserts with confidence, " Blessed is he that cometh in the name of the Lord." And further still, beyond all consolatory reflections, he is what he is and does what he does independently of recognition. He is come in his Father's name, not in his own. He seeks his Father's honour, not his own. And he is not really abandoned, for his Father has not left him alone.

With respect to his general relation as a man to the men around him, there is a no less interesting human-ness presented by our material. He is plainly very affectionate, and he craves for affection from those about him. He craves for companionship and sympathy, and he is most tenderly appreciative of any kindness. In one incident after another his nature, in this aspect, flashes forth. We may recall, for example, his inquiries of his disciples about their thoughts of him when others are opposing him or deserting him, his aggrieved outburst when he is forced to turn from his family and find in his disciples " brothers, sisters, and mother," and his sayings in connection with the rich young man on the way to Jerusalem. What pain, further, is suggested in the way he speaks of Judas, reserved as his remarks are ! What yearning to meet his friends again breathes through the sayings at the Last Supper ! But here also his humanness is met and glorified by divineness. In the hour of his trial he requests that those who care most for him may be permitted to go from him. In the hour of his agony he thinks of the welfare not of himself, but of those he loves most. And his consola-tion for himself is in this saying regarding his friends, " They shall never perish, neither shall any . . . pluck them out of my hand. My Father which gave them me, is greater than all; and none is able to pluck them out of my Father's hand."

Reverently analysing this character a little further, however, and comparing it with other characters, what is first to be noticed is an Intelligence, great enough to be said to be above being measured. This intelligence is of what is usually called the introspective order; that is to say, it does not find its objects of attention in material embodiments and their relationships, but fixes itself on the spiritual essences or first principles. And yet at once there is to be said also in regard to it that it is of a concrete character nevertheless. It does not much deal with spiritual essences abstractly or as separate objects of thought, but discerns the spiritual all through the material, and, looking always at the ordinary world, sees all to be spiritual. Being of this nature, it penetrates to the very centre of things ; it makes the ruling and all-pervading ONE the object of its perception, and applies categories and descriptions to that One as thus brought under knowledge.

Introspective in intelligence Jesus certainly was, seeing the spiritual essence in the material. Does it seem a discrepancy to maintain this when we further find he had a considerable knowledge of the things of nature, leading him to speak of the ways of birds and beasts, and giving him a command of the scientific idea of Growth ? He certainly knew nature as, for example, his great apostle did not know it ; and there is the greatest contrast between his treatment of sacred truth and that of Paul, just in the fact Cp. above, p. 310.
that, while Paul reasoned from the relations of

abstract ideas themselves, Jesus verified all by the
ways of nature as experienced. There is, however,
no discrepancy between saying this and saying that
Jesus was in intelligence introspective. It was the
divine essence in nature, not the particular relations of
the things of nature, to which he attended and in
which he interested himself. The occurrences in
nature were to him examples and illustrations. And
while such a combining of an introspective perception with a knowledge of nature was indeed a quality
of his intelligence, it only brings out that it was an
intelligence unusually organised, and the more commanding.

The character of Jesus viewed on its *moral* side was
a character devoted to the Divine Presence. His
spirit, first perceiving and knowing with a commanding
intelligence the Divine Presence, came to be unwaver-
ingly devoted to the Presence thus known by it. It
may be that this state of matters was a simple case
of cause and effect, and that the moral side of his
character was just the development of the intellectual
side. It may be that a spirit so organised intellectually
could not but have developed itself in enthusiastic
desire and aspiration in regard to the Reality that
it had come to know. Bringing the character down,
however, into comparison with ordinary human characters, for the sake of more clearly understanding it,
it is advisable to distinguish a moral side in it. We
must accordingly say, Jesus in his intellectual side
perceived always and everywhere the Divine Presence,
and in his moral side was devoted always and everywhere to the Divine Presence.

This combination in him of intellectual perfection

with moral perfection gives so much of an explanation of the position which he came to take as the
Founder of a new religion, or the Creator of a new
circle of moral and religious ideas; and it gives so
much of an explanation of how it was that he became
the Prince of all religious leaders. All, indeed, that
is to be believed as having brought about the position
of Jesus in regard to religion, is not in this way to
be summed up. There can legitimately be brought
to bear on this general subject investigation and
speculation of a kind that goes beyond the historical
work specially belonging to this book. And we shall
see something of the conclusions to which such
investigation and such speculation certainly lead in
next chapter. But so much of what made him become
the supreme prophet for our world is to be connected
with the quality of his character which is now before
us. The combination in him of a commandingly
strong and clear introspective intelligence with a
faultless moral purity and religious fervency, brought
about that he took up quite a unique attitude in
relation to the subject of Truth. It was an attitude
so far like that of many *reformers* who have appeared
in the world's history; but no mere reformer of an
old system has assumed quite the attitude which he
assumed. He took up an attitude of complete independence in regard to the embodiments of truth which
prevailed in his time and in his nation. He saw that
these embodiments had become so corrupt that they
no longer represented the real truth. He likened them
in his speeches to dead things. And turning away Mt. xxiv.
from them altogether, he appealed to truth as truth, 28.
and made truth as truth supply guidance for his

Cp. end
of c. vi.
thought and for his action. That Jesus did assume
this attitude in relation to the subject of truth, his
teaching as it remains to us itself declares. We find,
See espe-
cially
xviii. 37.
however, also that he claimed to do so. The Fourth
Evangelist has given the most complete record of his
dealing with the idea of truth; and while the Fourth
Evangelist evidently understands him to have given
to the idea of truth the narrow range of a new dogmatic
embodiment, it is plain to criticism that this is a misunderstanding on the evangelist's part, and that Jesus
himself thought of truth as truth, or truth as it
recommended itself to reason. This state of the case
is made more certain by an unintentional witness, so
to speak, in the Gospels of Mark and Matthew.
In both of these gospels, without the subject being
directly dealt with, there is record of certain men,
who were trying to lead him into difficulties, having
alluded to his devotion to " truth." The words in
Mk. xii.
14. Cp.
Mt. xxii.
16.
Mark recording this are as follows : " And they send
unto him certain of the Pharisees and of the Herodians,
to catch him in his words. And when they were come,
they say unto him, Master, we know that thou art
true, and carest for no man ; for thou regardest not
the person of men, but teachest the way of God in
truth : Is it lawful to give tribute to Cæsar, or not ?
Shall we give, or shall we not give ? " It is involved
in that remark made to Jesus—and its testimony will
have great weight with any candid student—that Jesus
had spoken much about " truth," and had meant truth
as truth, the truth that recommends itself to reason.
Combining, then, this testimony with the testimony of
the Fourth Gospel, and with the indirect testimony
which is borne by Jesus's own whole course of life,

as we have become confidently acquainted with it, it
is certain that Jesus claimed to turn away from the
prevailing embodiments of truth, and to find his
guidance in truth as such, or in the fountain of truth.
And this much is certainly to be explained by that
combination in him which we have just recognised,
of a commanding intelligence with a perfect religious
and moral enthusiasm. In fact, without going into
the question of how he had the power to get a new
circle of ideas from truth itself, and only thinking of
how he had the impulse to do so, we may reverently
apply to him a rule which will hold good also for the
multitudes of thinking men who have in all ages taken
up decided positions of more or less antagonism to
popular embodiments of religious truth. The rule is
that it is a combination of very strong intelligence
with very strong moral enthusiasm that has distinguished such men. Strong moral natures, whose
intelligence has not been in keeping, have often, we
know, been content to cling to embodiments full of
error. And we can see that, on the other hand, strong
intellectual natures, whose moral sense has not been in
keeping, may also at least have tolerated such embodiments, because manifestly they may have known things
were wrong and yet have not cared. And even what
might seem to be exceptions to the rule must be
explained by slight failings in the one factor or in
the other. One's own consciousness, for example, of
limitation either in intelligence or in purity of moral
purpose, has no doubt in many cases been a deterrent
from interfering. And many, again, have been deterred
by certain flaws in the one factor or in the other—
moral flaws, such as laziness or fear; or intellectual

23 *

flaws, such as non-recognition of the importance of religious matters. But none of these things held in the case of Him who has been the King of rebuilders and the Founder whose work all others can only help to restore and can never improve. In his perfect heart and perfect mind he has been an example to whom the rule purely applied. And even in the uniqueness of his case the rule is still to be seen. For if his case is beyond parallels, is not that in great measure to say that his intelligence was beyond parallels, that his moral purity and power were beyond parallels, and that the combination was beyond parallels? In the balance of his spiritual qualities his royalty is to be seen. He knew the Truth. He knew that the embodiments of truth which prevailed in his time had totally lost the power to represent the truth to mankind. He knew that it is man's duty to recognise the real truth and fear no consequences. He accordingly set up THE TRUTH against the prevailing embodiments, and as he did so, created fresh and new ideas which all men would accept.

So the character of our Lord Jesus opens up to us, under the treatment of criticism, in all the sublimity that has been ascribed to it by that Impression which has come down to us through the ages. By means of a fair estimation of the documents in which it is made known, influenced only by a reverence which the general facts justify, and aided by a legitimate synthetic judgment, it has come before us as a distinct reality, consistent all through, and winning us into a unique admiration.

CHAPTER XXIV.

THE DIVINITY OF JESUS.

It now only remains to bring into greater distinctness how the doctrinal association of Jesus with what is above the human is, in its essentials, placed on the more secure basis by this work and all similar work.

We have seen that Jesus was conscious of a relationship with the Divine Presence so close and so complete that he expressed it as *sonship*. This he professed to share with mankind in general; but at the same time he recognised in himself a certain prophetic initiation, and indeed was so keenly assured of this that, when first there suggested itself to him and afterwards was urged on him by others his fulfilling the hope of a " Messiah " or Divinely Commissioned Deliverer for his people, he admitted the office and name of the Messiah to be his own. His early followers, and with them the whole western world, have not only recognised along with himself the prophetic initiation, but have much more particularly estimated it. They have seen in him the first, or more correctly the One, who has *realised* the relationship of Son to the Eternal

Supreme,—realised it in virtue of something special
in him. They have thus apprehended that his work
has been not merely the work of a teacher, but the
work of a communicator, and that he has become
worthy not merely of gratefulness, but of worship.
They have found in him not only their Prophet, but
also their Priest and their King. They have called
him in all respects Divine. The meaning and significance of this process of thought which has taken
place is what must be inquired into in this last
chapter.

The idea of the Divinity of Jesus in its essentials
means, to begin with, that in Jesus there was a quite
unique indwelling of God. It has also, however, a
reflex signification caused by the idea of what God is.
In accordance with the idea of what God is, it means
that above and around ourselves there lives what
specially dwelt in Jesus. It means that what specially
dwelt in Jesus is the Ruling Eternal Presence. It
means that, in spite of many natural phenomena which
might seem to declare the contrary, what we see in
Jesus is the ruling Power in the universe.

The idea rests first, for all ordinary minds, like the
knowledge of his perfect character, on the Impression
which Jesus made on his own and the succeeding
generations by his personality. The details of the way
in which this impression was created are to many
minds somewhat uncertain; but the Impression itself
is a fact remaining for all. This Impression is, for all
ordinary minds, sufficient to make plain that there
specially dwelt in Jesus that which has Power, and
prevails in the universe.

There has, however, come about a practical confirma-

tion of the idea through the *Experience* of countless
individuals. A sense, within the human being, which
perceives the Divine above us and around us, has
certainly been awakened for multitudes through the
contemplation of Jesus. This sense, indeed, is not to
be supposed as having been altogether unawakened
before the time of Jesus's earthly life. That it was previously awakened is, without inquiring into the religious
condition of the ancient world in general, sufficiently
evident from the whole Psalm literature, as, for example, from such an exclamation as this, "Whither Ps. cxxxix.
shall I go from thy Spirit? or whither shall I flee from
thy presence? If I ascend up into heaven, thou art
there: if I make my bed in hell, behold, thou art there.
If I take the wings of the morning, and dwell in the
uttermost parts of the sea; even there shall thy hand
lead me, and thy right hand shall hold me." But for
the world at large there has been quite a special
awakening of the sense through contemplation of Jesus.
The human soul, face to face with Jesus, has recognised
God in him. And the sense which perceives God,
being thus awakened, has gone on to perceive what it
found in Jesus extended through time and space,
whispering in moments of quiet, prevailing in the world
in general, governing, chastening, and encouraging the
personal life. The case has been something like that
of some curious antique writing on ancient stones;
the eye unaccustomed to detect the writing sees only
the stone, whereas the eye that has had attention
called to the writing in some special way not only
reads the writing in one spot, but is ready to find it,
as experience goes on, again and again. A better
illustration of the case, however, is found in that of

some ordinary human virtue, as, for example, kindness.
Just as some child who has been starved and beaten
from infancy may not be able to detect kindness even
when in its presence, and may impute its outcomes to
other motives, so many a soul may go through the
world deaf to the voice of God and blind to His glory;
but as the down-trodden child, having on some
occasion met with a resplendent and unmistakable
instance of kindness, ever after has new eyes to look
for it, so the soul that has perceived God in Jesus has
had awakened a new sense, which is ever repeating its
discoveries. It is thus that rightly the name of Jesus
has come to be used for what is above the human. It
is thus that the Christian, as such, possesses a peculiar
heritage.

Thus any person whose religious experience has
been at all full and rich will never entertain the
possibility of any study being able to interfere with
the idea of the Divinity of Jesus in this its essential
meaning. There has, however, been thrown on the
idea a certain confusion or darkness, through the
development of discriminating thought in modern
times. Two discoveries have caused disturbance for
a large number of minds. On the one hand, it has
been discovered that the documents which alone
contain representations of Jesus's earthly life are in
their particulars not beyond criticism, either as laying
claim to tell what really happened, or as consistently
arousing adoration. With respect, indeed, to the
latter point there is this curious phenomenon, that one
criticises the particular representations of Jesus by the
very idea of Jesus which one possesses. On the other
hand, it has been discovered that life goes on dis-

closing its Author and calling forth new wonderment, not only in ways of which no account is taken in the documents telling of Jesus or in the systems which have been built on them, but also in ways of which a literal reading of the documents seems to be somewhat contradictory. This confusion is dispelled, and more than dispelled, the essentials of the idea are re-established and more than re-established, by the work of Biblical Criticism, or Biblical Science. Literal reading of the gospels is helpless to face the confusion, being itself, indeed, one of the causes of it. Criticism accomplishes what Literalism fails to accomplish.

How does Criticism do this? What aid does it give towards maintaining the conception of the Divinity of Jesus for all classes of mind?

To begin with, recognition must be given to the fact that modern critical study as a whole is helping the unconscious assent to the conception, in that it bears witness to the unique attractiveness first, and afterwards the retaining power, of Jesus's personality. It is to be carefully recognised that, though criticism throws doubt on the question as to what was the exact nature of the phenomena which were witnessed in connection with Jesus's life, it leaves one "miracle" untouched, and that is Jesus himself. By leaving that miracle untouched, it brings that miracle into relief; it emphasises the conclusion which, as we have seen, the ordinary mind must draw from the Impression made by Jesus on the world. It leaves us with this position : Let criticism go its greatest lengths, there remains to our contemplation in certain history a Figure establishing complete ascendancy over the western world, a Figure truly supernatural.

Modern critical study of the life of Jesus, looked at
in the aggregate, is surely, both in its first effort and
in the reverent and worshipping spirit which it main-
tains, an expression of adoration not to be decried
or slighted. The early ages of the Christian era
glorified Jesus in their own way; the age of science is
not behind them in the degree of its homage. The
work of modern students, taken all together, as they
earnestly follow the footprints of the Sacred King,
bears witness in the most powerful way to the fact
that there was something in Him of whom the gospels
tell which, beyond what is seen anywhere else, fasci-
nates and yet hushes into reverence the world of
thought. The whole body of work, first approaching
the subject in fervent absorption, then traversing
freely the outer ground, and then stopping at one spot
where criticism in relief and delight yields to worship,
will take a distinct if modest place, along with the
Cathedrals of Europe, the Poetry and Music and
Pictures of generations, and the assemblies of men in
hall and street-corner in every western city, as obeying
God in contributing to Jesus's exaltation.

More definite and more positive aid than this, however, is rendered by criticism towards maintaining the
conception of the Divinity of Jesus. What the conception really depends on is the question whether in
his life as it was in history there is to be seen a
perfectness which leads us to centre on it our highest
thoughts of the Divine. That question is the same as
the question, whether out of all the perplexing elements
presented by the four gospels, there proves itself as
having peculiarly lived in Jesus a *character* which is the
highest ideal. Those particulars in the gospel documents

which cause confusion, as arousing criticism in regard
to credibility or ideality, cease to disturb if it be proved
that, distinct from the representations in the gospels,
there was certainly realised by Jesus himself an ideal
character, with such fulness and consistency that he
himself stands above criticism ; then these particulars
become swept away as insufficient efforts to depict his See App.
character. And those appearances in the advance of life, I. (13, 23).
telling us of the government that is really over us, change
their attitude completely if what we bring to compare
with them is no mere body of theories, either in regard
to natural science or in regard to the possible ways of
attaining to goodness and purity, but is a historical
character, which historically was unrestrained in
assent to everything to which the human mind, when
true to itself, bows, and in its own achievements was
more commanding than any other appearance that
meets us. The important question, therefore, is,
Whether there was such a character so realised in
Jesus. And this question has here been answered confidently in the affirmative in last chapter. From last
chapter it is but a short step to the position : In Jesus
there was a quite unique indwelling of that Living
Presence that is the eternal Son of God, one with the
eternal Source of life, the end towards which life is
moving. Or, stating it precisely, Jesus in history,
through the royal character which we have discerned
as having belonged to him, is the *Revelation* or the
Unveiling to us first of God, Redeemer and Creator,
and then of the High Destiny of man.

What exactly is meant by saying that Jesus in
history is the Revelation or Unveiling of these
Realities ?

There is meant, to begin with, that we recognise his character to be just the same as that which we otherwise know to be the Divine, and just the same as that which we otherwise know to be the human ideal. So that when we would describe the Divine, or describe the human ideal, we can turn to Jesus and say, There it is.

But there is more than this implied in saying that Jesus is thus a Revelation. There is implied that he has given us a conception with which to enter on experience. For us the union between his character and the Divine character has this special significance, that he has been the first to bring the Divine character perfectly before our minds. He has given a glimpse, as it were, that arrests the otherwise unawakened vision, and it is this glimpse, properly, which, as we have seen above, is to be verified by further perception and by experience. Perfect knowledge of God has come to the world in knowledge of Jesus. Jesus has through his own character provided us with a conception of God.

And what a conception it is! It is the conception of a character that actually values infinitely and loves infinitely every personal life. If it is a true conception, then overshadowing us, grasping us, making us, is One to whom every soul of us can appeal. If it is a true conception, then we can, each and all of us, appeal from the hard laws of nature to an eternal Soul that calls us children of the eternal, and promises us life in the midst of death.

And it is a true conception this that Jesus in his character has given us. We can dare to say it is certain that the Supreme Being is such as we see in Jesus.

Scientific certainty, indeed, may seem to many to be as yet only partially established; but even that is on the way to being established. It waits now for its complete upbuilding on the further development of Modern Theology, the greatest of the sciences; now under tutelage, but growing surely; ever approaching the time in which it will put restraints aside, and assume its position at the head of all the great sciences that have come before it and are heralding it. It is a science having to do with what is involved in all our life, and with what is to be perceived in all our life. It is a science based on the Present, the Living, and the Eternal.

Meanwhile, however, there is for one and all of us a certainty not less valuable than scientific certainty. And that is the certainty of experience. Experience of the Divine " Christ "—of the Eternal Divine Presence that was the inner soul of Jesus—is alive among us. It is to many the most certain of all realities. So real and true a thing is it that, like any other thing of life, it is assuming multitudinous varieties; and zealous professors of orthodoxy are bound to, it may be, men the most negative in profession by a common experience of One near them who is both a personal strength and the source of all purity and kindness.

The doctrine, then, of the Divinity of Jesus as amounting to the conclusion that there was a unique indwelling of the Supreme Being in Jesus, and that as Jesus's character was, so God is, is confirmed by our critical study. A further element, however, has been recognised in the doctrine by the consciousness of Christendom—namely, the conclusion that it was the *purpose* of God to dwell in Jesus, and that that purpose

of God arose from the gracious intention of both mani-
festing Himself to man, and saving man from the
corruptions of his nature.

This further element, this purpose, brings God before
us as not only full of care for the individual, but also
acting in behalf of the world in general, coming as the
Eternal Son, or Living Ideal, into a human life, and
becoming in that life a centre of faith and a spring of
action for the succeeding ages of the world's history.

It will be plain to the reader that this further
conclusion arises naturally out of the recognition of
the fact that God specially dwelt in Jesus. So that
reaching that fact, as we have done, through study of
Jesus's character, we go at once beyond it to this
sacred conclusion. Critical study, finding in its object
a supernatural presence, ends in worship; then comes
contemplation, which discovers in the supernatural
presence a condescending and gracious purpose. The
mind begins by seeing the Divine in the human; it
ends by rising to a higher plane of thought, and
discerning what is involved in the Divine itself.

A logical distinction, indeed, comes to light in the
course of the contemplation, and for the student and
for the teacher this distinction is of vast importance.
It is the distinction between the historical and the
Transcendent. The Transcendent, in all ages, is the
Divine; the historical has for us bodied forth the
Divine. The mind, recognising a unique indwelling of
God in our Saviour, must also recognise that God, who
dwelt in Jesus, transcends the historical appearance.
Revelation must leave a still-remaining incomprehen-
sibleness in what is revealed. So again, the mind,
recognising the very actions of God in Jesus, must also

recognise that the actions in their essence transcend the human movements which occurred in time and space. This also is involved in the category of revelation. We say, In Jesus there was God ; but inasmuch as it was God indeed that was in Jesus, what God did for us in Jesus is in its reality an eternal doing, and Jesus in history bodied forth that eternal doing. This distinction is demanded by the very idea of God. And it is of the highest importance both for religious faith and religious practice. It is the legitimate development of what is stated both in Bible and Church formula. It may not come into clear consciousness for every mind ; but it ought not to be forgotten by the student and the preacher.

The conclusion, then, is for us no less than this, The Most High, in His wisdom and love, has manifested Himself to us by dwelling in a unique way in our Lord Jesus. God manifested in Jesus His whole self in its relation to us. And so we are to understand the atonement. In the sacred death of Jesus there was bodied forth the eternal submission of the Son to the Father, of Life in glorious Finality to the Author of Life ; and in the action of Jesus, in which he gave himself freely when he was called to die, we are to see bodied forth the Soul of One who sympathises with the afflicted everywhere, feels for each and all of us in our shame, and makes our pains, our burdens, and our losses His own—a Divine Son, and behind that, a Divine Father who is one and the same.

A special inspiration reading a great circle of truth in relation to God and human destiny was occasioned by the manifestation of God in Jesus. And of that inspiration the New Testament is the fruit. For many, indeed, when Jesus was no longer seen " after the flesh," there was awakened the sense that perceives the Divine. Many perceived around them and above them the Transcendent Reality that ·had been bodied forth in the historical.   Many perceived around them and above them One who was Son, first, an Ideal of life that was a Living Presence, a Strength, a Heavenly Friend, then also Father, a Fountain of Care, a " faithful Creator."   But for a few the awakening was so special that they became, as we must say, specially inspired, so as to rank with the older prophets and surpass them in the glory of their perceptions.   From these, or it may be only some of these,· came the New Testament. Their inspiration was special ; but they conveyed what they learned in it through human conditions, of country, of mode of thought, of time, of individual tendency.   They conveyed to us the message that God had been in Jesus; that his suffering and death had bodied forth to us the transcendent dying for us of the Son of God ; and that, as the Son and the Father are One, there had been manifested a Love which would deliver us from every enemy.   This message is not obscured, but made the clearer through critical reading of the medium which has conveyed it to us down the ages.

The earliest attempt which remains to us in the way of expressing the truth of the Divinity of Jesus, is in the narrative preserved by all the gospels, of how the Holy Spirit was seen descending on Jesus at the time of his first public appearance among the followers of John.   We have seen that it is possible there may have been at the root of this narrative some definite psychological experience ; but, whether that be so or

Above, p. 18.

not, the chief significance of it lies in its expressing the idea now under consideration. Soon this way of representing the idea was not enough for the popular imagination, and there were provided the two stories which introduce the Sacred Life in the Gospels of Matthew and of Luke respectively. The advance which these stories brought was that they portrayed the special element which must have been in Jesus before his birth. They conveyed the fact that his was no mere reception of prophetic fire as his mind became susceptible, but a heritage of the Divine, a sacred inner self. What need for us to follow the inquiry as to whether these stories had also external evidence and external facts to support them, seeing we discern what they really mean, and see that in their real meaning they are absolutely true? As an expression, however, of the truth, they are obviously, at least in great part, poetical and figurative; and to neglect to notice this is to make them do violence to the idea, instead of expressing it. A much greater advance is found in the next later representation, that of the Fourth Gospel. Here poetry is abandoned, and philosophic accuracy is aimed at. Here also the danger is avoided of materialising the conception of the Divine Nature or of limiting to the earthly phenomena the revelation which had been granted. In the Fourth Gospel the state of the case is expressed as having been that the Eternal "Logos," or Reason, the Divine Being who is *in* the world, as distinct from the Divine Being who is invisible and at the beginning of all things, was "made flesh" in Jesus. It is to be said that, while the philosophical view of the universe on which this representation was based has been enlarged with the increase of knowledge,

Cp. Lk. i. 35 w. Jn. i. 1 and 14, note the " there-fore " in Lk. (*dio*) seeming to make the son-ship to God begin at the birth of Jesus.

Jn. i. 18.

24

yet the essentials of **both** the general view and this particular representation are sound, and call for recognition to this day. Finally, added to all these attempts to express the idea **of the** Divinity **of** Jesus, **there has come** down **to us, in a** book written, **in all** probability, earlier than any of these attempts **took form,** another contribution of thought which was needed for completing **the** understanding of the subject. In the Epistle to the Galatians the Apostle Paul told of how the **gospel** had come to him by the "revelation" (*apokalypsis*) of Jesus Christ, and of how it had pleased God to "reveal his **Son**" in the apostle himself. **He** thus brought into use the category which, revived by the idealistic theologians in **general of** modern times, has been here employed **for explaining** how it can truly be said that One who is rightly **called the "only begotten Son "** of God was made known to the world in Jesus. The sum of all this expression in the New Testament is that the Supreme, the Omnipresent, the Incomprehensible, as Son first, then as Father, was unveiled in the human soul and **the** historical life that have been the subject of **our** reverent study.

Cp. also Rom. viii. 19 (Greek, or Revised Version), 1 Cor. i. 7 (Gr. or Rev. Vers.), 2 Cor. xii. 1-4; Ephes. iii. 3-5, &c. See App. I (21)

The further course of this conception and the outgrowths from **it, as** the Christian Church took form— the doctrine of **three** " personae " or *figures* in the Godhead, all equal **in** substance, **power, and** glory; the popular anthropomorphisings of **this** doctrine; the **reactions** into Unitarianism; the practical importance of recognising the Sonship as well as the Fatherhood in **the Deity ;** the historical thoughts regarding secondary embodiment of the Son-" **Person," the** early thought of an embodiment in **all** creation, **then the** thought of an embodiment in a miraculously gifted Church, then

Broadly distinguishable as the thoughts (a) of the early Fathers, (b) of the Catholic Church, (c) of the Protestant creeds, and (d) of modern Christian speculation.

the emergence of a distinction, for this respect, of an
invisible from the visible Church, then the looking for See App. I. (24).
embodiment in an ever-improving human society—
all these developments from the conception of the
Divinity of Jesus, not yet by any means left behind,
more truly not yet come to maturity, are beyond the
sphere of consideration belonging to this book.

Meanwhile the Heavenly Friend unveiled in Jesus
remains held fast in the knowledge of an ever-living
experience. And this experience, awakened through
the gracious unveiling which has been before us, is
in a greater degree than critical study the anchorage
of our hope of that gospel message which the unveiling brought being still read and ever more clearly
read. This experience not only places all the earnest
among us above the need of an exact science, but is
itself bringing the nearer the triumph of such a science.
As in early times, so now, experience of the Christ
Presence has really more to do with advance in religion
than education of the intellect. Early Christianity
was established, under God, through the experience
of many, from Paul to the humblest martyr who faced
violence and death, seeing the care of God in the midst
of them and beyond them. Protestant Christianity
was established similarly; and Luther himself has left
sure indications that but for such experience he would
have succumbed under the fury of his enemies. And
in our own century experience of the same Eternal
Reality, advancing in clearness, has been quietly
victorious. Great men in Scotland, in the earlier
days of the century, bore witness, in the strength of
this experience, to a Father and a Redeemer that
are One indeed, mercy being greater than intention

24 *

to punish with the first as with the second. Illustrious men in both parts of our island have since
added to this testimony. And now, when Biblical
Criticism has come with its forces, removing the
dead weight of Literalism which hampered even those
teachers and opposed distrust to their perceptions,
who will limit the achievements of that still living
experience? It will advance still, and it will repeat
the conclusion of the earliest great prophet of the
Divine in our Lord Jesus : " I am persuaded that
neither death, nor life, nor angels, nor principalities,
nor powers, nor things present, nor things to come,
nor height, nor depth, nor any other creature, shall
be able to separate us from the love of God, which
is in Christ Jesus our Lord."

APPENDIX.

I.—General Notes.

1. *Birth Narratives.*—I have purposely avoided, in this form of my work, all detailed criticism of the narratives in the opening chapters of Matthew and Luke. Let worshippers, all who will, take such encouragement as may be afforded them from these passages. One thing only is necessary to say here in a note. It is that for those who find the essence of the Christian idea most fully realised under the belief that Jesus, as " very man," was born a man in a way that requires some free reading of these passages,—who, it may be, especially love to think of Him as having sanctified ordinary, honourable wedlock as He did all that is healthfully human, there is strong evidential support in the New Testament. The course of the accounts in the first three gospels, as they proceed, cannot be said to disturb the view of such persons, nor can that of the Fourth Gospel, read all in all. They may also appeal to Mt. i. 1 ; Mk. iii. 21, cp. vers. 31-35; Lk. i. 27, cp. i. 69; Lk. ii. 48; Lk. iii. 23, cp. i. 69; Jn. i. 45; and along with these, to Acts xiii. 23 and Rom. i. 3, in which there is no trace of either author entertaining the idea afterwards held by the Fathers, that the descent from David came through Mary. It may be added that at least against the view of such persons the unbending literalist can hardly claim a monopoly of the orthodox Christian doctrine ; in the Christian creeds the matter is stated in a way

under which the view just alluded to may be defended.   Is not, indeed, the literalist in danger of falling into "heresy"?   Did Origen, for example, not fall into heresy when he spoke of Christ's body as "like to our own, *differing in this respect only,* that it was born of a virgin and of the Holy Spirit"? (De Princ. Pref. 4.)   The difference, as stated in our creeds at least, is only that Jesus, being like us otherwise, was "without sin."   Cp. the commentary of so conservative a writer as Dr. Meyer, translated by several of our Scotch professors—who, however, do not commit themselves to his views.

2. *Jesus and Baptism.*—Mark x. 38 has no weight for show-ing that Jesus made a special point of baptism.   Baptism there is used as a mere illustration for Jesus's own consecration. The very using of it for the purpose of mere illustration suggests that it was an institution very familiar to Jesus and to his hearers, but also that it had not itself a place among Jesus's more sacred thoughts.

3. *The Temptation* Stories.—Very eminent scholars (Holtz-mann, Pfleiderer, Wittichen, &c.) have been inclined to look at the lengthened account of the "Temptation" found in Matthew and Luke as being purely legendary (though *symbolically* his-torical), and that on the grounds of most valuable investigation, along with a wide consideration of the subject.   For similar views upheld in English, see Carpenter, "First Three Gospels," pp. 163-164.   I prefer the interpretation which I have given in chapter 3, while finding in the presentation of these scholars much that throws light on the narratives as they read in our received gospels.   A specially interesting point is the explanation by Holtzmann of the "pinnacle of the temple" reference as having its probable origin in the later throwing down of "James the brother of the Lord" (Eusebius ii. 23).

4. *Jesus's dwelling in Capernaum.*—The "his" in Mk. ii. 15 (*autou*) may refer either to Levi or to Jesus.   Looking carefully at the text alone, the reference seems to be to Jesus; but the other is admissible.   In the corresponding passage in Matthew the disciple Matthew seems to have followed Jesus to the house of Jesus; but in the account in Luke it is distinctly stated that Jesus was entertained by Levi.   Taking all things together, the

reference of the pronoun is too uncertain for a confident conclusion to be based on this verse ; but Luke has much weight.

5. *Jesus's words in John v.* 19, 20.—In the gospel the words are exactly, " The Son can do nothing of himself but what he seeth the Father do," and so on. The change made here only substitutes, in regard to two phrases, the well-authenticated language of Jesus himself for the philosophical language in which the evangelist has set all his presentation.

6. *Jesus and the Publicans.*—Mt. ix. 13 (first half) may also have been part of Jesus's saying to his disciples on his being charged with associating with " publicans and sinners "; but seeing these words are found neither in Mark nor in Luke, their authenticity is hardly certain. A justification from the Old Testament seems always to be demanded by the author or originators of the First Gospel ; and this procedure of Jesus, in view of the purpose of the gospel to declare a new moral law would so very specially demand a justification in their eyes, that if there was no justification from scripture at hand, one might be searched for and inserted.

7. *The Leaving Zebedee.*—The deduction made in chapter vii. from the account of James and John leaving Zebedee with the " hired servants," is the more supported when we compare Mk. i. 20 with the parallel passage in Matthew (iv. 22). The misplacing of the " straightway " (*eutheos*) shows the advance of the account from being that of a general leaving of Zebedee with no one helping him but hired servants, to being mixed up with the dramatic calling itself.

8. " *Matthew* " and " *Levi.*"—We may believe that the First Gospel was neither in error nor carried away by indirect motives when it changed the " Levi " of the story in Mk. ii. into " Matthew," thus letting it be understood that Levi was identical with Matthew the apostle. The account of Mark very strongly suggests that Levi would become an apostle (1) through naming him at all at this early stage of the ministry, and (2) through recording that he was a son of " Alphæus," who had at least one other son that became an apostle of Jesus. Besides this, the words, " And he arose and followed him," seem to indicate prominence on Levi's part among Jesus's disciples (Mk. ii. 14).

9. *" Kingdom of God" and " Kingdom of Heaven."*—The explanation given in chapter viii. is quite in accordance with the view of the origin of the different gospels followed in the Introduction.   The writer or originators of the First Gospel, having at hand the notes of Matthew, discover that *" ton ouranon "* (of heaven) is the favourite expression of Jesus, and so bring it in as a corrective of Mark each time.   Mark, on the other hand, having not so full a collection of the sayings, but only the shorter account that has come in great measure from Peter (though through other channels doubtless also), uses the popular phrase.

10. *The Dead-raising Stories.*—The stories of Jesus raising the dead must in modern times not be taken literally.   It is becoming impossible to take them literally.   At the bar of Reason we modern Christians cannot maintain the accounts of such violation of all experience and all scientific ideas on the trifling evidence which we possess.   We have, indeed, no evidence that does not crumble away in our own hands.   The three stories of the kind that the gospels contain have no organic connection with the rest of the narrative; the other events recorded seem in no way affected by the tremendous circumstances which these stories relate.   Their being historical, therefore, is inconceivable.   It is not conceivable that Jairus, who was actually " one of the rulers of the synagogue," should have done nothing in defence of Jesus throughout all the attacks made on him, if Jesus had really brought back his child to life ; still less is it conceivable that the raising of Lazarus by Jesus should have made the authorities decide to put Jesus to death. On the other hand, the origin of the stories comes before us most palpably.   The origin of them is in Jesus's teaching. Thus, in the Nain story, it is recorded that the people came to speak of how a great prophet had appeared among them (Lk. vii. 16).   This is no doubt a notice of real history.   What led to this happening among the people was no doubt Jesus's authoritative teaching, especially regarding a resurrection.   The evangelist, however, or his precursors (having likely the ancient stories of Elijah and Elisha in remembrance, as advanced scholars are right in pointing out), supposed an actual miracle had brought about that the people should speak in this way.   In

this and in the other two cases a raising of the dead in faith and in promise has assumed the form of a story of the preternatural.

It is to be said further, however, in regard to these stories, that taken literally they are perplexing rather than helpful to religion, and that taken critically they are of the highest value to religion. When we take them literally, they only tell of accidental experiences of three persons in an age long gone by, which only gained them a short extra span of life in this world of struggle and then left both them and mankind generally exactly where they had been as regards hope of anything more. And to this must be added the disturbing thought of the persons having been required to pass twice through the dire experience which a merciful God, for ends of wisdom, requires of all of us once. When we take the stories critically, on the other hand, they tell plainly of two things: first, that our Lord Jesus had a power to speak clearly and convincingly of a life which ends not with the grave; and, second, that it is natural for the human mind to believe in such a life. It is plain that in great measure Jesus gained his ascendancy through assertion and exposition of that great truth; and it is also plain that that truth, having been once asserted in boldness and with intelligibility, fascinated mankind, brought a new interest for life, and gained gradually universal belief.

11. *Luke's Account of the Nazareth Visit.*—Luke iv. 25-27 must be genuine, so perfectly does it fit in with Jesus's whole line of thought as it is discerned from the records in general read critically. The passage presents a most interesting parallel to the " Jonah " reference (Mt. xii., Lk. xi.).

12. *The Syrophenician Woman.*—The account given in the tenth chapter, based on the story of the Syrophenician woman, will recommend itself. The story has the marks of having a historical original, and yet that original could not well be what the story literally relates. That a woman actually of the country to which Jesus had withdrawn came up to him and sought to have her daughter healed by him, that he compared her to a dog in relation to the Israelites, and that she accepted such a comparison and adroitly turned it to advantage, has not the appearance of truth. On the other hand, it is highly likely

that the adroit remark was made by a woman from among
Jesus's own followers, and an uncritical evangelist would very
easily fall into or adopt the mistake of making her out to be a
woman of the country into which Jesus had gone. Cp. Lk. iv. 26.

13. *Three Curious Cases in the Fourth Gospel.*—There are
three cases where comparison between the Fourth Gospel and
the earlier gospels tempts one to believe that the Fourth Evangelist, in his carelessness about historical accuracy, has actually
contradicted the original report—no doubt, unconsciously—
namely, vi. 26 (cp. Mk. vi. 52, Rev. Ver. viii. 12), vii. 27 (cp.
Mt. ii. 5, also cp. Jn. vii. 42), and viii. 42-44 (cp. Mt. xxiii. 9).

14. *Getting the Child-nature again.*—It is interesting to see
how Jesus's teaching about getting back the nature of a child
came first to be supposed to mean being " born again " (Jn. iii.
and Justin, Apol., i. 61), and then came in popular use to have
the directly opposite signification from its original signification,
and to mean getting rid of all that is to be found in a natural
child. This has not been a real development. The idea is
profounder and more beautiful in the original teaching.

15. *Marriage, &c., and Mt. xix. 12.*—Mt. xix, 10 and the
first sentence of verse 12 must be connected as both belonging
to the objections of disciples, as obviously verse 12 is in a completely different line of thought from Jesus's sayings in verses
5, 6, and 9. Probably neither what is in the one verse nor
what is in the other was brought before Jesus by his immediate
disciples ; it is likely that both (and what is in verse 12 most
certainly) are expressive of later questions arising from per-
plexities occasioned by the growing belief in the virtue of
celibacy, which Jesus's words seemed hardly to encourage.
Thus we are to notice further that verse 11 and the last
sentence of verse 12 contain the answer which was supplied
for such questions by the early Christian authorities who issued
the Gospel of Matthew—an answer of some prudence in the
circumstances, and having its origin in being an echo of real
words of Jesus (see Mk. iv. 9, &c.).

16. *Jesus and the Rich Man.*—" Trust in riches " (Mk. x.
24) is not found in either of the two best of the manuscripts
of the New Testament, and is therefore struck out by some

scholars. It is ably defended, however, by Meyer, a very competent authority.

17. *Jesus Riding on the Colt.*—Dr. Keim, in dealing with Jesus riding on the colt, which Keim, following Matthew, takes to have been an ass's colt, attributes Jesus's having done this (in accordance with Zechariah ix. 9) to his wish to show that his claim of kingship was not one requiring outward splendour, but was one joined to meekness. Keim further compares this to his adoption of the name " Son of man " (Eng. Tr. V. 103).

18. *The " Sheep " and the " Goats."*—It is also to be noticed about the " sheep " and the " goats " that, even taking the passage literally, the " sheep " are represented as beings of intense care for others, which is inconsistent with the idea in the picture that an everlasting separation of their brethren the " goats " from their power to help them would be pleasing to them—not to speak, also, of the idea that such would be the reward which the Ruler of all would have prepared for them. There is thus a thorough confusion in the picture as it stands ; and the benign Author of the teaching regarding that care for others that is attributed to the " sheep " could not have fallen into such a confusion, being, as it really is, a stumbling on the very threshold of his meaning. Here, as in the case of the parable of the Tares, the evangelist has given us first Jesus's parable, then a Church application.

19. *" After two Days," Mk. xiv.* 1.—There is a great looseness in the New Testament in regard to time. We can only in the different cases judge from the context as to the correctness of any statement on the subject, and also as to the degree of exactness which the author has really meant. It seems to have been a habit to use a number of days just to express a gap in the narrative, the extent of which is often unknown. The doing this would seem to have implied often more or less of a guess at the time ; but the guess seems in some cases to have had a certain amount of information to confirm it. Jesus's own " three days," founded on Hosea, is an instance of this habit ; and in that case, as the time alluded to is beyond the grave, the time stated is evidently purely figurative. In Mk. ix. 2, however, another instance, the time stated must be a

guess based on a real knowledge of the time that the events
took altogether; though in that case the guess so far fails
through the evangelist not having noticed that what he was
introducing was not a particular occurrence at all, but a general
occurrence, the time of which could not be so accurately defined.
Mk. xiv. 1, we may say, is another instance, and in it there is
a guess which seems to have been very accurate. Cp. Mk. ii. 1,
where, instead of any statement of exact time, we have expressed
in a simple way the same thing as the habit we are considering
really expressed; and on the other hand, compare the several
instances in the Fourth Gospel of the habit we are considering,
in which the statement of time is arbitrary and perhaps figurative.
(See also Luke ii. 46.)

20. *The Burial of Lazarus, Jn. xi.* 17.—There is great
variation in the manuscripts regarding the "already" and the
"four days" in this verse. Whatever may have been the
original reading in the gospel, we may confidently conjecture
that the verse has been based on a statement in the original
account from which the gospel was compiled, to the effect that
Jesus came, having last seen Lazarus about four days previously,
and found that he was "already" (*ede*) placed in the tomb.

21. *The Idea of "Revelation."*—The idea of "revelation,"
properly speaking, applied to the appearance of God in Jesus,
as indicated in chapter xxiv., might form the subject of much
interesting investigation. It was neglected by the early Catholic
theologians, who were content to *assert*, without *explaining*,
two distinct natures in Jesus (See Ambrose, on the Christian
Faith, ii. 7, 56). Still, the writings of these theologians are
not without premonitions of this explaining idea (See Augustine,
"City of God," x. 5, where he calls *sacrifice*, as among the
ancient Israelites, "a visible *sacramentum* or sacred sign (*id est
sacrum signum*) of an invisible sacrifice"). In regard to the
re-awakening of the idea in modern times, and its beginning to
be applied to the life of Jesus, these early words of Thomas
Erskine are interesting : "The gospel reveals to us the existence
of a fund of divine love, containing in it a propitiation for all
sin," and again : "I am led to regard the pardon of the gospel
as another name for holy compassion . . . and thus as a part

of the unchangeable character of God, rather than a particular act" ("Unconditional Freeness of the Gospel," pp. 116, 120). A looser, less sound notion called "revelation," which has prevailed more widely, must not be confused with the idea in its stricter comprehension.

22. *Hell-fire.*—The origin of the conception of hell-fire is indicated in Is. lxvi. 24, where there are prophesied a "worm" that "shall not die" and a "fire" that shall not be quenched for all who have transgressed against God. From Mk. ix. 49 it is plain that Jesus looked upon this fire as a reality, but as a reality to be experienced, more or less, by all ordinary men and women, and from ver. 50 it appears that he regarded the fire as purifying the individual soul from evil. In the Gospel of Matthew the influence of early Christian preaching has already been brought to bear on Jesus's words, and so given them at certain places that turn which suggests the everlasting burning of certain souls in their very selves. Especially this influence is found in Mt. xxv. 41. No soul can be everlastingly tortured at the hands of Him whom in all His transcendent benignity and anxious love Jesus declared and revealed. The hell-fire which Jesus really taught of is itself an instrument of love. May the good God give to the fire and to the worm all about us that is opposed to His purity and beneficence, and save ourselves in His great mercy!

23. *The Fourth Evangelist as a Disciple.*—It is very important to notice the entirely different aspect which some of the sayings ascribed to Jesus by the Fourth Evangelist come to possess when acknowledgment is made that the evangelist has himself given them their literary form. Especially to be considered with respect to this are three sayings in the eighth chapter, namely, those in verses 42, 44, and 55. What would have been so perplexing as the actual words of Jesus himself appear, when proved to be really the words of the evangelist, as the expressions of a just resentment on the part of an earnest disciple against the persecutors and murderers of his divine Master. In this aspect, also, the words become an important witness for the general Impression which Jesus made. "Children of the devil" seemed not too strong an epithet for

this zealous disciple to apply to those who had been the enemies of One so pure and so majestic.

24. *The Doctrine of the Trinity.*—By general agreement the Latin word *personae* has been translated by the word "persons" in statements of the doctrine of the Trinity. This is so far justified by the investigations of classical scholars in regard to the Latin usage. And yet the *conventional* sense of the word "person," or the sense in which it is applied to a human being, is by no means, properly speaking, the sense in which the word "persona," translated "person," is used in the traditional formulas. That is to say, it is not the doctrine accepted by the Catholic and by the Trinitarian Protestant Churches, to conceive of the three "persons" as three beings separated by limitations of knowledge in accordance with the self of each person, by different streams of experience, by independent and possibly disagreeing wills, and so on. Such anthropomorphism is, indeed, supported by some of the presentations of the very early ecclesiastical writers, as it is certainly also supported by the utterances of many who in modern times deal with the doctrine. But firmly against it are both the history of the doctrine and the formulas themselves as weighed and compared. The Church indeed narrowed to the thinnest line all qualitative difference between the three "personae," while, on the other hand, it was careful to maintain that the three were not *nominal*, nor even *apparent*, but *real* entities or figures, distinguishable for analytical thought within One Supreme Personality. See the Athanasian Creed, and cp. the illustrations in Origen de Principiis, I. 2, 12, and Tertullian, against Praxeas, cc. 8, 13, 22, and 27. Later than the writers just mentioned, Augustine, in "The City of God," expounded the doctrine in such a way that, so far from the three "personae" being likened to three human persons, every human person was supposed to have within a reflection of the Trinity; and in doing this Augustine was careful to distinguish his view from that of the Sabellians, who agreed with him in the matter of the Trinity being reflected within the human being, but did not ascribe to the members of the Trinity the distinct reality which Augustine recognised.

II.—PASSAGES IN EARLIER GOSPELS CONFIRMED BY THE FOURTH GOSPEL IN EVIDENTLY INDEPENDENT THOUGH DOCTRINISED ACCOUNTS.

	MARK.	MATTHEW.	LUKE.	JOHN.
General relations of Jesus with the Baptist	i. 9-11	...	...	i. 6, 15, 19, 20
Return from Jordan to Galilee	i. 12-14	...	...	iv. 1-43
Motive of the return	...	iv. 8, 9	...	iv. 1
Hunger on the way	...	iv. 2-4	...	iv. 31-34
Association with Peter, &c., before Capernaum teaching	i. 16-20	...	...	i. 37-42
Choosing Capernaum to go to instead of Nazareth	...	iv. 13	...	iv. 44. 46-50
Settling down at Capernaum	i. 21	iv. 13	...	ii. 12
Objections to his teaching the Fatherhood of God	ii. 1-12	...	...	v. 17, 18
Not fasting like John the Baptist; objections and sayings	ii. 18-22	...	...	ii. 1-11
Objections to his conduct on the Sabbath	ii. 24; iii. 2	...	...	v. 1-10, 18
Extending of ministry	iii. 9; iv. 35; v. 1	...	...	vi. 1, 2
Incident on the mountain (choosing "apostles")	iii. 13-19	...	...	vi. 3
Visit of mother and brothers to Jesus at Capernaum	iii. 21, 31-35	...	...	ii. 12
The Pharisees asking a "sign," and his appealing to works	[iii.]	xii. 38 ff.	...	v. 36; vi. 30; vi. 42; vii. 2-9
Visit of Jesus to Nazareth	vi. 1-6	...	...	...
Second retreat from public notice (with hunger again) and sayings	vi. 31-44-viii. 27	...	...	vi. 5-13, 27
Simon Peter naming Jesus the Messiah	viii. 29	...	...	vi. 66-69
Rebuke of Simon Peter for worldly view	viii. 32, 33	...	...	vi. 70, 71
Quiet preparatory journey through Galilee	ix. 30	...	...	vii. 1
The journey to Jerusalem	ix. 30; x. 1	...	...	vii. 10
A man getting new spiritual eyesight at Jericho	x. 46-52	...	xix. 1-10	i. 44-50
Entry into Jerusalem	xi. 1-11	...	...	xii. 13-16
Seizing public attention in the Temple	xi. 15-18	...	...	ii. 13-16
Answering objections by naming John the Baptist	xi. 27-33	...	...	x. 40
Saying about Abraham in relation to truth of immortality	xii. 18-27	...	...	viii. 52-58

III.—PASSAGES IN EARLIER GOSPELS, &c.—continued.

	MARK.	MATTHEW.	LUKE.	JOHN.
The parable of the Good Samaritan	...	...	x. 30-37	viii. 48; xi. 54
Objections to Jesus on grounds of Galilean birth	xii. 35-37	...	...	vii. 26, 27. 41.42, 50, 52
Saying his teaching not opposed to Moses	...	xxiii. 2, 3	...	vii. 19
Teaching at Jerusalem the Fatherhood of God	...	xxiii. 8, 9	...	viii. 35-44
Calling the Pharisees blind	...	xxiii. 19, 24, 26	...	ix. 40, 41
Sayings about destruction of the Temple	xiii. 2	...	...	ii. 18, 19
Sayings about sufferings not punishments of special sins	...	...	xiii. 1-5	ix. 3, 7
Prediction about being recognised by his people after he will be gone.	...	xxiii. 39	...	vii. 33, 34; viii. 28
Two days' pause in visit to Jerusalem	xiv. 1	...	...	xi. 6
Supper at Bethany	xiv. 3-9	...	...	xii. 2-9
Characters of Martha and Mary	...	...	x. 39, 40	xii. 2, 3
The betrayal	xiv. 10-11	...	...	xi. 46
The Last Supper	xiv. 17-26	...	...	xiii.-xvii.
Saying about betrayal	xiv. 18-20	...	...	xiii. 21-26
The wine incident	xiv. 22-25	...	...	xv. 1, 2
Sending the disciples as "apostles" again in the midst of seeming defeat	...	x. 16	...	xvii. 18
Prediction of sufferings for disciples	...	x. 17-25	...	xiii. 16; xvi. 2
Promise of help from the Spirit of God	xiii. 11	x. 20	...	xiv. 16, 17, 26; xv. 26
Teaching of right behaviour of one called "Master"	...	...	xxii. 24-27	xiii. 1-15
Speaking of the disciples as his friends	...	...	xxii. 28	xv. 14 (cp. ver. 27)
Philip's misunderstanding, and teaching that God will dwell with those that do good	...	vii. 21, 22	...	xiv. 8, 9, 23
Speaking of scattering of sheep	xiv. 27	...	...	xvi. 32
A deed best for darkness	xv. 33	...	xxii. 53	xi. 9; xiii. 30
Before Caiaphas	xiv. 53-64	...	...	xviii. 13-24
Before Pilate	xv. 1-15	...	...	xviii. 28-xix. 16
The end	xv. 16-37	...	...	xix. 18-30

Note.—For simplicity's sake the parallels of the Synoptics, one with another, are not given here, unless in cases where more than one Synoptic notice makes the parallel with the Fourth Gospel the clearer.

III.—Outline of the Fourth Evangelist's own Treatment of his Material.

The Fourth Evangelist uses the material which has come to him (from the Apostle John, as we have concluded), to present in order the following doctrinal subjects :—

The eternal " Word," or Reason—the higher life for man—the higher birth—the Father and the Son—the lamb of God—the new " wine " of the gospel—the higher birth explained—the Father and the Son more fully—spiritual conceptions of God and worship—the living water—the meat that does not perish—eternal life in the eternal Son of God—the last three subjects more fully—the light of the world, and the taking away of blindness—the heavenly Shepherd—the resurrection in the power of the eternal Son of God—the New Commandment—the Way to Life—the Other Representative of the Father—the True Vine—the unity of separates, in the love of God—the kingdom not of this world — the Undying Redeemer.

(These subjects are all, to begin with, of a kind familiar to Alexandrian philosophy; and a full study of them would have to take account of the stages of that philosophy. Interesting for all readers, in connection with the Fourth Gospel, is the book of " The Wisdom of Solomon," found in the " Apocrypha " of the Old Testament. In that book there are three names which so far represent that Life in God introduced as "the Son " in the Fourth Gospel, namely *Sophia* (wisdom), *Logos* (word), and *Rema* (word; cp. 1 Pet. i. 25). See, *e.g.*, ix. 17, ix. 1, xvi. 26. The work of the Fourth Evangelist was to bring out, as he was right in doing, that that Life in God became manifest or intelligible in the life of the Saviour. See especially, for a proper exposition of this theme, Hausrath's New Testament Times, now in great part translated.)

IV.—Time and Place Notices in the Fourth Gospel Corrected by the Correct Notices in Mark, with Explanations of their Inaccuracies.

Passage in Mark	Telling	Corresponds to passage in John	Where the state of matters is that
i. 9	How Jesus joined the Baptist.	i. 29	The event is related with mystical accompaniments, but not inaccurately.
		and iii. 22	The same event is told a second time, as if it were a new event (owing evidently to the evangelist starting on a different account of the whole ministry), and the evangelist, led away by his desire to make a connected story, says that Jesus's "disciples" (whom really he had not yet met) went to the south with Jesus.
i. 12-14	How Jesus returned to Galilee on John being arrested.	i. 43	The event is related mystically, but not inaccurately.
		and iv. 1-3	The same event is told a second time (from the same cause as in the case above) with hardly any inaccuracy.
i. 21	How Jesus started his ministry at Capernaum.	ii. 1, 12.	The evangelist has somehow confused a place called "Cana" with Capernaum. and so says (wrongly) that Jesus was previously before the public in Cana, but then says (rightly) that he went to Capernaum, adding that his mother and brothers went to Capernaum also, an

Time and Place Notices—*continued.*

Passage in Mark	Telling	Corresponds to passage in John	Where the state of matters is that
		and iv. 46	event that really took place, but *later*. (See Mk. iii. 21 and 31.) The same event is told a second time (from the same causes as in the case above), the confusion of the evangelist between "Cana" and Capernaum is more evident than before, and again the evangelist is led astray into connecting this with what has gone before, by way of making a continued story.
ii. 23	(Indirectly) how Jesus's ministry at Capernaum had begun in the springtime.	v. 1	The evangelist reproduces an assertion to the effect that "a feast of the Jews" (evidently the "Passover") was going on, and adds what is impossible to be historical according to Mark, that Jesus *went* to this feast, which, however, the evangelist himself seems to neglect having said, as he soon after makes Jesus go "over the sea of Galilee," with no word of how he got back from Jerusalem. (Also, the events that he relates are palpably the same as those which Mark relates as having happened in Galilee.)
iv. 35, 36	How Jesus, having chosen "apostles," extended his ministry to the other side of the lake on which Capernaum stood.	vi. 1	The event is simply and truthfully recorded.

TIME AND PLACE NOTICES—*continued.*

Passage in Mark	Telling	Corresponds to passage in John	Where the state of matters is that
v. 21	How this first little missionary journey was soon brought to a close, and Jesus returned to Capernaum.	vi. 16, 17	The event is simply recorded.
vi. 1-5	How Jesus paid a visit to Nazareth.	vi. 42	The whole record of time and place has disappeared, but the sayings of the people of Nazareth about Jesus (as told in Mark) are preserved, and ascribed vaguely to "the Jews."
vi. 31 to viii. 27	How Jesus made a journey eastwards and then northwards, ending at Cæsarea-Philippi.	vi. 66-71	The whole record of time and place has disappeared, but a little conversation that happened near Cæsarea (as told in Mark) is preserved in a very distorted but recognisable form.
x. 1; xiv. 1	How Jesus left Galilee for Jerusalem at the time of the Passover.	ii. 13. and vii. 10, 14	The event is recorded simply and truthfully. A second account of the event is given, a little confused itself, and as if it were a new event (as in the cases above).
xi. 12 (cp. ver. 1, also ver. 19; and xiv. 3)	How Jesus while at Jerusalem spent the nights at a village called Bethany, near the Mount of Olives (cp. Luke xxi. 37).	viii. 1, 2	An instance of his going to the Mount of Olives and returning in the morning is simply recorded.

TIME AND PLACE NOTICES—*continued.*

Passage in Mark	Telling	Corresponds to passage in John	Where the state of matters is that
xiv. 1.	How there was a cessation of Jesus's teaching for about " two days."	x. 40; xi. 6	The evangelist relates (evidently rightly) that Jesus retired out of notice for these two days, but (quite wrongly) makes him out to have journeyed away " beyond Jordan " (through a confusion, in the evangelist's mind, with a going away of Jesus, *in what he said*, related in Mk. xi. 30).
		and xi. 54	The evangelist gives a new statement about this going away, as if Jesus had gone away again (having found, evidently, in his material, the event asserted a second time in a new connection), and (mistakenly) speaks of him going to " Ephraim," probably through a traditional account of the going away to the Ephraim country *in · thought* or *in speech* which is related in Lk. x. 30-33.

N.B.—vi. 4 may be interpreted as a purely *didactic* remark, intended by the evangelist as an introduction to his own eucharistic teaching which follows. The nearness at hand of the Passover alluded to cannot have been a greater nearness than that of about eight months; but that was sufficient nearness for the didactic purpose of one who cared nothing about time and place as such.

V.—Some Evident Touches of Real History in the Fourth Gospel, in Passages where it is no Longer Possible to Read the History Clearly.

ii. 24, 25.—Something having to do with Jesus's withdrawals?

iv. 45.—An account of Peter and the other Galilean hearers of John having in some way introduced Jesus at Capernaum?

vi. 14, 15.—An indication of Jesus having told his disciples plainly that he was glad to be recognised as a "prophet," but did not wish political associations to be connected with him?

vii. 22.—Some further reasoning on the subject of Sabbath-observance?

vii. 45, 46.—The officers of the priests, &c., actually refused to arrest Jesus at first?

xi. 48.—An indication of some of the authorities having sought to justify the death of Jesus to his disciples on the plea of danger from the Romans?

VI.—Some Cases in which the Fourth Evangelist comes back on a Phrase, Making one Believe that he has Received the Phrase, and is Himself Enlarging on it.

i. 31, 33.—"I knew him not" (the historical truth pointed to).

v. 25, 28.—The hour coming when the dead "shall hear his voice."

vi. 27, 33, 51, 58.—Bread giving life, bread from heaven.

vi. 37, 44, 65.—Coming to Jesus through God drawing one, &c.

vii. 16, 18, 28, 29, 33; viii. 16, 18, 26.—Jesus referring to One who "sent" him, and saying that He is "true."

vii. 34 ; viii. 21 ; xiii. 33.—Jesus saying that his countrymen
will " seek " him after he is gone. (Note the obtuse
remarks attributed to " the Jews " after each of the first
two cases—viz., vii. 35 and viii. 22.)

x. 7, 9.—Jesus the " door."

x. 11, 14.—Jesus the " Shepherd."

xii. 23 ; xiii. 31.—The hour for the Son of man to be " glorified."

xiii. 16; xv. 20.—The servant not greater than his lord.

xiv. 14 ; xvi. 23.—Ask and it shall be given.

viii. 29; xvi. 32.—Jesus not left alone.

xvii. 21, 23.—Belief, or knowledge, of the " world."

VII.—Reminiscences of Jesus in the Four Great Pauline Epistles.

GALATIANS.

    i. 4 recalls Jesus's general giving of himself.

    iii. 26 ,, (indirectly) his teaching of the Fatherhood of God.

    iv. 4 ,, (indirectly) his claiming to be Son of God.

    iv. 19 ,, (perhaps) his saying about the future life (Jn. xvi. 21).

    v. 14 ,, his saying to the earnest scribe (Mk. xii. 29-31).

    vi. 2 ,, the same.

1 CORINTHIANS.

    iii. 10 ,, (perhaps) his saying about himself and the Baptist (Jn. iv. 35-37).

    v. 6 ,, sayings about leaven (Mt. xiii. 33, and Mk. viii. 15).

    v. 12, 13 ,, (perhaps) his recognising a *special charge*, and leaving the rest of the world to God (Jn. xvii. 9, &c.).

    xi. 24, 25 ,, his sayings at the Last Supper.

    xiii. 2 ,, his saying about faith (Mk. xi. 23).

1 CORINTHIANS.

xv. 3, 4 recalls his dying, and his own and other teaching connected.

xv. 36, 37 „ his saying about the corn of wheat (Jn. xii. 24).

2 CORINTHIANS.

i. 5 „ his sufferings.

iv. 6 „ his sayings about light (Mk. iv. 21).

iv. 10 „ his dying greatly.

iv. 14 „ his being confidently believed to have risen again.

ROMANS.

ii. 19 „ his sayings about blindness (Mt. xxiii. 17, &c.).

ii. 28 „ (perhaps) his saying to Nathanael (Jn. i. 47).

xii. 20 „ his general teaching (Mt. v.-vii.).

xiii. 9 „ his saying to the earnest scribe (Mk. xii. 29-31).

xiv. 10-13 „ his general teaching (Mt. v.-vii.).

VIII.—THE OTHER EARLY CHRISTIAN WRITINGS, IN RELATION TO THE LIFE OF JESUS.

The Acts of the Apostles,

the most purely historical of all the books in the New Testament, and very reliable when read critically, deals with events that happened after Jesus's death, and therefore does not give direct information regarding him, but also gives through spontaneous allusions indirect evidence for the facts of his life, of a most trustworthy and important kind. It gives emphatic testimony, with no qualification, to the fact that Jesus belonged to Nazareth (iii. 6, iv. 10, vi. 14, x. 38, xxii. 8, xxiv. 5, and xxvi. 9). It expresses the belief that he was inspired by the " Holy Ghost " (i. 2, and x. 38; cp. Mk. i. 10). It gives a saying of Jesus not recorded in the gospels, but of the same tenor as the gospel sayings (xx. 35). It sums up the names of the enemies that he had in his short public life (iv. 27). It gives indirect

testimony to his remark about the *times* of the good to come in
the future not being known (i. 7; cp. Mk. xiii. 32). It echoes
his saying about sheep and wolves (xx. 29; cp. Mt. x. 16).
It bears witness to the fact that Pilate wished to let Jesus go
(iii. 13). It testifies to his having been crucified (ii. 36).

The Epistle to the Ephesians,

dealing with the subject of the Church, has a reminiscence of
Jesus's saying about marriage (v. 31).

The Epistle to the Philippians,

dealing with practical religion based on belief in Jesus, has a
reminiscence of Jesus's sayings about light (ii. 15).

The Epistle to the Colossians,

like Ephesians in subjects, has perhaps a reminiscence of Jesus's
saying about the "treasures in heaven" (iii. 2).

The First Epistle to the Thessalonians

expresses a very early Christian attitude. It looks for a dramatic
"second coming of Christ" (for example, i. 10, iii. 13, iv. 16).
It has a trace of the general impression made by Jesus, centering
religion on brotherly love (iv. 9; cp. Mk. xii. 31). It has also
what is perhaps a reminiscence of Jesus comparing the persecution of himself to the persecutions of older prophets (ii. 15;
cp. Mt. xxiii. 29 and 37).

The Second Epistle to the Thessalonians,

being similar in subject to the first epistle, is very materialistic.
It seems to have a materialised reminiscence of Jesus's saying
about the Temple and its worship (ii. 3-5).

The First Epistle to Timothy,

having to do with oversight of the Church, has a simple reminiscence of Jesus's appearance before Pilate (vi. 13). It
shows that difficulty had arisen over the subject of marriage (of

which Mt. xix. 12 is likely also an outcome), but does not contain any decided trace of Jesus's own teaching recorded in Mk. x. It emphatically repeats Jesus's teaching about love of neighbours (i. 5; cp. Mk. xii. 31).

The Second Epistle to Timothy and the Epistle to Titus,

similar in subject to First Timothy, do not, either of them, give any important contribution.

The Epistle to Philemon

gives no important contribution.

The Epistle to the Hebrews,

an exposition of early allegorising doctrine, shows a little of the tradition, or of the account, of the real life, in speaking of Jesus having *prayed* (v. 7).

The Epistle of James and the Epistles of Peter,

dealing with practical Christian religion, introduce spontaneously some of the *ideas* of Jesus's teaching, and so bear witness unconsciously to these ideas having been expressed by him (for example, Jas. ii. 5 and iv. 10; 1 Pet. ii. 25; 2 Pet. iii. 10).

The Epistles of John

bear testimony of a very important kind to Jesus's teaching. While dealing with metaphysical subjects that Jesus himself certainly did not enter on, they professedly take their start from certain *themes* which are only accidentally brought into connection with their metaphysical line of thought. Now not only the want of connection between these themes and the general line of thought in the epistles, but also the fact that these themes are elaborated in a far narrower way than the same themes are handled in the teaching of Jesus in the Synoptic gospels, make it plain that the writer has taken the themes from some source beyond himself which he reverences, and is trying to convey them, with devotion to the author of them, even while he does not understand them. Such is the theme of the importance of following truth as truth, in the way that Jesus did (1 Jn. ii. 21, iii. 18; 2 Jn. 2, 4; and 3 Jn. 3, 4), which the writer manifestly hardly understands (see 1 Jn. ii. 22, iv. 6). Such, again, is the theme of brotherly love, the "new commandment" of Jesus, running through these epistles, which the writer has clipped down till its spirit is almost gone (see 1 Jn. ii. 22, iii. 10, iv. 5, and v. 16; cp. also 2 Jn. ver. 5 with ver. 10, and cp. 3 Jn. ver. 6 with ver. 10). And such also is the theme of all being "light" about God and religion, made much of by Jesus, sounded by the writer of these epistles (1 Jn. i. 5) only to be abandoned without any force having been given to it. Small details also may be found in the way of showing otherwise the influence of the teaching of Jesus (for example, cp. 1 Jn. iii. 15 with Mt. v. 21, 22).

The Epistle of Jude

gives no important contribution.

The Apocalyptic Books—

that is, the " Revelation " in the New Testament, along with 2 Esdras, the Book of Enoch, &c., otherwise translated—depend as evidences on the way the question is to be decided as to how far they are Christian writings and how far they are earlier writings adapted to early Christianity. It may be said, however, confidently, that the book in the New Testament, with all its startling fancy, bears witness both to the new hold on immortality and resurrection brought about by Jesus, and also to the general spirit of Jesus's teaching (see especially vii. 13-17); and it may also be said that 2 Esdras contains a most notable echo of Jesus's really detailed ideas regarding the life to come (ii. 31 and iv. 40-43).

The First Epistle of Clement,

a very commonplace writing based on slavish dealing with Scripture, though evidently by a heroic man, gives independent and very substantial confirmation of several points regarding Jesus. They are these : His teaching regarding mercy and forgiveness, &c. (c. 13) ; the Parable of the Sower (c. 24) ; his teaching that he was sent from God, and that his disciples were to be "sent" (*apostoloi*) from him (c. 42) ; and his teaching regarding " offending " " little ones " (c. 46).

The *Epistle of Polycarp*

has some of the teaching found in the Sermon on the Mount, in an evidently independent, or at least freely quoted, form (c. 2).

The Epistle of Barnabas,

an allegorising writing like the Epistle to the Hebrews, but more anti-Judaistic, has an independent echo of Jesus's saying about the "first" and the "last" (c. 6; cp. Mk. x. 31).

The other early writings do not give much particular testimony of any importance; but they witness to the general grandeur of Jesus's personality, and also echo some of Jesus's ideas in such a way as to confirm their being universally recognised, in the time of the writings, as Jesus's ideas. This is especially the case with " The Shepherd of Hermas." As we come to writings of slightly later date than those mentioned, their importance if lost by their evidently using our received gospels. Some quote from authorities now lost, as a " Gospel of the Hebrews " and a " Gospel of the Egyptians "; but the added information thus offered does not materially increase our knowledge of Jesus.

INDEX

G. NORMAN AND SON, PRINTERS, FLORAL STREET, COVENT GARDEN.

www.ingramcontent.com/pod-product-compliance
Lightning Source LLC
Chambersburg PA
CBHW021334110726
47900CB00005B/1460